The Tiverton Staghounds

Richard Lethbridge

Richard Lethbridge

ISBN 1 -898546 -43 -6

First Published December 2000

2nd Edition Published February 2001

Tiverton
Staghounds

Richard Lethbridge
Sunnymead
Chittlehamholt
Umberleigh
North Devon
EX37 9NS

Contents

		Page No
Introduction		7
Foreword		9
The History So Far		11
Chapter One	Sir John Amory's Staghounds (1896–1911)	23
Chapter Two	Captain Harry Amory's Staghounds (1911–1915)	72
Chapter Three	Charlie Slader and the South Molton Staghounds (1915–1919)	75
Chapter Four	Memories of the Yandles (1919–1945)	88
Chapter Five	More memories of the Yandles, including the days of Ken Webber, Percy Pennington and Aubrey Besley	113
Chapter Six	Walter Ash, Ray Giles, Ray Burrow and Ray Dart	152
Chapter Seven	John Norrish	185
Chapter Eight	Harbouring	192
	Deer of the Tiverton Staghound country	195
Chapter Nine	Chester	203
Chapter Ten	The followers of the Tiverton Staghounds	214
Chapter Eleven	Bruno	247
Chapter Twelve	Tiverton Staghounds motorbikers	250
Chapter Thirteen	Tiverton Staghounds cappers	255
Chapter Fourteen	Hunt characters	257
Chapter Fifteen	Whist drives and dances	269
Chapter Sixteen	Point–to–Points	284

Colour Photo Section between pages 160 and 161

I dedicate this book to my mother
Diana Mary Lethbridge

ACKNOWLEDGEMENTS

I would like to thank everyone who has helped me with the making of this book, especially Aubrey Besley, Tom Yandle, Colin Yandle, Robin Nelder, Denzil Shapland, Steve Martin, Victor Mock, Stafford Babbage, Brian Seward, Sally Luxton, Betty Palfrey, Walter Ash, Ray Giles, Ray Burrow, Ray Dart, Walter White, Evelyn Waldron, Philip Lashbrook, Mrs Amory snr (Hele Manor), *North Devon Journal*, *Mid Devon Gazette*, Mandy Ridd, Lazarus Press, Luke Harvey, Neil Harris, Geoff Boundy, John Burgess, Johnny Kingdom, John Norrish, the late Arthur Parker, Tina Snell, Jack Broom, Fred Clarke, Jane Pearce, Pearson Publishing (*Baily's Hunting Directory*), Ken Blackford, Ruth Ure, John Lake, Norman and Joan Ellis, Jenny Hayes, Walter Reed, Lewis and Iris Bright, Gillian Stevens, Mrs Mary Greenslade, Michael Sagar (Editor, *Hounds* Magazine), Halsgrove Productions.

Thanks also go to all those who provided photographs: John Burston, Steve Rendall, Philip Lashbrook, John and Pat Ellicott, Michael Jackson, Ginnie Beard, Oliver Harvey, Julie Millman, John and Sally Luxton, John and Simone Williams, Mrs Jim Cole, Aubrey Besley, Baths Photographic, Mr Hessman at Scenic Prints, Walter Kingdon, Ruth Ure, Robert Venner, Norman and Joan Ellis, Bill Pennington, Walter Reed, *Mid Devon Gazette*, Lewis and Iris Bright, Lady Kennard, Jane Taylor, Eric Gibbs (Race Course Photography), Michael Heathcoat Amory, Ray Burrow, Mary Brady, and the late Arthur Parker

My apologies go to anyone I have not mentioned.

Introduction

I have followed the Tiverton Staghounds since the early 1970s, first on a push-bike and then later on, when I was old enough, I progressed to a motor bike, and have used the same sort of transport ever since. With numerous books written on the Devon and Somerset Staghounds over the years, to my knowledge there have been none on the Tiverton Staghounds. To bridge that gap I decided to put something in print.

This book contains old hunt reports, photographs and people's memories, giving everyone an everlasting dialogue of this hunt's history so far. Today's huntsman, John Norrish, shows good sport along with Guy Loosemore as whipper-in and two excellent Masters, John Lucas and Stuart Kelland. Together with a hard-working team of fund-raisers and many loyal followers, this hunt goes from strength to strength.

Richard Lethbridge

FOREWORD

In 1990 I took early retirement from my job as NFU Group Secretary. A year or two later, with its hundredth anniversary coming up in 1996, I wrote to my two cousins, Jim and Tom, to say, "I'm going to write the history of the Tiverton Staghounds". However, I became involved in other things, so that's as far as it got. I am therefore delighted that Richard Lethbridge has, of his own volition, decided to write the story. And what a hunt he has had! After some preliminary tufting in the West Country, the line has taken him far afield, casting in London, Cambridge and elsewhere to follow up sightings.

My family had the Tiverton Staghounds for over a quarter of a century, from the end of the First World War to the end of the Second. My father, Jack, was the eldest of four farming brothers, so they made him Master when they started. Percy took turns to hunt the hounds with Bert, who was Jim's father. Ernest, Tom's father, whipped in. They were all good horsemen and knew the ways of the deer and became a legend between the two wars. I remember my sister, Cherry Stapledon, who was the first lady whipper-in to the Devon and Somerset Staghounds, asking my Uncle Ernest what the Tiverton did when it was foggy. "Let the hounds go and keep hollering," he said. Well, they could holler all right – some said they could be heard two miles away. With the knowledge of the four of them, one or other was almost bound to see the deer. I remember messages being passed up and down the Barle Valley by them.

I was 12 when the Second World War started, being the eldest of us three cousins, and I am so glad to have had a glimpse of the pre-war life and hunting. I am indebted to Richard for doing what I should have done – write the history of the Tiverton Staghounds.

Colin Yandle

*The History So Far**

By the end of the 19th century red deer herds of Exmoor had not only increased in size but had spread beyond the boundaries of Exmoor and the country hunted by the Devon and Somerset Staghounds. In seeking more plentiful and readily available grazing, unacceptable damage to farm crops was now being experienced as far south as the Stoodleigh area and elsewhere in the verdant Exe Valley. This resulted in complaints being made to the Devon and Somerset Staghounds by farming landowners who thought that the deer population should be reduced to more tolerable levels. Following these protestations, Sir John Heathcoat Amory of Knightshayes Court, near Tiverton, agreed to keep a pack of staghounds to hunt the Devon and Somerset country to the south of the then (now defunct) Taunton to Barnstaple railway line. The pack was known as Sir John Amory's Staghounds and was hunted from 1896 until 1911 by Sir John's son Ian (later to be called Sir Ian), assisted by his two other brothers Harry and Ludovic.

Although Sir John Amory was the Master of these hounds, some of the hunt reports mention Ian as Master; more than likely Sir John took a back seat and let his son take charge of the day-to-day running of the hunt.

Newspaper reports tell us that it was a private pack funded at Sir John's own expense and no subscriptions were asked of the followers but some of those who enjoyed the sport contributed towards the deer damage fund.

* with extracts from *Hunts and Huntsmen from the Southwest* (Bilographer Press,1908)

Sir John Heathcoat Amory who started Sir John Amory's Staghounds (now known as the Tiverton Staghounds) in 1896

The kennels were at Hensleigh, Tiverton, and at the time of starting, Sir John had already got his own pack of harriers which he established in 1859. They were known as Sir John Amory's Harriers, and hunted the hare. He was also the Master and hunted these hounds himself for 20 years, then his son Ian hunted them for 15 seasons, followed by Sir John's son-in-law, Charles Carew. Reports do not tell us which year the Harriers were disbanded, but there is no record of them after 1913 in the *Baily's Hunting Directory*.

Sir John's grandfather John Heathcoat came to Tiverton and started a lace factory in 1816, which is still running today, although they now make other things including air bags for cars, dress veiling and Jersey-knitted fabric to name just a few of their products. It's nice to think the factory still retains his name (John Heathcoat & Co.). Long may it continue. One man who worked for John Heathcoat was Samuel Amory, a London lawyer and banker, who married John Heathcoat's daughter Anne. On John Heathcoat's death in 1861, in default of a son, the Amorys' son John (Sir) was the first to use the amalgamated surname Heathcoat-Amory and some of the family still retain this in their name today. When John Heathcoat died, Sir John was a natural successor to inherit the now well-established business which at the time provided employment for 1,100 workers. Today they have a workforce of around 600.

52 John Heathcoat (1783-1861). Driven from his factory at Loughborough, Leicestershire, when the Luddites broke up his machines, he set up again at Tiverton where his brilliant invention, the new bobbin-net machine, together with a willing workforce, quickly brought success.

Right: John Heathcoat (Sir John Amory's grandfather) who came to Tiverton in 1816 to start up the lace factory

In 1911 Ian Amory was persuaded to take on the Mastership of the Tiverton Foxhounds from his uncle Ludovic Unwin and to hunt them as well. A swopping around of kennels for both packs of hounds now took place, Ian Amory taking the foxhounds from their kennels at Bolham to the staghound kennels at Hensleigh, which is still their home today, and Ian's brother, Harry Amory, took the staghounds – of which he had become Master – to be kennelled at Bolham. From then on the staghounds were known as Captain Harry Amory's Staghounds.

In the meantime Harry had Hele Manor near Exebridge built for himself and his family, and we see from the 1913 *Baily's Hunting Directory* that they were then kennelled there.

Ludovic Amory died while fighting in the First World War and Sir Ian Amory continued hunting the foxhounds until December 1930 when, hunting at Witheridge, Ian's horse caught his hoof in a rabbit hole, throwing him off. On 4 January 1931 Sir Ian died from his internal injuries.

By 1915 Harry Amory was called up for an overseas posting in the services and Mr Charlie Slader of Hacche Barton near South Molton agreed to keep a pack of staghounds which consisted of hounds from several packs including the Devon and Somerset Staghounds. This assorted pack of staghounds, harriers and foxhounds proved to be highly successful.

Legend has it that Charlie Slader had a sheepdog called Jack who invariably turned up at the meets 'accidentally on purpose', and who could always 'wind' a deer at greater distances than any of the hounds. At the time these hounds were known as the South Molton Staghounds. In Chapter 3 there is a photograph of one of the heads that was killed at Wixon in 1916.

The retirement of Charlie Slader in 1919 saw the start of a 26 season involvement by four members of the Yandle family, the kennels being at Duvale near Bampton. Jack, Percy, Bert and Ernest were Joint Masters from 1919 to 1945, Percy and Bert hunting hounds on alternate days. The pack was renamed the Tiverton Staghounds.

At the end of the 1945 season, the four Yandle brothers gave up and Percy Pennington and Ken Webber hunted the hounds, hunting and whipping-in on alternate days. At the time the Yandles gave up, Mr Ernest Ellicott was the Master and the hounds were kennelled alongside the Eggesford foxhound kennels. In 1948 they were taken to Ken Webber's farm at Hill Town, Mariansleigh. Later, Mr Ellicott's two sons Charlie and John shared the whipping-in and, with Percy Pennington only staying a season or two, Ken Webber became the sole huntsman.

Mr Ellicott continued as Master until 1951 when he was succeeded by Tom Pennington, and in 1957 Mr Pennington was joined in the Mastership by Ken Webber. With Charlie and John Ellicott giving up the whipping-in, Dennis Boyles came along in 1954 and stayed for a season or two and later went on to become huntsman for many years with the Devon and Somerset Staghounds.

When Dennis Boyles gave up the whipping-in, Jim Cole was taken on as whipper-in for the Tiverton Staghounds and continued when, in 1958, two new Masters were appointed: Mr Aubrey Hosegood and Mr Aubrey Besley. The 15 couple of hounds, a blend of staghounds and foxhounds, were hunted by Aubrey Besley and kept at his Loxbeare home near Tiverton.

In 1964 Jim Cole left to be succeeded by Ivan Webber as whipper-in and at the end of the 1968 season, Mr Hosegood gave up the Mastership and Mr Besley was joined by his wife Mary for the following season.

In 1969 Mr and Mrs Besley and Ivan Webber, the whip, stepped down, and Mr Sidney Gillbard and Mr Robin Venner were appointed as Masters, with Walter Ash as huntsman and Ray Giles as whipper-in. This combination continued until 1975 when Walter Ash left to become huntsman of the West Somerset Foxhounds. Ray Giles took over as huntsman and Raymond Burrow moved down from the Duke of Beaufort's hunt to be whipper-in.

At the end of the 1978 season, Mr Sidney Gillbard stood down as Master and was succeeded by Mr John Lucas. In 1979 Ray Burrow left as whipper-in to be replaced by Ray Dart. Ray Burrow then spent one season as kennel huntsman at the Stevenstone before coming back as huntsman to the Tiverton Staghounds in 1980 when Ray Giles left.

In 1984 a hind went into Ray Dart's horse causing him to come off and injure his back. Laid up for a while, Ray got back into whipping-in, but at the end of the 1985 season he found it hard going with his back and stood down together with Robin Venner who retired after 16 seasons as Master.

A family photograph.
The opening meet of the Tiverton Foxhounds, 30 October 1911 at Knightshayes Court, Tiverton.
By this stage Captain Harry Amory had taken over hunting the staghounds and Ian Amory had started hunting the foxhounds.
Left to right: Ian Amory, Charles Carew (son-in-law who hunted Sir John Amory's Harriers), Sir John Amory, Ludovic Amory, Harry Amory.

Mr Frank Turner was then appointed Joint Master to join John Lucas, with David Ford as whipper-in. Due to ill health, Mr Turner was forced to relinquish the Joint Mastership after one season. At the same time, David Ford also gave up.

At this stage, John Colthorpe was appointed Master with George Milton as whipper-in. George took up office but left before the hunting season started with Graham Thorne taking his place. Before the end of the 1987–88 season, Graham had an injury to his hand so David Ford came back to stand in.

In 1988 big changes took place with John Lucas and John Colthorpe standing down as Joint Masters, to be replaced by Jane and John Pearce. From then on John Pearce hunted the hounds, bringing in Tony Allibone (Bones) as whipper-in, and sadly Ray Burrow and David Ford had to retire. Graham Thorne, at this time, had already left.

In 1993 Tony Allibone left. He then went as whip to the Dulverton East Foxhounds and now hunts them. Tony Allibone was replaced by Martin Blackmore who did not stay long, and then Sharon Mogford was taken on as whipper-in, wearing a red coat, and Andrew Sexon came in as kennelman and did some whipping-in too.

In 1995 Jane and John Pearce gave up the Mastership and John Lucas came back to take on the Chulmleigh end of the country, with Stuart Kelland and Ivan Webber as Joint Masters for the Tiverton end. John Norrish was appointed as huntsman with David Ridge as whipper-in. After one season Ivan Webber was forced to give up through back trouble, and David Ridge also left. John Norrish's son Peter then took over as whip for two seasons and was replaced by Guy Loosemore. This combination of Masters and hunt staff is still in place today enjoying good sport from this pack of hounds and bringing the history of this hunt up to date so far.

§

The 1900–1901 *Baily's Hunting Directory* gives an account of Sir John Amory's Staghounds, and also his Harriers

SIR JOHN AMORY'S STAGHOUNDS

Master – Sir John Amory, Knightshayes Court, Tiverton, Devon.
Secretary – Lewis Mackenzie, Esq., Tiverton.
Huntsman – Ian Heathcoat Amory, Esq.
Whippers-in – A. de las Casas, Esq., and J.C. de las Casas, Esq.
Harbourer – T.C. Yandle, Esq.
Twenty-five couple of hounds.
Kennels – Hensleigh, Tiverton (telephone from P.O. Hensleigh).
Telegraph Office and *Railway Station* – Tiverton, 1 1/2 mile distant.
Days of Meeting – Wednesday and Saturday.
The country, which lies in Devonshire, covers an area about 30 miles long by 20 miles wide; it consists of about 40 per cent pasture, 50 per cent moorland, 5 per cent plough, and 5 per cent woodland. There is no wire. The Tiverton, Mr Bathurst's, the Dulverton and Mr Tremlett's Foxhounds hunt portions of the territory.
The best centres are: Tiverton, Dulverton, Witheridge and Bampton.
A private pack, the property of the Master.
Sir John Amory's Staghounds were established in 1896, at the suggestion of the Master of the Devon and Somerset, to hunt the country into which the deer were spreading, and which lies beyond the limits of the Devon and Somerset regular territory; the latter pack not being able conveniently to hunt it.

SIR JOHN AMORY'S HARRIERS

Master – Sir John Amory, Knightshayes Court, Tiverton, Devon.
Huntsman – Charles Carew, Esq.
Whipper-in – Ludovic Heathcoat Amory Esq.
Kennel Huntsman – E. Harris
Eighteen couple of 20-inch pure harriers (entered in *H&B Stud Book*)
Kennels – Collipriest, Tiverton.
Telegraph Office and *Railway Station* – Tiverton, 1/2 mile distant.
Days of Meeting – Monday and Friday.
Sir John Amory's country lies within the limits of the Tiverton and Eggesford territories in Devonshire; it consists of about 50 per cent pasture, 35 per cent plough, and 15 per cent moorland. There is no wire.
A private pack owned by the Master.
The pack was established in 1859 by Sir John Heathcoat Amory, and has been in his possession ever since. The hounds are all white or badger-pied, and have no touch of foxhound blood.

A meet of Sir John Amory's Harriers
at Black Dog on 29 March 1904
(*Mid Devon Gazette*)

The meet at Black Dog on Monday last of Sir John Amory's Harriers brought a successful hunting season to a close, exactly the same number of hares having been killed in the previous season. The total of 96 in fifty days hunting, testifies to the generous support and careful preservation of hares by the farmers over whose land the harriers hunt, as also to the sportsmanlike forbearance of shooting tenants and landlords. Last Monday Mr Salters' farm (Emlett) was first tried, and though the day was almost too fine and dry for scent to lie, hounds struck well to the line, and after about an hour they were able to run into their hare. The next one was found on Emlett and went across Brownstone Moor towards Washford Moor and was lost. Mr George Selley had plenty of hares on Washford Moor, one was killed after a short run, and a good run with another, past Puddington and around by Henceford Moor, bringing the day's proceedings to a close. On Tuesday the farmers who had walked puppies were, as in preceeding years, entertained by Mr Carew to luncheon at Colliprest, and judging by the smart appearance of the next season's entry, there is every prospect of good sport in the future.

THE TIVERTON STAGHOUNDS 1999–2000
Baily's Hunting Directory as it stands today

Distinctive Collar: None. Evening Dress: Red, red facings.
Acting Jt Masters: (1995) S Kelland, Pipshayne, Bampton, Tiverton, Devon EX16 9DT. Tel: 01398 331448; (1995) J Lucas, Lakehead Farm, Chulmleigh, Devon EX18 7AG. Tel: 01769 580339
Hon Sec: (1987) Mr T Laman, 66 Brewin Road, Tiverton, Devon. Tel: 01884 259421
Point-to-Point Sec: (1995) Mrs G Mock, Bircham, Burrington, Umberleigh, Devon EX37 9JW. Tel: 01769 520203
Huntsman: (1995) John Norrish
Whipper-in: (1998) Guy Loosemoor
Kennels: Mouseberry Farm, Worlington. Tel: 01884 860577
Meet: Saturday and Wednesday
Subscription: Single mounted £175; family £250; car £80. Cap: staghunting £25; hindhunting £15. Car £3.
The country, which lies almost wholly in Devon, is lent by the Devon and Somerset Staghounds, and lies south of the Taunton-to-Barnstaple railway. All, or parts of the following foxhound countries are hunted: the Tiverton, the Eggesford, the Dulverton (East), Dulverton (West), the Torrington Farmers and the South Tetcott.
The Pack, which hunts red deer, was established in 1896, at the suggestion of the then Master of the Devon and Somerset, to hunt the country into which the deer were spreading, and which lay beyond the limits of the regular Devon and Somerset territory. Best centres: Tiverton, Dulverton, Witheridge, Bampton and Chulmleigh.
Former Masters: Sir JH Amory, Bart, 1896–1911, Capt HH Amory, 1911–15. C Slader, 1915–19. J Yandle, 1919–34. Mr P, E and Mr A Yandle, 1934–45. Mr EJ Ellicott, 1945–51. Mr T Pennington, 1951–57. Mr T Pennington and Mr K Webber, 1957–58. Mr AL Hosegood and Mr AHP Besley, 1958–68. Mr and Mrs AHP Besley, 1968–69. TRS Venner and S Gillbard 1969–78. Mr TRS Venner and Mr PJ Lucas 1978–85. Mr PJ Lucas and WF Turner 1985–86. Mr PJ Lucas and JM Colthorpe 1986–88. Mr and Mrs JR Pearce, 1988–95. I Webber, S Kelland, and PJ Lucas, 1995–96. S Kelland and PJ Lucas, 1996–2000.

Below is a list of people who have taken office as Secretary, Treasurer or Chairman during the Hunt's history.

Secretary	Treasurer	Chairman
1896–1901 Mr L Mackenzie	Mr E C Nicholetts	Mr Benjamin Hurford was Chairman at some point between 1945 and 1958
1901–1904 Mr T O Lazenby (Eastfield)		
1904–1918 Mr Frank Dunsford (Ashley)		
1918–1928 Lieut Col H Amory (Hele Manor)		
1928–1945 Mr J Follett Pugsley		
1945–1958 Mr Tom Pennington		1959–1981 Jack Adams
1958–1964 Wing-Cmdr Ernest Mortimer		
1964–1967 Mr Geoffrey Sellick	Mr A L Hosegood	
1967–1968 Mr Geoffrey Sellick	Mr A L Hosegood and Mrs D E Sellick	
1969–1972 Mr Geoffrey Sellick	Mrs D E Sellick	
1972–1975 Mr Geoffrey Sellick	Mr H M Southcott	
1975–1983 Mr H M Southcott (Joint Sec and Treasurer)		1981-1988 Mr Geoff Hurford
1983–1986 Mr H M Southcott	Mr Frank Turner	
1986–1987 Mr H M Southcott	Mr N Webber	
1987–1988 Mr H M Southcott and Mr T S K Laman (Joint Sec)	Mr N Webber	1988–1992 Mr Robin Venner
1988–1993 Mr T S K Laman (Joint Sec and Treasurer)		1992–1993 Mr Derek Cole
1993–2000 Mr T S K Laman	Mr M J Webber	1993–2000 Mr Robin Venner

The first recorded Chairman was Mr B Hurford.

We must assume that the people who were Secretary without a Treasurer beside them took on that job as well.

TIVERTON STAGHOUNDS, 1947–1948
BALANCE SHEET

Receipts	£	s	d
Subscriptions	125	7	6
Mr J Parkhouse	206	16	3
Hunt Balls	428	9	0
	£770	12	9

Expenditure	£	s	d
Cash – bank	674	15	4
Cash in hand	1	1	0
Balance	94	16	5
	770	12	9

Hunt Balls	£	s	d
South Molton (Miss R Hancock)	125	0	0
Creacombe (Mr M Greenslade)	70	0	0
Chulmleigh (Mr M Lake)	69	15	0
Witheridge and Worlington (Mr G Greenslade)	64	0	0
Chawleigh (Mrs J Parkhouse)	54	10	0
Lapford (Mr W Smaldon)	32	10	0
Week (Messrs Hammet and Mock)	17	12	0
Field Glasses (Mr J Parkhouse)	5	2	0
	438	9	0

Collected – Mr J Parkhouse			
Mr and Mrs E Yandle	5	5	0
Mr G H Potter	5	5	0
Mr A Webber	5	0	0
Mr C M Elworthy	5	0	0
Mr R J Bowden	5	0	0
Mr Norman Walter	5	0	0
Mr A W Nash	5	0	0
Mr F Moor	5	0	0
Mr P Pennington	5	0	0
Mrs F Smyth	5	0	0
Mr and Mrs Pratt	5	0	0
Mr F Lake	5	0	0
Mr N Slade	5	0	0
Mr H Bowden	5	0	0
Mr C Stocker	5	0	0
Mr E Ford	5	0	0
Mr T Snell	5	0	0
Mr R Northam	4	0	0
Mr L Baker	3	3	0

Payment			
Eggesford Hunt	530	0	0
Mr F Moore	86	17	6
Mr R Hannaford	5	12	6
Mr W E Sanders	3	14	0
Mr P Matthews	10	10	0
Licences	9	7	6
Mr J Sanders	15	15	0
Mr Masland	2	13	2
Mr Northcote	4	7	2
Mr R Jury	2	2	0
Mr W Gill		12	6
Telephone/Postage	3	0	0
Cheque-book		4	0
	674	15	4

T Pennington, Beechleigh, Chulmleigh,
Hon Sec and Treasurer.

Chapter One

Sir John Amory's Staghounds (1896–1911)

Before the formation of Sir John Amory's Staghounds the Devon and Somerset Staghounds would from time to time come and hunt the country. An example of this is shown in a report below from 1882 when they met at Eggesford, no less than 300 horsemen being present including the Rev. John Russell.

The following pages contain hunt reports courtesy of the *North Devon Journal* and the *Mid Devon Gazette.*

> For the last five or six years some few of the red deer of Exford have showed a decided inclination to migrate into the cultivated lands of Mid-Devon. The first explanation of this is doubtless the fact that they have increased very much in numbers on the borders of the forest, the valley and woods of the Bray offering them a quiet and fairly safe retreat, within a short distance of their native haunts. A few have been seen at Castle Hill, and Bremeridge Wood has several times been known to contain a warrantable deer, many a good run having terminated a kill near the viaduct. But within the last two or three years these lordly animals have been out on a still more daring front by making the large covers around Eggesford their home. Here they have remained pretty much in quietness, thanks to Lord Portsmouth, but must have caused that nobleman some trouble and annoyance during the foxhunting season. Early in the last season an attempt was made by Lord Ebrington, with his splendid pack, to dislodge these deer and drive them back to their native woods, but the success of his efforts was only partial.

The cultivated lands of Devonshire, with enclosures and big fences, and intersected by innumerable roads is not the country best calculated for staghunting. On Monday last a second meet took place at Eggesford, and although the morning promised anything but fine weather the assembly was a large and brilliant one, not less than 300 horsemen being present. Among the number were the Master, Lord Ebrington M.P., Sir John Shelley, C.H. Bassett, Esq, Rev. John Russell & C. A five year old stag was soon found in a wood near the station. He showed little inclination to hurry himself, at first, doubtless thinking it was Charlie with his foxhounds. He was soon undeceived though, and when he found business was meant he pointed straight for Castle Hill, giving his pursuers an hour and twenty minutes of the fastest run for the season, barely keeping himself away from view of the hounds, and only about ten horsemen being anywhere near them. In his line he passed near Lee House, through Chulmleigh and Colleton, leaving King's Nympton to the left and pointing for Meshaw, then to Alswear, where he evidently soiled. Scent after this became indifferent, growing from bad to worse and he was finally abandoned by Arthur Heal the huntsman about two miles South West of South Molton.

On 25 April 1896 a meeting was held at Tiverton Town Hall to discuss plans for the formation of Sir John Amory's Staghounds (to be known from 1919 as the Tiverton Staghounds).

A meeting was held in the Tiverton Town Hall on Tuesday in support of the movement for the formation of a pack of staghounds for Tiverton and district. Mr J.R. Holland presided and there were also present Messrs Ian Amory (MH) W.C.L. Unwin (MFH), L. Mackenzie, T.O. Lazenby, A.M. and L. De las Casas, H. March Phillips, Major Braddon, Messrs T. Clarke, C. Carew, Jarvis Bailey, and many others. Thanks to the active support of landowners and tenant farmers in the Stoodleigh country, deer had greatly increased there of late years. Mr Dunning realising that, in the interest of his tenants, this rate of increase could not go on indefinitely and asked the Masters of the Devon and Somerset Staghounds to hunt the country more regularly and to undertake to kill a certain number of deer in each year. Mr Sanders, the Master, after consulting the committee found himself unable to do this owing to the demands made on him by the rest of his large country. He then asked Ian Amory if he would undertake to hunt the country south of the Devon and Somerset railway. Mr Dunning and the other landowners having expressed approval gave most generous subscriptions towards the funds which will be necessary to raise for the compensation of farmers whose crops may be damaged by the deer. Ian Amory had been lucky enough already to have been given four couple of very good looking young hounds, most of them presented by Mr Unwin. There were as yet very few stags in their country old enough to run, so that it would not be necessary to begin hunting until well on in November, when they would start hind hunting and probably keep at them until the beginning of the April following, after two or three weeks they could then start hunting the stags. Tiverton would not be called upon to subscribe towards any of the ordinary expenses of hunting the country, but he hoped those among them would who had the interest of hunting at heart would subsribe such a sum as would enable the committee to guarantee the farmers to whom they owed so much against any loss they might suffer by preservation of the deer. Mr Unwin in proposing that a committee be formed, said he did not think stag hunting in the district would interfere with the foxhunting. Mr L. Mackenzie pointed to the fact that Sir John Amory and his son Ian would bear the whole of the cost of the pack. The following committee was then appointed, Sir J.H. Amory, Messrs C. Carew, N. Chichester, H.J.W. Coulson, G.J. Cruwys, T.C. Daniel, E.H. Dunning, F.B. Dunsford, J.R. Holland, A. De las Casas, L. Mackenzie, E.M. Mole, E.C. Nicholetts, J.F. Pugsley, General Spurway and W.C.L. Unwin. Mr L. Mackenzie was elected Secretary and Mr E.C. Nicholetts Treasurer.

§

6 October 1896
The first meet of Sir John Amory's Staghounds

The opening meet was held at Stoodleigh Court, the residence of E.H. Dunning, with the new Master, Mr Ian H. Amory and his two whips Mr Albert and Manuel De las Casas, who arrived punctually at ten o'clock with 14 couple of hounds. A large number of staghunting friends assembled, and a most warm and hospitable welcome was given to everyone by Mr and Mrs Dunning. The day promised to be fine and a balmy south west wind and heavy dew seemed signs of a scenting morning. The harbouring had been excellently performed by Tom Yandle, and a warrantable stag was found within a few minutes of the tufters being thrown in Stuckeridge Wood, just above the old kennels opposite Black Copse. Hounds at once began to bustle along, driving through this long cover down to Chain Bridge, and from thence opposite Duvale, away to Cove Bridge and leaving Emmerford on the left, nearly to New Bridge. Here the tufters were stopped and the hounds, which had been left at the new kennels were soon fetched, and rattling down to the Stoodleigh Drive, were put in just below Hatherland Wood North. Soon after getting into the wood hounds divided, and a hind was seen to be the cause, after some delay Ian Amory got his hounds together and laid on the stag, which had been seen making his way back to Stuckeridge. Passing down the iron mill stream we crossed the Exe to Wonham House and away as if for Bampton, but turning back through Highleigh Wood South to Wonham again and the Stuckeridge Coverts, where he turned up four fresh deer. This proved fatal to sport and as hounds had been running for four hours and the ground was seriously foiled, they were called off and taken home. Mr Ian Amory who acted as huntsman is to be warmly congratulated on his first day's sport with a fresh pack, only five couple being old hounds, everyone was pleased with their day's sport with the new venture.

§

A Letter to the Editor of the *Tiverton Gazette*, 6 October 1896

Dear Sir
Sometimes farmers and other friends of hunting take in and feed stray hounds, will you allow me through your columns to make known the fact such a proceeding is a mistaken kindness on their part. It makes a hound that is inclined to be lazy too ready to put up at the first farmhouse he comes to instead of travelling home to kennel. I shall be much obliged, therefore, if anyone from whom a stray hound attempts to beg his supper and a night's lodging, will, unless the hound be ill or injured, ruthlessly drive him away from the house.
Yours Truly
I.H. Amory
Hensleigh, Tiverton

§

20 October 1896
The First Kill

There was a fairly good meeting of Sir John Amory's Staghounds at Stoodleigh Court on Monday, and a hearty reception was accorded to all by Mr E. H. Dunning. The day was well suited for the field, and most of the hunting and the kill – the first stag killed by the Tiverton pack – took place close to the main road. Three couple of hounds and tufters commenced operations about 10 o'clock but Town Wood was drawn blank. Mr Moyle shortly afterwards tallied at

Stuckeridge and when just about to inform the Master Ian Amory another stag came up close to him. Two hounds bayed him, and he then made off over Stuckeridge Lawn, where he jumped the lawn tennis net. He crossed by Stuckeridge Bridge, where Mr Moyle turned him back, he then got into the main road, and ran up and down until turned by a stone cracker into the cover by Stuckeridge Bridge. Only one hound was on all this time, old Remus, and the stag kept on baying him. At about 11.30 am the pack was laid on by the orchard adjoining Duvale House. Here he bayed all the pack in the cover, and crossed the hams by Half Penny Bridge. Into the water and up Duvale Wood to Cove was his next move. He stayed in the water at Emmerford for about 20 minutes, and then jumped out amongst the field. He made off towards Stoodleigh, and crossed by Half Penny Bridge again into Duvale Small Wood, but the scent was good, and he was soon at bay again standing in an opening by Chain Bridge, he took up a good position under a Holly Bush. He then jumped the Mill Leat and right into the River Exe, where he remained for over half an hour before he was killed at about 3 pm. This grand old stag was very powerful and big about the body, and had all his rights and four atop one side and three the other. The head was presented to Mr E. H. Dunning and the slots to Mrs Mackenzie, Messrs De las Casas (the two whips) and Mr Amory the Master.

§

3 November 1896
Ian Amory in a Fall While Hunting his Father's Harriers

On Saturday at Sloe Pool, near Cullompton between 40 and 50 well known followers of Sir John Amory's Harriers assembled for a day's sport in that neighbourhood. The run had commenced only about a quarter of an hour, however, when a regrettable accident occurred to the Master, Mr Ian M. Heathcoat Amory who, it appears attempted to clear a bank, when his horse slipped, and fell backwards. The rider was unseated, and in the fall his left arm was badly fractured above the elbow. As soon as the mishap occurred, the hounds were taken home. A messenger was dispatched to Cullompton in search of a medical man, but unfortunately none was at home. Mr Potter's lady assistant was however driven to Wheatcroft Farm, where Mr Amory was, and rendered all possible assistance until the arrival of a doctor. Mrs Mackenzie of Tiverton, who was summoned by wire, was soon on the spot, and attended to the injury, after which the Master was conveyed to Hensleigh House in Sir John Amory's carriage.

2 March 1897
Sir John Amory's Staghounds

On Wednesday a small field met these hounds at Ash Cross, Stoodleigh, which included Misses Chichester (2), Miss Amory, Messrs H. Amory, De las Casas (4), J.R. Holland, F. Dunsford, J.F. Pugsley, J. Blake, T.W. Charlton, Jarvis, Baily. No reliable news of deer being harboured that morning being to hand. Mr Amory drew the Coverts towards Bickham and when Stileham Wood was called on a good hind and yearling were quickly out towards Rackenford Moor, the tufters were stopped on the edge of the moor, and we waited until the pack were laid on at 12.15. The deer had stopped in a cover a little way on, and when hounds worked up to them they ran a circle back to Stileham and down the valley to Wheatland, when they turned sharp to the right up the Coleford Bottom towards Gibbett Moor, it now began to look like a gallop, and we were not disappointed. The Tiverton Turnpike was crossed by Tidderson Moor, through the Hill Town Coverts, over the Dart, straight on to the large ponds at Bradford. Here our hind soiled, but went like a giant refreshed leaving the field, who had by this time become quite select, to follow as best they could, passing under the right of Witheridge, we rode over the moors towards Rose Ash and Meshaw, the hounds flitting like passing shadows ever in front, until we reached the valley of the Dart, when our hind stuck to the long line of Coverts between Affeton Castle and Chulmleigh. Never going far from the water, she was finally killed at Chulmleigh at 6 o'clock. Those present at the death were Messrs Manuel De las Casas (whip) and T.W. Charlton. The line led over some of the best of the open moors in the hunt, and the pace was so severe that all the horses were beaten, and only the two above mentioned were able to see the finish. The extreme points on the ordnance map show 14 miles, but the distance actually travelled by the hounds must have been very great and was a fine performance for a pack in its first season "snaffle".

§

13 March 1897

These hounds met for the first time at the Gidley Arms Inn near Meshaw, on Saturday, March 13th, the interest taken in staghunting by the farmers and others living in this part of Sir John Amory's new country was made clear by the number of horsemen who assembled at the meet to welcome Mr Amory and his sporting pack, who had already made so good a reputation for themselves. This must be the first time the staghounds have met in this country for very many years, and though a curiosity to see a new pack may have had something to do with the number of the field – certainly not fewer than 200 horsemen being present, 170 were counted as they passed down one road, and anyone who knows a field of Devonshire staghunters will be ready to swear that there were certainly a good many knowing men waiting on the tops of the neighbouring hills, that it was not curiosity only was clear from the way in which the majority of the field settled down to ride, when the pack was laid on. The hounds were trotted to Prescott where Mr Nott made arrangements for kennelling the pack.

Two couple of tufters were taken out to draw Meshaw Wood, where they could apparently just own the stale line of a deer through the Covert and across a field or two into another small larch Covert. A hind was then viewed by Mr De las Casas, leaving at the further end, one of those long, lean, thoroughbred-looking hinds that do not seem to have known the troubles of a family for the last year or two at any rate, and then can go on galloping for the greater part of a week without feeling the worse for it. From Meshaw Wood with the pack on we galloped as hard as we could induce our horses to go over some miles of rather open moors. Coming to Ash Moor Gate we crossed the South Molton Turnpike road, and finally past Creacombe on to Rackenford Moor. The whippers-in had considerable difficulty in stopping their hounds, and in catching up the Master and the leading hounds who by this time had taken their deer through Bickham Wood, Wapsley and the Stoodleigh Coverts down to the Exe by Chain Bridge. Coming out of the water here she ran the Stoodleigh chain of woods past Cove, up to Steart, back to the Exe by Emmaford, and down the stream almost to Worth, leaving the water and passing close to Washfield where we had our serious check – she went into Courtney Farm over Slade Moor and into Rifton Wood where hounds ran into a herd of fresh deer and were with difficulty stopped and laid on the line of what was believed to be the hunted deer, down Coleford Water to Spurway Mill and down the valley of the iron watermill stream to the Exe by Duvale, across it and up the other side, going nearly out to Bampton and on past Coombe Head, down to the Exe again, not far from Exebridge, where hounds were stopped at 6.45. It is almost impossible to say how far hounds actually ran, as the last half of the run was not straight, and it is therefore difficult to measure, but from Meshaw Wood to Chain Bridge is 13 miles, measured straight across the map, and this was done at racing pace without the semblance of a check. Then taking six other points, and measuring the distance between them on the map, we got a further 12 miles. Hounds had 13 miles to the meet and 10 home, so a staghound's life must be rather a wearing one. Where we changed deer as we must have done I cannot say, but suppose it must have been in Rifton Wood, as I believe we took our hunted deer into it. That it may not be long before we see this capital young pack and its very sporting Master out here again is our hearty wish.

§

28 September 1897

Stoodleigh Court, the residence of Mr E. H. Dunning, J.P. presented a lively appearance on Saturday morning, for the opening meet of Sir John Amory's staghounds. Shortly before eleven, the time fixed for the meet, horsemen, crowded vehicles of almost every description, cyclists and persons on foot began to arrive, and a few minutes after that hour the spacious courtyard was packed with mounted ladies and gentleman, the number on horseback being estimated at close on a hundred and twenty. A few minutes before the appointed time the pack, numbering nineteen couple, arrived in charge of the Master (Mr Ian Amory), Messrs A. and M. De las Casas (whips) and Ernest Hellard the popular huntsman. At every available point in the yard on the sloping green upwards of a dozen photographers had taken up their positions and were busily engaged until the assemblages filed out to begin the day's proceedings. Before leaving the Court, the company were kindly entertained to lunch by Mr Dunning, after which a move was made to Wormsworthy cover, about half a mile distance. With three couple of tufters the Master, whips and huntsmen were soon busily engaged in working this cover while most of those on foot and on wheels took up their position in a field above Champells Farm. For nearly an hour this and the adjoining cover of Champells were tried but without result, so the tufters were taken into Town Wood, situated close by Champells. After a few minutes a couple of hinds were seen to leave the cover, but after running a short distance doubled and re-entered the cover. As a couple of stags had lately taken up their abode in Walsley Wood, a considerable time was spent in trying to discover their whereabouts, but all efforts seemed to be in vain. At length, about two o'clock a stag was observed in the act of breaking away, but like the hinds altered its mind after proceeding a few yards. A second stag was afterwards observed dodging about in this wood and the tufters having had enough work were taken to Stoodleigh Moor where the pack was kennelled and another half dozen set to work. For nearly two hours these tufters worked the cover without succeeding in bolting either of the stags and it looked as though the proceedings would terminate without a run. At length a three year old stag got away in the direction of Chain Bridge. This animal was considered hardly old enough, but the Master desirous of giving the field a run had the pack unkennelled and laid on the foil near Hangman's Hill. The line first took them to Chain Bridge then visiting Half Penny Bridge and Highwood, travelling through Stoodleigh, carrying the line down to the iron mill stream. The pack then visited Chain Bridge again and in reaching this spot were called off, darkness setting in. Scent was very bad and the run was one of the worst experiences since the formation of the pack.

§

5 October 1897

Staghunting is indigenous in Devonshire, the love of it is in the blood of the people as surely as the earth consists largely of red sandstone, and the immense popularity of the sport is somewhat due to the infectious character of this blood disorder, so that all who come near the West Country get a greater or less share of the excitement stage. At all events many of the labourers and artisans are quite as full of stag lore as the hunters themselves. I saw with these hounds (Sir John Amory's staghounds) on Friday, a working man with a capital pair of field glasses, and he informed me as to the size and character of the quarry we were running, and of the hinds and male deer he was seeing in the immediate neighbourhood. Breathless with interest he was having a birds eye view of all going around him. The meet of Sir John Amory's staghounds at Rackenford on Friday last went far to prove the words I have written. There were some old farm hands, crippled with age, with labour, and with exposure, dozens of bright-eyed chubby-cheeked children out from school for quarter of an hour, at the meet (who knows what a wholesome stimulus to their little brains this must have meant!), old women, young women and all sorts and conditions of men, all full of interest and as keen as the Master himself. The absence of that good sportsman Mr Frank Yendell, owing to illness, was the cause of a generally expressed regret, and many were the enquiries about him. The hounds, 18 couple and a half, were kennelled at Cruwys Haye, and the tufters drawn and taken to Rackenford Manor.

After half an hour a stag was moved with two hinds from the south-east corner making away for Sydeham, the pack was laid on just by Spurway Mill, taking the line to Coleford Water, where the stag (two on top each side) was fresh found, he made for

Littlewood and Greatwood crossing the mill stream and leaving West Cott Barn on the left, we reached Spurway Wood, where our stag lay low, and careful hunting ensued. After some delay and a fresh find we ran away to Pinkworthy and Nethercote Wood and across to Champles Wood. Here our stag put up more than one hind, and deer seemed generally plentiful. After a short check we could hear 'Windsor' carrying the line towards Hangmans Hill with a voice which seemed to assure us that he had quite made up his mind he was on the hunted stag, and indeed he was. For the pack shortly joining him they rattled their quarry above Black Copse and Down Copse, for some half an hour, now onto Chain Bridge and crossing over South Stuckeridge covers turning up a fresh stag. Mr Tom Yandle was ahead in time to tell us that our fresh found stag was none other than the grand old veteran known amongst the officials of the hunt as 'Old Bill' and after a fruitless attempt to fresh find our hunted stag Mr Amory decided to give the welter one a run. Running round the old kennels and across the iron mill stream through Holmingham Wood this stag made towards Cove, and was fresh found by Mr Amory. With the pack just above Half Penny Bridge, turning downward he crossed the swollen Exe just below Duvale Barton, and ran down towards the old Turnpike Gate making for Higher Barn, hounds pressing closely, past Druids, Haye and away to West Brook plantation. Here Old Bill reached the River Batherum about half a mile south of Bampton and was killed here. How many times this old gentleman has beaten hounds it is impossible to say, but roughly speaking, I should say he was 12 years old, and carried the finest beam and antlers that I have ever seen. He had brows, no bays, trays, and three on top each side, and the largest slots by a great deal that most of those present had ever seen.

§

12 October 1897

Of late years deer have been increasing in number in the valley between Barnstaple and Arlington, and in consequence, they have been doing a considerable amount of damage to the farmer's crops adjoining the large covers on Sir Arthur Chichester's property. For seasons past the Devon and Somerset have put in an occasional day and some fine runs have been experienced from this neighbourhood. But the deer are now so numerous that it was thought desirable that more hunting should take place along the valley. Mr Basset having made a representation to the effect to the Master of the Devon and Somerset, the latter kindly permitted Mr Basset to invite Ian Amory to come down with the Tiverton Pack which he did on Monday last, ample accommodation being provided for horses, hounds and servants at Pilton stables, while the Master and whips (Messrs De las Casas) were entertained at Westaway by Mr Basset.

§

14 October 1897 – Stag hunt near Barnstaple
A Kill in the Taw

Sir John Amory's Staghounds concluded their complimentary visit to the west side of the Devon and Somerset district on Friday, when they had a very successful run from Loxhore Cot, where the pack was to have met on Thursday, the meet, owing to the severity of the run on the previous day being postponed to give horses and hounds extra rest. It being Barnstaple market day, and the meet only three miles away, there were not so many present as there would otherwise have been, although the attendance included quite 60 on horseback, while many came by carriage or bicycle. The introduction of cycles at a stag hunt was too much for one of the thoroughbreds. At the sight of them the animal became restive, and, eventually bolted, knocking over several cyclists, besides causing the upset of a trap party, although happily no serious injuries resulted. Among the company present were the Master (Mr Ian Amory), Mrs Amory, Messrs De Las Casas (whips), Miss Hibbert, Miss Hurst, Sir Arthur Chichester, Mr C.H. Basset, Mrs Hugh Toller, Miss Smith and Miss Crang (Eastdown), Mr A.F. Seldon, Mr W. Penhale, Mr R. Lake, and Mr Speeke. Among those on wheels were Mrs Chichester and party and Mrs Seldon and party. Two stags had been harboured, one by Sir Arthur Chichester's keeper in Youlston, and the other by Mr Litson. The latter, which was lying in Woolywood, was selected as being close at hand, and it did not take the tufters long before they had aroused a fine four year old stag, which at once pointed its head towards Barnstaple. The scent was so good and the tufters had gone such a pace that it was impossible to stop the whole of them. The pack was therefore taken by Mr Basset and Mr De Las Casas to Cross-tree, three miles from Barnstaple where they quickly took up the line by Blakewell Mills to Tutshill, where they turned into the wood to Westaway, where the stag was in full view, crossing Mr Basset's grass land to Raleigh, Frankmarsh and Stoneyard. Here it was thought the stag must have returned to the large covers by the River Yeo, where deer are known to be very plentiful, but refusing this shelter, he turned to the right, the hounds carrying the line across the Lynton and Barnstaple road, sinking into the valley by Maidenford and crossing the Devon and Somerset Railway at Bishopstawton, where, after crossing Whitemere it got down to the tidal waters of the Taw, exactly underneath Tawstock Court. The stag was killed here, it proving to be that of a powerful specimen with brow and bay, two on top one side, and one on the other. Thus concluded about as successful a week as any the Tiverton pack has had. Mr Pile, of Eastdown, had a nasty fall during the run, fracturing his ankle.

§

2 December 1897
Sir John Amory's Staghounds in the Barnstaple District

Amongst the followers of the sport of staghunting in the Exmoor Country including the district of Barnstaple, the presence of many staghounds in the Loxhore Valley and woods belonging to Sir Arthur Chichester, Bart, is viewed with great satisfaction. Sir Arthur, a few days ago caught sight in his park one of of the finest stags he has ever seen, and Goss, the keen harbourer to the Devon and Somerset Staghounds has given his opinion that it is the biggest in the Exmoor Country. Sir John Amory's Staghounds have been invited down from Tiverton and they are now being kennelled at the farm of Mr C. H. Basset, Westaway, near Barnstaple, who was a former Master of the Devon and Somerset Staghounds. A meet took place on Saturday at Chelfham near Barnstaple. The tufters were taken to Woolley Wood, opposite Loxhore Cott. On the way the tufters broke off after a big stag and a young male deer. Eventually they found their hind and raced down a stream of water to the bridge at the bottom of Bratton Hill, where she crossed the road and made for Smithapark Wood, the pack was there laid on, and as the deer was taking the line generally taken by deer for the forest, the field were hopeful of a moorland run, but this was not to be. Scent was good, and at a fast pace the hounds carried the line over Smithapark and Riddle to Loxhore village. The deer bore away to the right and again down to the River Yeo, near the point where she first left it, and she held a course to Chelfham Mills, down the water to Coxleigh Wood, hounds carrying the line to Kingdon Gardens. They broke out over the top on to Coxleigh Farm, and through Brightley Cott down over the hill, crossing the Shirwell road into the valley leading down to the Playford Paper Mills. Hounds were now racing very hard, the course now to Roborough overlooking the town of Barnstaple. Her she rested amongst some shrubs at the back of Raleigh

House, now turning left handed and came down underneath Mr Basset's farm, Westaway. Here the field had some capital galloping over Mr Basset's meadows, racing the hind in view as far as Bradiford from where she followed the stream to the Braunton road close to Barnstaple. She held the road for some distance down, and just before reaching Strand House she broke over the fence and crossed the Barnstaple–Ilfracombe railway. She was slotted to the water edge of the River Taw, where further there was none. The dangerous river for fording here is well known, but a bold adventurer, Mr Speke, led the way at a point just below Sir William's Salmon Weir. The bulk of the field followed, but on the other side there was no trace of the deer. She must have been gifted with the same forethought as Robert the Bruce, and successfully waded or swam some distance down the river. At any rate the line could not be recovered. Rain came on just now and the Master was reluctantly compelled to abandon the pursuit.
Red Coat

§

2 December 1897

The deer which eluded Sir John Amory's Staghounds on Saturday by swimming away in the Taw near Strand Houses was captured in Appledore Pool on Sunday. Some men walking on the sand hills at Instow disturbed the deer, which bounded into the water and swam towards the pool. The capture was effected by fishermen, who placed their prize in a shed at the Beaver Inn.
Mr Vigors

Mr C. H. Basset, of Westaway, telegraphed on Monday, and on Tuesday the deer was forwarded to Barnstaple, afterwards being transferred to Tiverton. At Appledore the animal was photographed by Miss Pike of Richmond House.

§

7 December 1897
Accident to Mrs Amory

These hounds met at Stoodleigh on Friday, the pack were kennelled at Stoodleigh Manor, while several couple of tufters tried Champells Wood. Several stags were roused but failing to find, the hounds were taken to a cover near Gibbet Moor. The tufters, however, settled on one which took them near to where the pack were kennelled. At this point a regrettable accident put a stop to the day's proceedings. Mrs Amory was galloping round a corner when her horse slipped on some ice with the result that she was thrown on her head. For nearly ten minutes she remained unconscious, and a conveyance being procured from Stoodleigh Court. She was taken to the Court and medical assistance sent for. Mr L. Mackenzie was promptly in attendance to her head and shoulder. We are glad to learn that she is now making favourable progress.

§

21 December 1897
Grand Run and Exciting Finish
Plucky Action by Tiverton Lad

A large field assembled at Knowstone on Saturday. Those present little expected such a run was in store, while the finale was such as has never been witnessed since the formation of the pack. Three and a half couple of tufters were put into Knowstone Wood, where three or four deer were set afoot and after singling out a hind the tufters were stopped at Moortown Farm close to where the pack was kennelled. Hounds were put on the line on good terms with their quarry and carried it at a rapid pace across Rackenford Moor and through Bickam Cover. From here the hind directed her course to Waspleigh Wood (Mr Coles' preserve, where so many deer have been found both this season and last) and down to Chain Bridge. Here she turned, and after travelling some distance up the iron mill stream went over the ridge past Stuckeridge and away down to the Exe opposite Wonham. After proceeding down the river for about half a mile the hind travelled through Westbrook Wood, then went out over the top and pointed as if for Bampton. However, she soon changed her mind and re-entered Westbrook. Leaving here the hunted one led hounds to Duvale, then went up the valley to the Batherum, almost into Bampton. Turning left-handed the deer paid a second visit to Wonham, then going round the hill she ran the whole length of Westbrook Wood with the hounds following the line down to the Exe near Half Penny Bridge. Keeping close by the river the deer led the pack at a rattling pace until almost opposite Cove House then crossed to the left bank she passed close by the house and hounds ran fast into Bickleigh Wood, Cove. From here the line left over an earth into which the Tiverton Foxhounds had just driven a fox, and seven or eight couple of that pack, as well as a number of the field, joined in pursuit of the deer. The foxhounds however, after travelling a short distance, refused to follow the line, but not so the sportsmen who had just joined in this chase. Emerging from Bickleigh Wood, Cove, the quarry next went down to Fairby and up to the fishponds. Going out over the hill to Marley the animal went on to Knightshayes and across to Chettiscombe. Here the line turned and coming back over the park crossed the railway line between Bolham and Tiverton. Crossing the volunteer range and the Bolham road, close by the turnpike gate, the deer entered the Exe near Worth. Going downstream she landed at the Castle gardens and jumped a high wall into Captain Moore's stable yard. Here the animal was cornered and as she was in close proximity to the town the Master took the pack some distance away and had the quarry liberated in one of Mr Bidgood Haydon's fields. As soon as she was free the deer struck out across the volunteer range and over the railway line near Bolham. Returning she made for the Exe and on carrying the line into the race field hounds caught a view of their prey in the water. The deer again swam down as far as the Castle where she was killed. Then followed a novel and exciting scene: the animal continued to float downstream when a lad named John Stuckey, who was in a field by the side of the river known as Ham, endeavoured to bring the carcass ashore. He lost no time in divesting himself off his clothes and dived into the water opposite Mr Watkins' garden. At this spot the water is of considerable depth and the current was much stronger than usual. From here to Exe Bridge is a distance of from a hundred and fifty to two hundred yards, and the plucky lad swam the whole way before he caught up to the animal. The body got caught in a snag, but Stuckey managed to free it when it again floated with the current. Meanwhile a large and excited crowd had collected on Exe Bridge who could see the lad was becoming exhausted. A number of people shouted to him to endeavour to land, but on getting below the bridge he managed to get hold of one of the animal's ears not far from mid-stream. He then made his way to a landing known as Broads Court, West Exe South, towing the deer. This was no easy task with such a strong current, but the plucky little fellow managed to accomplish it with the assistance of a couple of residents in the Court, Mr Land and Mrs Grant who held out a line prop which the lad when near enough was able to grasp and he thus landed, dragging the dead animal and closely followed by several hounds. Stuckey was taken into Mrs Grant's house where everything was done to prevent his catching cold. Meanwhile Mr C. De las Casas had obtained a boat from Mr O. B. Chown, and rowing to the spot, took charge of the deer. Stuckey's clothes were soon afterwards brought to him, and after dressing he was able to leave Mrs Grant's house, feeling nothing the worse for his emersion. The carcass was afterwards taken to the estate office, here the lad was complimented by the Master – who in addition to others rewarded him for his plucky action. People frantically shouted for a boat to be sent out to him, and several entered the yard of the White Ball Hotel to go to his assistance in a boat belonging to Mr Chown, which was moored behind his premises. The lad John Stuckey, whose exhibition of pluck is on everybody's lips, is a son of Mr John Stuckey, a factory operative of Melbourne Street. He is just sixteen. Relating his story to the *Tiverton Gazette* afterwards to the following effect. "At about 3 o'clock I was near Mr Farrant's stables when I saw the hounds hunting the deer which was then making for the Exe. She entered the river just above the Black Bridge in the race field, then with several others I went down to the leat just above Loughborough Cottages, we crossed the bridge and got on the banks of the Exe where we followed the hind to Exleigh. When opposite Mr Watkins' garden I took off my clothes and dived in after the deer but was unable to get at it until just under the Exe Bridge where the carcass was stopped by some brambles. I managed to set it free when it was again carried on by the current. On the other side I managed to get hold of its ear with one hand and with the other struck across to the back of the gardens at Broads Court. Here I was assisted by Mr Land and Mrs Grant who had obtained a line prop which I managed to get hold of when near enough. I was then taken into Mrs Grant's house where everything was done to guard against my catching a cold and my clothes soon after being brought to me, I dressed and have felt nothing the worse since."

§

14 February 1899
Sir John Amory's Staghounds

On Wednesday these hounds met by invitation of Mr Sanders at Chipstable Cross in the Devon and Somerset country. Hounds and horses were conveyed by special train from Tiverton, and in spite of the torrents of rain that was falling, a large field turned up at the fixture to welcome this sporting pack upon its first visit to this part of the country. Deer have been lying in Mr Capel's Coverts for some time, and upon Mr Amory's arrival Goss was able to report to him that two hinds had been in the big Covert close to Bulland Lodge in the early morning. Hounds soon picked up the line and ran steadily across the moor and into the young larch plantation on the opposite side of the hill. There they ran up to the deer, and, coming away in view of two magnificent hinds, they ran them at racing pace across some heathery moors into St John Davies Coverts at Bittiscombe, where the deer separated, and hounds stuck to one of them and pushed her, still almost in view, through these steep Coverts out on to Skilgate Moor, and along its entire length into Haddon. They gave her no time to dwell here, but ran her up on to Haddon Moor and as hounds passed Goss's Cottage, Mr Amory, without the loss of a moment, had out the other half of the pack that had been kennelled here, instead of being taken to Wiveliscombe, and laid them on with the leading hounds. On over the length of Haddon Moor they raced, horses having all they could do to live with them to Wynne Corner, down through the Covert and across the water, and up to Baron's Down into the Exe valley, and so into Exe Cleave. Here unfortunately, they ran into fresh deer, and drove the herd before them into Pixton Park and through the whole herd of Lord Carnarvon's fallow deer, out of the Park and back into Exe Cleave. The leading hounds stuck to the hunted hind and ran her through Exe Cleave, up over Court Down, and along the top of the hill to Red Cleave, through it, and to Winsford village, here she turned and came down the Exe valley, now in the water, and now along the overhanging Coverts, until, between Hele Bridge and weir, they killed her at 3.30. She proved to be a very large hind, and must have been an uncommonly strong one, as she stood before the hounds from 11 o'clock until 3.30, and the pace at which they ran her most of the way was a caution to those who, like myself, without anything more than a superficial knowledge of the country, and without any great knowledge of this most fascinating and wildest form of hunting. Great credit is due to Mr Amory who hunts these hounds himself, for the quickness with which he rode up to his hounds, across the almost unridable (in the ordinary acceptation of the word) country, and for the perseverance with which he worked through all the difficulties which confronted him until at length he had the satisfaction of bringing his deer to hand. I was astonished also to find the pace of which these great hounds get over the ground, they seem to be travelling at their ease over the heather, and not to be going at their best pace ever, and it is not until one tries to keep pace with them over the big moors that one realises the speed at which they are actually getting over the ground

West Somerset in the field

§

14 March 1899

On Saturday the meet was at Spurway Mill. Miles, the harbourer, reported that a herd of deer were moving on towards Rackenford. Hounds being kennelled, Mr Amory trotted off with three and a half couple of tufters and laid them on. A line just beyond Broadmead Cottage came up with a herd of 13 deer lying in Withy Croft, they made off over Lower Meadown on to Sydenham, where they divided, four of them turning back towards Meadown Cover, where the tufters ran. One deer now singled out and ran through Trowcombe Wood, Warbrightly Covers to Aldridge Mill, where the pack was laid on. The deer pointed for Coleford Water, but turning, ran back to the valley under Aldridge Mill and right down to Chain Bridge, through the covers to Cove, where he ran a ring back to Duvale turning sharp back to Cove again on to Newbridge, through Washfield Covers, taking the water at Fairby, he ran down the river to Lithecourt and on under Worth House, through the lawn, skirting Palmers village, on to Lurley. Then over Mr J Butts and Courtenay Farms, pointing for Loxbeare Barton, through which we ran close by the farmhouse, then on to Gibbett Moor down to Blatchworthy Cover, under Rifterwood to Coleford Water, going down stream to Aldridge Mills, again running down to Chain Bridge, where our deer went to water and was killed after one of the best runs of the season. Time three and a quarter hours. One of the most prominent during the run, and who was also in at the death was the worthy Master Sir John Amory.
Whalebone

§

11 April 1899

These hounds met again in their own country on Saturday last after some weeks hunting in the Devon and Somerset country, where they have been very successful, having killed I hear, no less than 20 deer, north of their own boundary. A large field numbering between 80 and 100 horsemen, turned to welcome them on their arrival at West Worlington. At 11 o'clock the Master appeared with the hounds, who looked in the pink of condition and certainly none the worse for the hard work they have been doing lately. The harbourer reported seven stags to be in Weekson Wood, and thither hounds were taken, being kennelled at Week Farm. The deer were soon found, and tufters settled on to a fine stag and ran him in full view of the whole field to Week Corner and back to Bycott. Here tufters were stopped and the pack was brought on, and getting away on good

terms with him they ran him at a pace that was too great for many of those who were out by Stone Moor, Chawleigh Barton Wood, Chulmleigh, to the big covers opposite Eggesford House, the residence of Lord Portsmouth. When he had led us almost to the end of these covers, he seemed to change his point and turned sharp back. Hounds were not to be put off the line by this manoeuvre but, working out the double as closely as a pack of harriers, they drove him back past Eggesford Station, across the river, and away to Chulmleigh. Here the pace was even faster than ever and it was all that most of us could do to see which way the best mounted members of the field were going, and they in their turn were hard put to it to keep the Master in sight, and how he managed to keep in touch with all his hounds at the pace they were going, over the most difficult country, was a matter of wonder to all of us. However he did manage to do this, and after the fastest two hours run that it has ever been my good fortune to ride through, he reached the River Mole with his hounds by South Molton Road Station, and found the stag in the water in front of them. The stag went down the river for about a quarter of a mile and so into the Taw, here he was taken. The next business was to get home, hounds must have had over 20 miles back to kennels and your correspondent not less.
Mid Devon Editor

§

24 October 1899

Sir John Heathcoat Amory's staghounds were last week hunting the Quantocks being kennelled at Quantock Lodge, the seat of Mr E. J. Stanley MP. It was a cold cheerless morning when Mr Ian Amory brought his hounds up to Triscombe Stone at eleven o'clock on Monday morning and there was at that time a large field to welcome him, but by the time the pack had been kennelled at Quantock Farm and the tufters brought out there was quite a big muster. Amongst the earliest arrivals were the Messrs De las Casas, in pink, acting as whips, the hounds having previously arrived at Mr E. J. Stanley's. Barber reported deer in various places, and it was decided to put the tufters in Cocker Combe and almost immediately they roused a big stag, with three and four a top, which broke over Flurry Down in full view into Great Wood. Whether the hounds got on a fresh line, or whether he turned back under Quantock Lodge is not quite certain, but the hounds took a deer back to Cocker Combe. After a considerable time a good stag was viewed again across Flurry Down, and this time he set his neck straight across for the Stowey road side, sinking the various Coombes without a check. The tufters were stopped in the Stowey road and the pack laid on. They took up the line at once, and ran well through a wood over Woodlands Hill by Haymands Pond and up over Hare Knaps. Here there was a check for a few minutes, but the hounds soon picked up the line, and raced him again over Alfoxton and Pardleston down to the fields pointing for Quantoxhead, where he took to the beach and ran by the tide for some distance towards St Audries, but climbing the cliffs, he took up position and defied his pursuers. A rope was obtained, and whilst an attempt was made to throw it over his head he dodged his pursuers, and ran further down the cliffs, but was eventually taken after considerable trouble. He proved a five year old deer, with brow bay and two long points a top on each side. On Tuesday nothing was done, the meet was again at Triscombe Stone, many deer were on foot but it was not until very late in the afternoon that a warrantable stag could be got away. He went in the direction of Halsway but no kill was affected.

§

13 February 1900

On Wednesday these hounds met at Gidley Arms, the weather had been so severe that no one imagined that the hounds would be able to hunt. However at 12 o'clock Mr Amory determined to make the attempt, and hounds were taken to Mr Murch's at Mouseberry and there kennelled. The field was not a large one, consisting as it did – in addition to the two whips – there was only Mr Renton, Mr Dunsford and Mr John Selley of Hilltown – a very different sized field from that which generally turns out to meet these hounds when they hunt in that part of the country. Miller had harboured three young stags in Week Cover, where tufters quickly found them, and, after one turn around by Odam Moor and the Gidley Arms, they drove one of them through West Week and in the Weekson Wood where they were stopped, and at 1.30 the pack was laid on. Hounds soon settled onto the line and in Bycott Wood fresh found their deer. They went away over Horridge Moor, and leaving Chulmleigh on the left made for South Molton Road Station and on through King's Nympton Park, across the River Mole to the village of Chittlehamholt. There they swung right handed and made their way straight to Lord Fortescue's coverts at Castle Hill. In the River Bray which runs through the park they fresh found their stag and raced him through the deer park with its herd of fallow deer to Filleigh Station and down beside the Devon and Somerset railway to Swimbridge near which they crossed the line, and going by Fenscott and Stoke Rivers found themselves

in the country usually hunted by these hounds during their visit to Barnstaple. It was now rapidly becoming dark and it seemed probable want of light would again – as it did just a week ago – put an end to the run before the stag could be killed, but in this instance so unsatisfactory a finish was not destined to take place. Hounds were heard (at the time it was hardly possible to see them) to be baying their stag in the River Yeo, and at 6.30 he was killed at Bratton Cross in exactly the same spot as the last stag that was accounted for in the Autumn when the hounds were at Barnstaple. He proved to be a young stag with brow, bay and uprights. Hounds were now 30 miles from their kennel, so it was decided to stay the night at Barnstaple. The run was a wonderful one, lasting as it did from 1.30 till 6.30 and covering such an extent of country. How many miles were traversed by hounds in the course of the run it is impossible of course to estimate, but the distance measured straight across the map from the point where the stag was found to the place where he was killed was 15 miles, and anyone who is accustomed to riding up and down Devonshire coombes, whether along the roads, on a bike, or across the fields on a horse will know how much be allowed on this score, in addition to which, naturally, the stag made many points in the course of the run, which were considerably out of the straight line, from Week to Bratton Cross.
Roadster

§

16 March 1900
Staghunting near Barnstaple

Dear Sir – Will you kindly allow me through your columns to say how sorry I am not able to hunt today at Chelfham Bridge and tomorrow at Loxhore Cott.

I have received a telegram yesterday evening – too late to make the news generally known – saying that Miss Chichester definitely forbade either hounds or horsemen to cross any part of her Arlington property, and requiring me – under threat of an immediate application for an injunction – to give an undertaking that her wishes in this matter should be observed.

Under these conditions, hunting the Barnstaple country becomes an impossibility, and no alternative was left me but – most reluctantly – to abandon the meets.

I am, Sir yours truly
Ian H Amory
Hensleigh, Tiverton, Devon

22 March 1900

Owing to action taken by Miss Chichester, of Arlington Court, the meets of Sir John Amory's Staghounds arranged for Friday and Saturday in the Barnstaple district were abandoned. Two years ago it became known that Miss Chichester wished to provide a "sanctuary" for wild deer on her estate, notice being given that hunting would not be allowed on any part of the demesne. This embargo stopped the meets for a time, as the Arlington coverts are situated in the heart of the staghunting district on the Barnstaple side of Exmoor. But the sport is so popular in the locality that it was decided to have meets and trust to the hunted stag keeping outside the prescribed area. Several splendid runs were enjoyed, and in the hope that fortune would be again favourable four meets were arranged for last week. Unfortunately, both on Tuesday and Wednesday the quarry entered Arlington grounds, the stag hunted on Tuesday being actually brought to bay and killed in the Arlington pond. Miss Chichester promptly communicated with her solicitors, who on Thursday gave Mr Ian Amory, the Master, notice that unless he gave an undertaking that the Arlington estate should not be trespassed upon an injunction would be applied for. This practically left Mr Amory no alternative, and so he cancelled the remaining fixtures. He was unable to give a public intimation to this effect, and consequently large numbers of persons made their way on Friday to the rendezvous – only to find there was no meet. Many ladies and gentlemen came to Barnstaple from Tiverton, Bideford and elsewhere with horses in the hope of participating in the sport. And so it is scarcely surprising that the incident has caused great irritation in hunting circles throughout the district. Experts consider that so long as Miss Chichester takes this stand there is no hope of Barnstaple becoming a recognised staghunting centre.

§

17 April 1900

Sir John Amory's staghounds met at Haddon on Saturday. The weather was delightful, and a large field on horseback, on wheels, and on foot met Mr Ian Amory on his arrival punctually at 11 o'clock. Goss, the harbourer, had left word at the meet that it was necessary to go and hunt a large herd of deer that had for some time past been doing great damage near Chipstable. However, as the chances were so very strong that when found, these deer would come back to the Haddon Coverts

– their natural and abiding home – Mr Amory took only a few hounds with him on his five mile trot, and left the pack and the hunt horses at Goss's Cottage on Haddon, together with many members of the most constant and most knowing of staghunters. It was agreed by the latter that those who were left would not have to wait more than an hour before they would have the whole panorama of the hunt unfolded before them. First the deer, then the hounds, and then finally those (in their opinion) deluded sportsmen who had made up their minds to take the necessary 10 mile journey to Chipstable and back, would be observed toiling along far behind the hounds and wishing that they had had the whit to remain quietly on the vantage point at the further end of Skilgate Common.

The best laid schemes O' mice and men
Gang aft agley;
And leave us nought but grief and pain
For promised joy

For it would seem that the above plan had not been submitted for the approval of the hind, or if so that she did not fulfil her part of the bargain. For no sooner had the tufters found her in one of Mr Capel's large coverts near Bulland Lodge than she set her head deliberately east instead of west, and passing close to Wiveliscombe crossed the Devon and Somerset railway about a mile to the west of that town, took a sweep out into the country beyond, and crossed back again about halfway between Wiveliscombe and Milverton. From this point she led the hunt over some intricate country and was finally killed at 2.30 within half a mile of Crowcombe Station, after a fine run of two and three quarter hours and about 15 miles from the meet. The inspiration which seized this hind to go out into that country was a most unfortunate one for all those who had gone up to Haddon and waited there, but in hunting, the deer has the choice of routes, and where he goes the hounds must follow, sometimes he decided well, but sometimes, as in this case, badly for those who had come out to see him.
Easter Egg

§

1 January 1901

These hounds met in spring-like weather by invitation at Haddon on Boxing Day. The pack was kennelled at Goss's Cottage and with five and a half couple of tufters Mr Amory drew the deer park for 17 deer seen there in the morning. These were bustled about up and down Haddon Woods and several were gone away to the allotments and back across Skilgate Common into Harford Cleave, where the Master laid on the pack on three hinds. After running down to Bury and back to the deer park, one hind went away for Skilgate Common onto the Bittiscombe Coverts, away to Chipstable passing close to Waterrow and straight onto Wiveliscombe. Through Wiveliscombe town and on for a couple of miles to some mills where this fine hind was taken soon after 2 pm. The run was a grand one, and it was only the best mounted who were able to live with them, it was a 10 mile point and much further as hounds ran. The pack was trained from Wiveliscombe.

§

8 January 1901

On Wednesday hounds met at Gidley Arms, Meshaw. The harbourers had found seven stags in Stone Moor plantation, and as they were unable to report that any hinds were to be found in that district, the Master decided to run one of these stags, the more readily as they had already made rather a long stay upon the farm of these good sportsmen, the Messrs Cobley at Bealy Court. Accordingly hounds were kennelled at Bealy Court and with two and a half couple of tufters Mr Amory soon raised the stags who came out to Mouticombe Moor in full view of the large field of farmers who had assembled. A good six year old deer soon separated himself from the others. In a moment all the tufters were stopped from the others and laid on to this line and Mr De las Casas had gone back to Bealy Court for the pack. After running for about a mile on to Winswood Moor, the tufters were stopped and in about twenty minutes the pack arrived and was laid on. It was now 11.30 and until 4.30 we were hard at work, engaged in what may truly be called one of the great runs of staghunting, a run worthy to be handed down in history as one of the historical chases of that wildest of sports. They ran across Winswood Moor into East Cheldon Wood across the valley and up the opposite side over Affeton Moor, and through Affeton Cover into the valley of the Dart by Worlingon village, down this valley hounds ran for a mile or so with hardly a pause, sometimes in the water and sometimes out of it, then left-handed they swung up through Burridge Wood and out over the hill at the top and across the Chawleigh and Witheridge road. A right-handed turn brought us after a few miles into the Lapford Covers, down through which hounds ran at a racing pace as if they would drive him straight across both river and railway, but close to the latter he turned again to the right, and threading the Eggesford Covers he crossed the River Taw under the railway bridge close to Chawleigh Week Mill.

Here occurred our first check, and most of us were not very sorry for a few minutes in which our horses might recover their wind. But by casting down one bank of the river, which was in full flood and back the other, Mr Amory soon hit off the line and away we went up the Rashleigh Valley and on to Beechington Cover, Labdon, and Bransgrove to Winkleigh Wood, where another short check unfortunately took place. But hounds finally worked out the line where the deer had gone up a stream and back again, and had left the cover on the same side upon which he had entered it. Then followed some slower hunting which was perhaps fortunate, for the field much reduced as it was in size, and without anyone who had ever crossed this somewhat intricate country before, on by Herdwick to the Taw, just under Bondleigh village. Here our stag had gone downstream for half a mile or more, but hounds, without any waste of time, hit off the line and began to run hard again, showing that we were a bit nearer to him than we had been for the last few miles. On they went over some very difficult country to Ashridge House, less than a mile from North Tawton and within about four miles of Dartmoor. Here they fresh found him and raced him back to the Taw where he had crossed it before and at 4.30 was taken. The field was then fairly select, for besides the huntsmen and whips, out of all those who started there were only four present. It is impossible to give any accurate idea of the distance traversed during this run but that the hounds and the hunt horses did a good day's work will be evident from the fact that from Ashridge House, where the stag was fresh found, to the kennels is 27 miles by the shortest road, so that they had merely gone straight there and straight back they would have covered 54 miles, but the place at which they met is far out of the straight line, and it goes without saying, that the various points made by the stag during the run were many miles apart and in many different directions. At the finish of their day's work proper, hounds, horses, huntsmen and whips had a trot of twenty five miles back to the kennel which was reached at 11.15 pm, hounds and horses having left at 7 am that morning.
West Country Man

§

26 February 1901
Deer Damage Fund

At a meeting of the deer damage committee connected with Sir John Amory's staghounds the resignations of the Hon. Secretary Mr Lewis Mackenzie and Hon. Treasurer Mr E.C. Nicholetts, were submitted and accepted. Mr Mackenzie expressed his regret that owing to the numerous claims upon his time, he was unable to continue the duties of his office and Mr Nicholetts explained by letter that his removal from the town necessitated his resignation of the position of Hon. Treasurer. Mr T.O. Lazenby, Eastfield was then unanimously elected as both Hon. Treasurer and Secretary. All claims therefore in the future for damage done by the deer must be addressed to Mr Lazenby whom also the subscriptions to the funds be remitted.

§

The James Jackson Ure Silver Slot

A while ago, Ruth Ure from Suffolk got in contact with me to say that she had a Sir John Amory slot with a silver top which she had inherited from her father, James Jackson Ure. As well as an inscription of where it was taken, there is also a monogram with his initials on the top. Ruth went on to say that although James had a brother, John Andrew Ure, she thinks it is her father's monogram as her father came to London from Scotland when he was quite young. The mount was made by Deacon and Francis, Birmingham, and the inscription is as follows.

Sir John Amory's Staghounds
2nd April 1904
Met – Haddon
Found – Deer Park
Killed – Wiveliscombe

§

2 April 1904, Sir John Amory's Staghounds

(The run in connection with the above silver slot and photographs on page 49.)

On Saturday there was a large field at the meet at Haddon, tufters drove a herd of hinds from Wind Corner back to the deer park, and up and down for a couple of hours or more. The pack was eventually laid onto a deer on Skilgate Common. Turning short back into the deer park she ran down past Harford Mill and into Venn Wood. Hounds raced her through Westhill and Upton Wood and back again through the deer park and onto Skilgate Common once more. Running the whole length of the common she entered Sir John Ferguson Davie's coverts at Bittiscombe and made a wide ring as if for Venn Cross, but turning back by way of Chipstable village and Waterrow she came close to the residence of that noted staghunter Mr Froude Hancock, fresh finding the deer was then taken close to Wiveliscombe.

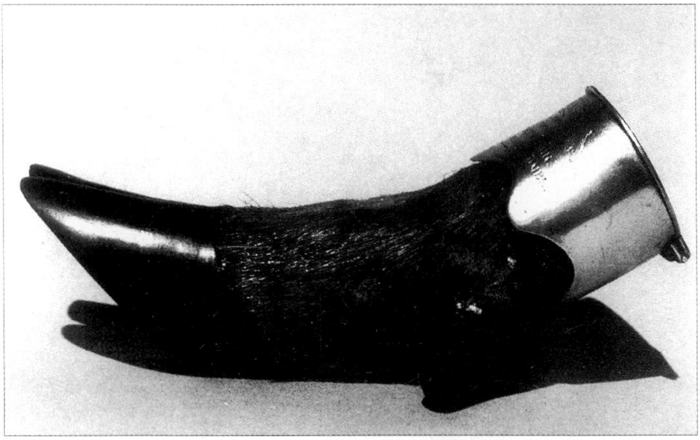

Right and above:
The James Jackson Ure
Silver Slot
2 April 1904

20 December 1904
Staghounds at Culmstock

Good days seem to be the rule with this pack this year, but Saturday's run will not soon be forgotten by those who rode through it. The meet was at Aldridge Mills and by reason of the fact that the Tiverton Foxhounds met at Hensleigh to draw Mr Amory's coverts the field was not a large one. It included only those who prefer a day with the staghounds to the rival attraction of a day's foxhunting. The pack was kennelled at Spurway Mills and Mr Amory drew Wormsworthy and Nethercott Coverts blank, but in Down Wood tufters soon found a young stag and as the time was getting late the pack was laid on and away they went with a dash. This young stag took quite an unusual line going away over the hill as if Anstey was his point. Soon changing his mind, however, he swung around right-handed and came back by Oakford, making for Stuckeridge and the Exe near Chain Bridge, then right-handed again by Bryants Copse and Highwood Plain down through the scrub, across the railway and river, then up by Cove and Marwood to Van Post and the Cobbacombe Coverts, then right-handed by Plushayes, where on his own farm we picked up Mr Blackmore Junior, who to judge by the way in which he rode through the remainder of this run bids fair to rival his father as a good guide to follow over the roughest part of any country. Away by Huntsham Wood and Bere Down to Ashbrittle, Appley Village, Greenham and Hoolacombe we reached White Ball, over which hounds ran as if they meant to go to Wellington monument, but the stag was evidently turned by a man who was ploughing and bearing right-handed we found ourselves in the neighbourhood of the Burlescombe Quarries. The stag soiled in the canal near here and led hounds straight through the big coverts by Maiden Down and over the Down itself, then down the valley by Prescott to Culmstock. Here hounds fairly ran up to him and catching a view raced him over the Vale and to the river where he was killed. The pack was laid on at 11.20 and ran with scarcely any check until 3 o'clock. The extent of the country covered must have been great, the distance from the point where the stag was found to the point where he was killed measured straight across the map is 14 miles, but if a measurement could be taken of the line hounds ran it would certainly be found not to be less than double the distance. It must surely be many years ago since the staghounds were seen in Culmstock village.

§

15 February 1906
Sir John Amory's Staghounds at Eggesford
Tufters Lost in Snow Storm

Kennelled overnight at the Fox and Hounds, 17 couples of these hounds, all looking in the pink of condition, and which have already this season accounted for close on 30 stags, met at Eggesford on Saturday. Up to a very short time ago stags were numerous around Eggesford, and it was only a few days since that 10 stags deserted Mr Vivian's Lapford Wood, having been disturbed there by a rabbiting party. Five stags and a fox also crossed the path in full view of Mr Augustus Luxton while shooting with Mr Martin of Collaton, a short time ago. Thus disturbed, the keepers could give out very little hope of a certain find in the near Vicinity. At 10.35 am however, Ernest Hellard (Kennel Huntsman) set hounds on the move in response to a wire sent him by the worthy master Mr Ian Amory to bring them on to the Chawleigh village where hounds were held up at the Barton. By this time harbourer Miller had arrived, having located a stag in the Molland Woods. It was however a most miserable morning, for in addition to the very keen wind blowing, rain and sleet fell heavily at intervals. Not withstanding this however a fairly large field turned out. On being laid on, the five tufters set to work at once by rattling over the hills to Rowsley, when they doubled back on to the ball cover. From here they turned right-handed over to the Cotton Hayes. By this time the field found themselves well into the teeth of a drifting snow storm of sleet and rain and a very thick mist also enveloped both Valley and hill, blotting out the view so much so that the tufters became lost. They had vanished but where no one knew. On the pack being brought up to Cotton Hayes no tidings of the tufters beyond that they had passed on an hour before, going then in the direction of Stone Moor, could be gleaned. Seeing this the worthy Master thought it best to make a by-cast, the pack being taken from Bearly Court through to Stone Moor to Chawleigh, from thence to Eggesford, where they galloped down the turnpike on to Hansford. The cast was made with the chance of hounds hitting the line off, but it proved unsuccessful and at 3.30 at Hansford the pack were held up and the field dispersed for home, leaving both tufters and stag somewhere unknown.

§

20 March 1906

Meeting at Worlington on Wednesday week, they found their deer near the Gidley Arms and killed near Yarnscombe, no one thought that another such day was in store for them the next time they were out. But this was so, and many of the followers of these hounds who were present at the meet at Worlington on Saturday had to cry off some time before the finish. The pack was kennelled at Mr S. Vicary's, Cheldon Barton, whilst Mr Ian Amory trotted the tufters off to draw Burridge Wood. The tufters ran merrily up the valley to Affeton old plantation, where they turned up through Cotton Hayes across the moor to Broadmoor, then in to the Wick Covert, turning up over the big Odam Moors and coming into Ball Cover. Crossing the road into Waterloo, he came down the valley through Wixon, into the Stone Moor covers, and crossed the Chulmleigh road. Mr Amory now let the pack go coming down to the Dart by the rifle range at Sydeham, hounds ran down the valley past Chulmleigh Bridge, turned out over into the Eggesford Covers, by way of Upcott and Southercott, then up the valley nearly to Chenson, on towards Foxes Covert, by way of Upcott and Southercott, then up the valley nearly to Chenson, on towards Foxes Covert and came back to the River Dart, with two deer in front, which separated in Chawleigh Barton Wood. One went away to the Stone Moor covers, the other ran down past Stone Mills, where hounds were laid on again, running up the valley, through Leigh Wood and Burridge, they crossed the road into the Lapford Woods by way of Pouncers, then down through Chenson Wood, Foxes Covert and Southcott, hounds ran past Eggesford Station to Chawleigh Week. Down to the River Taw and crossing the railway just by Colleton, our deer began to run short, back again we went into Bourne Wood, around which they 'scurried' him several times. Breaking at last, he crossed the road nearly jumping over the head of the Hon. secretary of the deer damage fund, and then went out over the top, after sinking the valley again, he ran over Bidivin Moor nearly into Ashreigney, through Ashwood then across still more enclosed country, he brought us to Burrington Moor. Leaving Burrington on our right, hounds drove along across several rough valleys, nearly to Roborough, then onto High Bickington. After running nearly through the village hounds turned away right-handed, it was now getting dark but hounds were still running hard, most of the field had cried off, their horses had had enough. From this point there was no one with the hounds except the Master and Ernest. Still running they went on towards Langly Ford, the furthest point hounds ran last Wednesday week. After crossing the stream they ran nearly into Yarnscombe, but keeping left-handed crossed the road into the covers at Cranford Cross. It was now 7.45, they went into Stevenstone Covers on past High Bullen, a holla forward luckily allowing Ernest to get to their heads as they were just crossing the road into Stevenstone Park where they were stopped. It was now after 8 o'clock and there began a long tramp back to Eggesford which was not reached until nearly midnight.

§

28 August 1906
Mr Ian Amory as Huntsman

A writer in *The World* has the following reference to Mr Ian Amory in an article on the Devon and Somerset and their history, just now the change of Masters is engaging everyone's attention in the west for the Master of the Devon and Somerset occupies a unique position. Mr R.A. Sanders though not connected with the West Country, except by marriage, had held office both long and successfully. He has been ably aided in Sidney Tucker his huntsman, though he was the first Master to hunt the staghounds himself. Mr Amory, a born huntsman with a rare knack of getting to his hounds in a strange county, now hunts Sir John Amory's staghounds pack from Tiverton, while Mr E.A.V. Stanley goes straight as a die when hunting the Quantock pack, between these two naturally lay the succession, but though the former's choice would have been universally popular, when he gave away to his younger Confrere staghunters congratulated themselves on having such an excellent second string to the bow.

§

6 November 1906
Sir John Amory's Staghounds Meet for the First Time in Tiverton

A bye meet was held at the Tiverton Town Hall by special invitation of the Mayor on Friday last, to hunt a stag that had been seen in the Exe Valley just below Tiverton on several occasions during the last few weeks. It was a first time that a meet of staghounds had ever taken place in the town, and as a result the event created a considerable amount of interest among the town folk. Regular followers of the hounds were more interested because the stag they met to hunt was believed to be the one which led a large field such a merry chase after the meet at Knightshayes Court last month.

Horsemen and pedestrians began to assemble outside the Town Hall at 12.30 pm and by 1 o'clock the hour fixed for the meet, there was almost as big a crowd in Fore Street as there was when the result of the Parliamentary election was made known in January last. The windows of the Town Hall, the Angel Hotel and all the houses in the locality were thronged with interested spectators, while all the photographers in the neighbourhood were busy taking snapshots of the stirring scenes being enacted in the street below.

Sir John and Lady Heathcoat Amory attended the meet in their carriage. Mrs Ian Heathcoat Amory and party came in a motor car. Among those on foot were the Mayor and Mayoress Mr and Mrs H. Mudford. Excitement ruled high when the kennel huntsman Mr E. Hellard brought 16½ couple of hounds from the Angel Hotel where they had been kennelled while the field was assembling. The Master made a brief speech to the foot people for whose convenience the meet had been held at 1 o'clock. He mentioned it was very kind of Mr Peace to allow hounds to go into the coverts within a few days of the holding of a shooting party, and expressed the hope that everyone would do their best not to disturb the game. If the field got a view of the deer he hoped they would not shout all at once or the hounds would not know which way to go.

After these few remarks the Master turned his horse into St. Andrew Street and the field moved off in the direction of Holwell Combe, where the deer had been lying all morning. The pack was kennelled at Mr Heard's farm while the tufters were thrown into the Combe where the deer emerged, a youth named Leonard Harres of John Street found himself much too close to be comfortable, the deer jumping clean over his head. After running in a ring around the farm the deer jumped into a turnip field, and made his way in view of a number of foot people, who had assembled on Exeter Hill, up the grassy slopes towards the road to Butterleigh. The ease with which he cleared the hedge into the road and the one on the further side was a revelation to those who had not seen a stag hunted before. With the pack on they streamed over the road and up the meadow to the left of Gogwell Lane, and thence to Higher Warnicombe crossing the road, hereabouts the deer lead hounds into and through Thorn's Copse and into the valley beyond leaving Brithembottom on the left and then bearing right-handed till he came to Morstone Barton.

Running on towards Cullompton railway station he crossed the railway near Five Bridges, and then took practically the same line as he did when last hunted. Reaching Bradfield Park he tried all sorts of dodges in the hope of shaking off his pursuers, but hounds stuck to him and eventually forced him out at the top end of the woods. Thence the line lay through Kentisbeare to the Black Down Hills, and over a furse clad moorland, where there was plenty of grief owing to horses putting their feet into rabbit holes. The field had become smaller by degrees and beautifully less when after galloping over this delightful stretch of country for several miles, hounds began to descend to the lowlands beyond. Of those who were still in the running very few had the slightest knowledge of the country they were riding through, as they raced on towards the Wolford Lodge estate and on between Honiton and Luppitt, the end came just as it was getting dark at Mohuns Ottery, four miles north east of Honiton.

Considering the distance traversed there were a fair number in at the end, including Miss Amory, Miss Wynter, Miss Chichester and Mrs Pugsley. After the morte had been sounded all who had stayed out this remarkable run rode on into Honiton where the arrival of so many horsemen and horsewomen caused no little excitement. One or two caught a train to Exeter, but the majority some 40 or 50 in number, came home by road leaving Honiton at 7 o'clock and arriving in Tiverton from 10 o'clock onwards.

'Greeting the Master' A meet at Chawleigh
(From the *Illustrated Sporting News* 12 October 1907)

"Mutual Surprise"
An incident with Sir John Amory's Staghounds, drawn by Lionel Edwards
(From *The Illustrated Sporting and Dramatic News* 5 October 1907)
(© By kind permission of the executors of Lionel Edwards)

Sir John Amory's Staghounds were established in 1896, at the suggestion of a Master of the Devon and Somerset Staghounds, for the purpose of hunting that country over which the deer were spreading in ever-increasing numbers, but which it was not convenient, owing to distance and other reasons, for the Devon and Somerset pack to cover. The incident depicted above took place in the long woods which lie on either side of the beautiful Lyn. A hunted stag, after giving a good gallop over Exmoor, "soiled" in the Lyn.

Refreshed by his bath, he climbed once more into the woods, cantering back along the path by which he had come. Turning a corner, he came suddenly face to face with some of the field. The surprise was mutual! The horses snorted and plunged, and the crowd hastened to give his antlered lordship the right of road. A stag, indeed, could give a man or horse a terrible wound with his sharp brow antlers, and such accidents, according to local gossip, have actually taken place. Horses seem to have a natural antipathy to deer. A tired hunter, or even the quietest old crock, will shy and plunge at the sudden appearance of a stag. In the present case, after surveying the crowd for a few seconds, the deer turned sharply to the left, and crashed downwards through the woods to the river again, where some twenty minutes later he was killed.

Sir John Amory's Staghounds at the Gidley Arms near Meshaw on 2 April 1907. The Gidley Arms is now a private residence called Gidley House

Photographs of the Gidley Arms Meet 1907.
Above is possibly Ernest Hellard (Kennel huntsman) or one of the De las Casas (whips).

Left: Mr Amory. A meet at Chawleigh (From the *Illustrated Sporting and Dramatic News* 12 October 1907)

Above: A meet of the Sir John Amory Staghounds at Chawleigh (from the *Illustrated Sporting News* 12 October 1907)

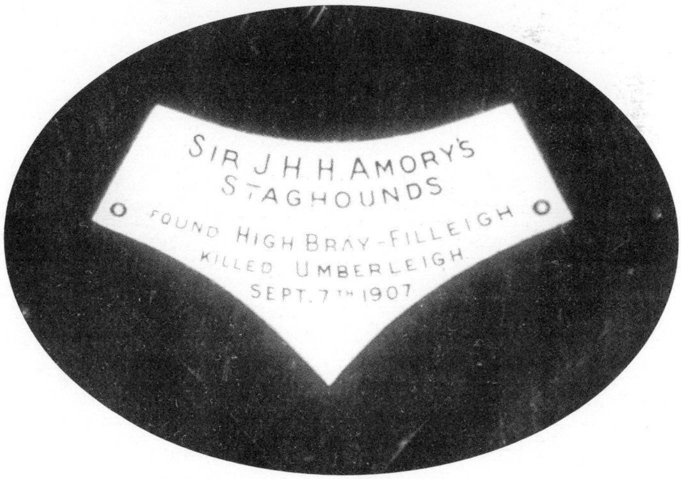

SIR J.H.H. AMORY'S
STAGHOUNDS
FOUND HIGH BRAY - FILLEIGH
KILLED UMBERLEIGH
SEPT. 7TH 1907

2 March 1909

There was much excitement in the neighbourhood at Culmstock on Wednesday when Sir John Amory's staghounds met at Culmstock Beacon for a day's hunting. It has been known for some time past that a stag and several hinds have made their home near the monument, and they have been carefully harboured, with a view to a hunt.

It is estimated that upwards of one thousand persons attended the opening meet on the Blackdowns, 300 of whom were mounted on horses. As soon as the stag was separated from the hinds he led a merry chase passing Clayhidon, Blackmoor, Forches Corner, Cuhead, Church Stanton, Churchinford, Lupit, and Blackborough, and finally reaching home again via Broadhenbury, the distance covered being many miles.

He proved to be too good a runner for his pursuers, and survived to run another day. It is too much to hope for the inclusion of Wellington monument or Culmstock Beacon in the regular list of meets of staghounds, but there is reason for supposing that the last has not been heard of staghunting on the Blackdowns.

§

A meet at Chawleigh. Mr and Miss St Hill (from the *Illustrated Sporting and Dramatic News* 12 October 1907)

Stag's head presented to Sir Lewis Stuckley by Ian Amory in 1910

Tiverton Foxhounds
Mr Amory Accepts Mastership

17 January 1911
Mr Lewis Mackenzie, Hon. Secretary of the Tiverton Foxhounds has received the following letter respecting the Mastership – Hensleigh, Tiverton, Devon. 11 January 1911.

Dear Mackenzie
I think I ought now to send you a definite answer to the invitation of the members of the Tiverton hunt to undertake the Mastership of the foxhounds. I shall be quite glad to do this, but only because I in common with other members of the hunt know that nothing will induce Mr Unwin to reconsider the decision to which he has come. We shall miss him very much, and if I can show the country half the sport he has shown during the 19 years of his mastership, I shall be well satisfied. I shall have to rely much upon the help of all who will give it, because my time on non-hunting days will be taken up by other things which cannot be put aside. It is because I feel sure that this help will be given, and that I may rely upon the same kindly welcome and hearty co-operation which the farmers have invariably shown me for the last 30 years, first with the harriers and then with the staghounds, that I am now willing to accept the invitation which has been so cordially given, and follow my uncle as Master of the Tiverton Foxhounds.

Yours sincerely
Ian H Amory

§

18 February 1911

Sir John Amory's Staghounds met in the main street of Wellington on Wednesday and proceeded to the Blackdown Hills. A move was made along the crest of the hill to the Honiton main road, five miles above Taunton, where on the Newton estate, a stag broke away at five minutes to one o'clock, and made across the Taunton Vale, disappearing from sight near Heatherton Park, the residence of Colonel Woodhouse. Eventually the stag was taken near the G.W.R. line at Allerford, Norton Fitzwarren. Last year the same stag was taken near the same place and released.

§

7 March 1911

Sir John Amory's Staghounds met in Fore Street, Okehampton on Wednesday in glorious weather. Hundreds of people on horseback, in carriages and on foot turned out. Just after 10.30 Mr Ian Amory and Ludovic Amory his brother, came on the scene with the pack which looked in fine condition. They had come from Tiverton by special train, quite a hundred ladies and gentlemen on horseback were present, including General Holley, Messrs J.D. Prickman, Luxton, Tattershall, Northley, and Matthews, Mrs May, Dr Burd, Major Newcombe, Colonel Edwards, Messrs E. Murrin, S. Horn, J.G. Heywood, R. Parker, P. Edgcumbe, Tapson, Palmer, Weekes, Harris, Northcott and others. The Mayor and Mayoress of Okehampton and many of the leading tradesmen were also present.

About 10.45 a move was made through the beautiful grounds of Oaklands to General Holley's woods (The Spryngets) where the stag had been seen on several occasions lately by the keeper and others. Four hounds were put into the copse. They very soon made it known that the stag was at home and presently it was seen trotting along between the trees and bushes. Hounds were then brought out, they rattled through the copse going towards Follygate. Eventually the stag made for Bowerland, going onto Ashbury Station and to Halwill. crossing back to Northlew and Highampton on its way to Hatherleigh. Just below Hatherleigh it took to the water in the River Lew, going some way down with hounds on its track. About a mile or so down the river going towards the Torridge, the stag came to bay. It was roped, taken back to Hatherleigh and stabled for the night.

§

4 April 1911
Hunt dinner at Chawleigh

Through the generosity of Mr Ian H. Amory a large number of farmers, sportsmen, and lovers of hunting were invited to dinner at Chawleigh (the Portsmouth Hotel). About 80 accepted the invitation. Mr Amory presided, Mr Ludovic Amory occupying the vice chair. They were assisted in the carving by Messrs E. Ford, E. Webber, and J. Tripe. Mr Ludovic Amory in proposing success to Agriculture emphasised its cast importance, remarking that much depended on its success. Owing to better prices for produce and the adoption of new methods times were certainly improving. Then Mr Thomas Baker in response, said he thought that parliament did not do much to assist agriculture. Taxes, for one purpose and another, were increasing. He considered that too much money was squandered on officials travelling the country. He trusted that in future MPs from agricultural constituencies would be influenced by the farmers union. Then Mr H. Smythe (Worlington) thought judging from the rosy faces around the tables, that very little depression existed among farmers. They must adapt themselves to the times, and introduce up to date methods. The hunting toast was proposed by Mr John Tripe who is a great lover of sport. He contended that real sport whether it be hunting the deer, fox, hare, otter, or shooting was of great benefit to agriculturists. Vast sums of money were annually spent in the purchase of foodstuffs alone, while it gave employment and enjoyment to thousands. All present would regret to hear that Ian Amory was about to retire from hunting the staghounds owing to his having taken over the mastership of the Tiverton Foxhounds. At the same time they were delighted to know that his brother Mr Harry Amory would succeed him. As long as any of the family came that way with their hounds they would receive a hearty welcome (cheers). Ian Amory's health was drunk with musical honours, Mr Amory in response said he had hunted with his father's harriers (15 years), and with the staghounds (16 years), never outside Devon had he experienced such hospitality and kindness as had been accorded him. No one had ever objected to his trying a covert or crossing a field. Just 500 deer had been captured in the district since he brought down the hounds. His brother was well known to them, and he felt sure they would extend to him that kindly feeling which he had always enjoyed. "My brother the Captain has made up his mind to give up a very good job in the Midlands in order to come home and take on the Staghounds, he will keep them in the kennels at Bolham." Mr Amory mentioned the able assistance rendered by Mr F. Miller the harbourer, who during the proceedings was the recipient, from his Master of a cheque in recognition of his services, songs were rendered by Messrs A. Cobley, E. Reed, and G. Drew, and a most enjoyable time was spent, the National Anthem brought a very pleasant gathering to a close.

§

15 April 1911

At the invitation of Mr Ian Heathcoat Amory, nearly a hundred followers of Sir John Amory's Staghounds partook of dinner at the Rackenford school room on Friday. Mr Ian Amory (MSH) presided, and the vice-chair was occupied by Mr Ludovic Amory (whip). Mrs Amory and Mr Jack Amory were also present. Mr Ian Amory said he had invited his friends, the farmers and tenant farmers, to dinner in order to say thank you before he gave up the staghounds at the end of the month. There were many present over whose farms he hunted 31 years ago. With the exception of Mr Bisset's Mastership of the Devon and Somerset Staghounds he believed he had been the longest of which there was any record (applause). For the past three years his wife had been unable to hunt with the hounds owing to an accident she recieved in the hunting field. His brother Captain Harry Amory was relinquishing an excellent position in the midlands under the Duke of Portland in order to come home and take on the Mastership of the Staghounds.

§

25 April 1911
Last Day for Ian Amory

On Friday the meet was at Worlington, the field was probably the largest that has ever assembled there, people had come from places as far apart as Exeter, Crediton, South Molton and Dulverton, as well as the usual contingent of staghunters from Tiverton. The local farmers had also turned out in large numbers, realising, no doubt, that this was the last day of Mr Amory's Mastership, and being determined to take a share in the final hunt. Miller had a deer harboured in Bycott, hounds were kennelled at Bealy Court, after the tufters had drawn Week and Ball Coverts to make sure that there were no deer there the young stag was soon found, in Bycott, and after one turn round the coverts towards Chulmleigh he made up his mind that Rackenford and Knowstone Coverts were to be his point. Tufters ran him very fast over the moors and were well stopped by Mr Tripe and one or two other good staghunters near Lutworthy Coverts. Mr Ludovic Amory had meanwhile gone for the pack laying them on the moor near the Gidley Arms. We soon found ourselves struggling over the intricate country by Creacombe, and near Ditchett Covert hounds came to their first check. They were soon put right, and sailed away over the big moors until they were again brought to a check on some newly sown fields near Beaples Hill. A wide cast round these fields put things right again, and hounds worked the line cleverly over a good deal of freshly burnt moorland into the top of Knowstone wood, through these large coverts, and away at the lower end. Hounds had evidently got on very good terms with their deer here, and it was all horses could do to live with them for the next hour. Away Northwards over the big moors, with plenty of boggy places in them, as two or three enterprising riders soon discovered, by Kipscott to Molland Station. Then right-handed and away by Anstey, Hawkwell and Upcott to Highleigh and down to the meadows under Riphay, across the River Exe, and away up through the Wonham Coverts, past Combe, almost into Bampton, down to the Exe by Halfpenny Bridge, and up the water to Chainbridge, where hounds caught a view and ran very fast up the valley to Hangman's Hill. Then turning, left handed they ran close past Stoodleigh village, down the long valley under Withy Cleave, and into the Exe under Hatherland. One cast down stream and hounds fresh found the deer and was killed above Worth House at 5 o'clock. So ends the season 1910–1911, the best season on record. So ends Mr Amory's 16 years of Mastership a day memorable on two accounts. First for the extraordinary amount of country traversed by what now turns out to be two separate deer. First a young stag, who came at any rate as far as Knowstone, and who there or thereabouts must have shifted his responsibilities onto the back of a very large hind, hounds therefore practically ran up two deer and in doing so hunted steadily and at times very fast over country which measured straight over the map from Bycott to Worth, taking Creacombe, Molland Station, Bampton and Stoodleigh as intermediate points. The day's hunting was noteworthy also for the points of interest to which the deer led hounds. The covert in which the deer was found is 14 miles from Highleigh, a property which Captain Amory the new Master has bought. Until this purchase was made and the property had thereby assumed close connection with staghunting it was apparently of no special interest to deer, for no record exists of deer and hounds having crossed it. But within a week of the Captain's purchase, deer, hounds and field swept over the very site of his new house. Then the last of Mr Amory's deer felt bound to visit the farm of the first of Mr Amory's staghunting friends (Tom Yandle of Riphay) the man from whom Mr Amory has been proud to learn the wiles and the art of this noble and difficult sport, the trusted friend and adviser of two generations of staghunters. It seems fitting also that the end of the day, of the season, and of the Mastership should have come within sound of Worth, the home of the Messrs De las Casas, all four of whom have at different times acted as whips to Mr Amory in the days before the work was undertaken by Mr Ludovic Amory, who has so often and so successfully during recent years hunted the hounds during Mr Amory's absence upon other business.

Since Ian Amory has been hunting the staghounds, those whose good fortune it has been to follow Mr Amory over the country declare him to be a born huntsman. More than once he has been offered the Mastership of the Devon and Somerset Staghounds.

Thanks to the fine sporting spirit of the Amory family the chase is within the reach of all classes.

Mr Ludovic Amory who in the past few seasons has acted as chief whip to Ian Amory will act in the same capacity for the Tiverton Foxhounds.

It is not at all likely that anywhere in this country or any other there are three brothers so closely associated in any form as are Messrs Ludovic, Harry and Ian. When hunting the Staghounds next season Harry Amory will carry on to run them as a private pack upon the same lines hitherto. Apart from being huntsman next season Sir John has also handed over the Mastership to him as well, making it a staggering 52 years as being Master firstly of his harriers which he formed in 1859 and still retains, but now given up the Mastership of his Staghounds which he formed in 1896.

Sir John Amory has put Tiverton into an enviable position in the hunting world, and it is sometimes spoken of throughout the West Country as the "Melton of the West". Long may it sustain its reputation. For the past 16 seasons Sir John's Harriers have been hunted by his son-in-law Charles Carew.

The following three books mention Sir John Amory's Staghounds.

An extract from *Staghunting on Exmoor* by Philip Evered, published in 1902 (Chatto & Windus, London).

A noble beast, from the Stoodleigh Coverts, taken by Mr Ian Heathcote Amory with Sir John Amory's Staghounds near Chain Bridge in the autumn of 1897, weighed, when cleaned and dry, no less than 333 lbs, which, reckoned according to the custom of the country, would amount to 16 score 13 lbs. This I believe to be the record weight, for the West Country at any rate, if not for the British Islands. The Scotch method of weighing being of course entirely different and would have included all that had been removed from this woodland giant. This stag's horn measured round outer curve from burr to tip the notable length of 39 1/2 inches.

§

An article on Sir John Amory's Staghounds from the book *British Hunts and Huntsmen* published by the Biographical Press in 1908.

In the five seasons following the formation of Sir John Amory's staghounds, they accounted for one hundred and fifty-one deer, of which fifty-seven were taken in the Country lent to him, while sixty-six were the result of a series of invitation meets in the Dulverton District of the Devon and Somerset Country, while fourteen were taken from the Barnstaple Coverts, and fourteen more from the Quantock herd. Since then Sir John Amory's pack, hunted by Mr Amory, has been at work regularly in its own country, and by invitation in the Dulverton district, and has long ago reduced the Stoodleigh herd to manageable proportions, but it no longer travels afield to the Barnstaple country or the Quantocks, the former being no longer hunted, and the Quantock hills having for the past six seasons owned a resident pack. In 1902 Mr Amory's level of good sport was well maintained, his season's record amounting to twenty-eight stags and sixteen hinds, and in the following year his total was almost the same, except that hinds preponderated. In 1904, deer had become somewhat scarcer, owing to several seasons of regular hunting, and only thirty-two were taken, but, at the Annual General Meeting of the Devon and Somerset Hunt Committee in May, 1905, which was a record year in the annals of wild deer hunting, Mr Amory's tally amounted to forty-six. In 1906, the numbers were somewhat less, and made a total of thirty-four deer. Throughout these years, Mr Ian Amory has carried the huntsman horn, and for the greater part of the time has relied on the services of amateur whippers-in, the Messrs De las Casas and Captain H Heathcote Amory being his chief supporters.

Mr Amory was the first to vary the time honoured custom of using only doghounds for deerhunting, on account of their superior size. So satisfactory did his experiment of using a mixed pack appear, that it has been largely followed by the Devon and Somerset, and other packs, in recent years. This pack has always been hunted without subscription, except for the purpose of providing a fund for the compensation of deer-preserving farmers, whose crops suffer from the ravages of deer, and the thanks of the countryside are due to Sir John Heathcote Amory, for the maintenance of an establishment which has kept wild deer hunting alive and prosperous in a wild district where it was threatened with discontinuance.

§

An extract from the book by Fred Goss *Memories of a Stag Harbourer*, 1894–1921 (H F & G Witherby, 1931)

Fred Goss was harbourer for the Devon and Somerset for many years. In 1931 he wrote a book of his memories. He also harboured for Sir John Amory's Staghounds of which he mentions below.

Long cross country runs have occurred especially after Christmas. I remember one deer we found in Hele Ball Wood above Jury, close to Dulverton, that ran to Milverton before being killed, a run of a good many miles, the run was with Sir John

Amory's staghounds and Mr Albert De Las Casas, who usually acted as honorary whip, he was hunting them on that day in the place of the Master who was ill. On looking back I think some of the happiest days in my life were those when harbouring was at its busiest and when hunting seemed at its zenith. It included a period in which, in addition to harbouring for the Devon and Somerset four days a week I was often employed in harbouring for Sir John Amory on the other two. In this way I have several times harboured six stags in a week. Meets for Sir John Amory's hounds were often held by invitation in the Haddon and other neighbouring districts, for these I was generally asked to harbour a stag. Later on, Miller and then Lang, the present harbourer for the "Devon and Somerset", used to harbour for them.

On leaving for military service Colonel Harry Amory gave many of his hounds to the Devon and Somerset, the remainder being looked after and hunted during the difficult war years by Charlie Slader of South Molton. On Mr Slader giving them up they became the Tiverton Staghounds of today passing into the hands of the Yandle family, sons of the late Tom Yandle, whose keen sportsmanship all country deeply respected. I have in my possession a highly valued memento of the five hundredth deer killed by the Sir John Amory pack, in the form of one of the stag's tusks mounted as a safety pin. And also another happy reminder of this period in the shape of a silver mounted blotter presented to me by Sir Ian Amory and Colonel Harry Amory, and on it inscribed, "In memory of many a good morning's harbouring and many a good day's hunting 1896–1915".

I remember in one spring staghunting season a young stag behaving with extraordinary coolness in face of hounds. The meet was with Sir John Amory's staghounds at Cuzzicombe Post, and I had harboured a young stag in West Molland Wood. While tufting for him I was riding through a wood just in front of Ludovic Amory who was that day hunting hounds, when I suddenly saw the stag I had harboured lying just below using an old charcoal pit. We stopped our horses to look at him and waited, expecting the tufters, which were close at hand, to put him up. Seeing he was observed and there being no undergrowth in the pit to serve as any sort of concealment, the stag got up but did not offer to move away. At that moment the tufters came level with the pit, but it so happened some ran above it and some below it, none of them chancing either to scent or see the stag. There the stag stood quite still watching the hounds passing him, realising no doubt that his chance of escaping their notice lay in not moving. So far as all those tufters were concerned the stag was not correct, but unfortunately for him one tufter had lagged behind and in following the rest he went straight through the pit thereupon he came right on the stag who then thought it time to leave.

Chapter Two

Captain Harry Amory's Staghounds (1911–1915)

Richard Stapledon's book *Exmoor Elegance and Rhythm* contains notes on Captain Amory's Staghounds. The article is reproduced below by kind permission of Richard Stapledon's granddaughter, Tina Snell.

> We used to enjoy very much going to meets of the Sir John Amory's Staghounds on our bicycles: everyone who did not own a horse in those days rode bicycles. Captain Amory (later Colonel, but even then always referred to as "The Captain") had taken over the mastership from his brother, Sir Ian. One day the Exe was running high and hounds had their deer in the water below Blackpool.
>
> The deer could stand in midstream, but hounds had to swim and were jumping into the river opposite the deer and naturally were being swept down by the current. Eventually one of the riders noticed this, caught hold of one of the hounds, took him a bit upstream and threw him in. The Captain happened to see what had been done – he was well over six feet, strong and well built. He strode up to the chap, seized his coat collar with one hand, with the other the seat of his breeches and threw him into the water after the hound. The man dragged himself out of the water onto the bank further down, soaked to the skin. Whereupon the Captain produced half a crown, gave it to him and said, "Now you know what the hound felt like!"
>
> During Capt. Amory's mastership he occasionally met at South Molton; this custom was carried on by the Yandles, when they took over the hounds. A special G.W.R. train was chartered, complete with passenger coach, horseboxes and hound van.

The train would stop en route at Anstey and Molland to pick up followers: we all paid our share.

I can vividly remember one of these days when the Captain was hunting hounds in this area. I was riding behind Mrs Turner, of West Molland Barton, who rode side-saddle, down a very narrow farm lane (but where has escaped me). As she came to a gate and was leaning over to undo the catch, the stag jumped over the gate, brushing her horse as he did so.

There was Bill Nott, whipper-in to Captain Amory's Staghounds, and later kennel huntsman to the Dulverton Foxhounds. One of the best raconteurs I have ever met. Wherever he went he invariably rode his pony. A bicycle, he repeatedly averred, did not know its way home. As Bill grew older his sight began to fail, which worried him because he was essentially an out of doors man. However, he never let it interfere with social functions, where on occasions his antics in playing an imaginary violin with his walking stick always brought the house down.

Shortly before one Christmas he attended the final night of skittles, which was for a silver cup. It was some evening and celebrations went on until after midnight. By that time Bill was a trifle "bossy eyed" – however, he was put safely on his faithful pony and set sail for home. After journeying for a mile, he reached the crossroads, but for some mysterious reason he turned left instead of right. His pony, knowing this to be wrong, became stubborn, but Bill was adamant and gave it one with his stick, only to find himself a few moments later in a cul-de-sac. He could not even turn the pony around. In despair he said in a loud voice, "Please can anyone tell me where I am?"

In a short time a light went on upstairs, a window opened and an irate postmistress poked her head out, "Yes, whoever you are, you're in my back yard, get out!"

§

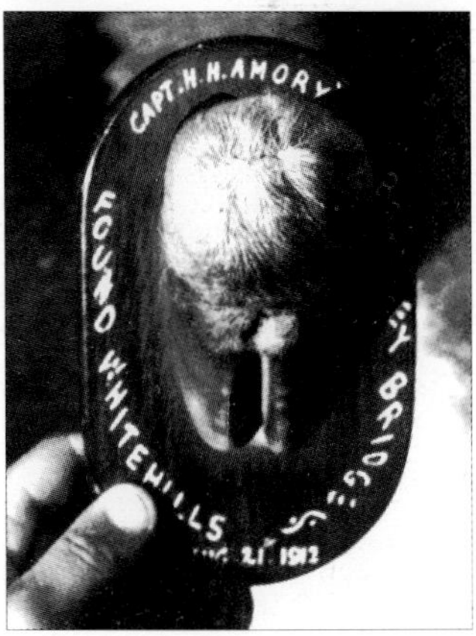

Right: Captain Amory Slot, 12 August 1912

5 September 1911
Captain Amory's Staghounds
Captain Harry Heathcoat Amory kills his first stag

Despite very adverse hunting conditions Captain Heathcoat Amory, who has taken over the staghounds from his brother, Mr Ian Heathcoat Amory, killed his first stag on Saturday. The meet was at Haddon and a deer harboured in King's Wood, was bustled by the tufters into Storridge, then over Baron's Down and back to Storridge again. Nothing would persuade the quarry to take to the open, and with the countryside parched and everything even in covert as dry as tinder, scent was wretched and nothing but the new Master's dogged perseverance and the help of those who viewed the deer, enabled the chase to be pursued. The deer at last went out over the top and down to the Exe, into Exe Cleave and Bury Wood by Windy Corner, up to Harford Mill, back to Windy Corner, over Baron's down and onto Exe Cleave again. Taking to water, there was another longish check, but Captain Amory, casting upstream again, got on terms with the deer at Barlynch, ran down stream to Hele Bridge and on to the big Pixton wood, where in the river at 5.30 the stag was taken. He had all his rights, and two a top each side. Capt Amory was congratulated on the successful issue of the hunt.

Chapter Three

Charlie Slader and the South Molton Staghounds (1915–1919)

In 1978, in her 84th year, Nora Clarke wrote a book called *My Four Feet on the Ground, Memories of Exmoor and Ballifants* (Rocket Publishing Co. Ltd, 1978). She was Arthur Heal's granddaughter, Arthur being one of the famous huntsmen of the Devon and Somerset Staghounds. In the book she mentions Charlie Slader who married Arthur Heal's daughter who then became her Aunt Ellen. Nora spent holidays with them when Charlie had the hounds at Hacche Barton near South Molton during the First World War. A family tree below starting with Arthur Heal and going down to Charlie Slader gives us an interesting insight into the family's history.

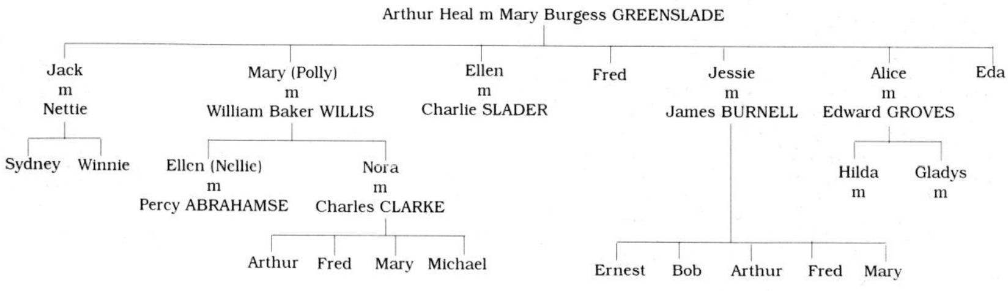

From Nora Clarke's book *My Four Feet on the Ground, Memories of Exmoor and Ballifants.* Reproduced by kind permission of her son Fred.

Charlie Slader, of Hacche Barton, South Molton, became our Uncle Charlie through his marriage to Arthur Heal's daughter, Ellen, my aunt.

A word about Aunt Ellen. When Arthur Heal's son Fred was three years old he fell into a pond and would probably have drowned if his mother had not heard his yells and jumped in to save him.

This plunge into cold water brought in the premature birth of Mrs Heal's daughter, Ellen. She was said to have been small enough to go into a quart pot and was brought up as 'delicate'. Yet she lived to the age of 93!

When war came in 1914 the red deer, increasing in number, were a trial to farmers with fields of roots and corn. Normally, farmers were all in favour of the fine and famous pack of Devon and Somerset Staghounds, but now they were discussing how they could protect their crops. They feared that poachers who occasionally shot a deer would not be watched and discouraged, as was usual. Once shooting commenced, one could never be sure where it would stop, and if not checked it might lead to decimation of the herds and even extinction.

The Devon and Somerset Staghounds kept very near their average of kills, but the staff were short-handed and could not go to the further district they were responsible for. So it was suggested to form a secondary pack which would deal with these neglected districts.

There was no criticism from the Devon and Somerset, who offered to give some surplus hounds to form the nucleus of the new pack. Mr Charlie Slader was asked to take charge and was even nominated as Master, but, modest man that he was, he refused to accept the title and nominated himself as Deputy Master, Lord Fortescue being the Master. Several other packs made contributions of a few hounds. Most of them had also to learn new words of command. Collecting these with Mr Slader made my holiday a very happy one.

Coming from different packs, the hounds varied much in size and colour, and their appearance was much criticised, but they did the job. The newcomers brought their names with them and I remember one, Warrior. He was the oldest and took it for granted that he was to be the leader. It was rumoured that it was on account of his "bossiness" that he had been sent to us. As younger members of his own pack had grown up and wanted to be leaders, fights had resulted.

Our little pack were mostly young and uncertain of themselves, and so accepted Warrior's leadership without question, and all was peaceful. Luckily, our winter reared calves were fit to go out to a field, which left their large house free for a kennel. It was close to the farm, but the hounds, being new to each other, did not 'sing' or very seldom. And never at night, which was as well, seeing our bedroom window was only 12 yards away!

The first few attempts at exercising the pack were hair-raising but we came back only one short and that one was brought to us by a neighbour. Mr Slader had a marvellous way with hounds and he very quickly taught them they were a pack and belonged together.

My sister, who had been seriously ill, made a wonderful recovery and was now able to ride with enjoyment, so she took on the job of whip (whipper-in) to the pack for the season. They killed their first deer on the second hunt and seldom failed on any subsequent hunt. In fact, one season they killed more than the Devon and Somerset themselves. About this we modestly remained silent.

Mr Slader had a collie type sheepdog, Sheppy, which was most devoted to him and followed him and his horse everywhere. He went on all the training outings with the hounds, and was very friendly with them. On the first morning hounds were taken to their real meet, Sheppy was shut in the stable and orders were given that he was to be left there. However, somebody did not hear the orders, or did not want to, and Sheppy was released. He soon caught up with his master and with what he no doubt regarded as his strange new flock. Whenever a car was heard approaching – a rare occurrence in those days – Sheppy got on the road side of the flock and hustled in any members who seemed likely to get into danger.

Uncle was a bit embarrassed but at the same time he released Sheppy was being very useful. The dog stayed with them throughout the hunt and whatever the farmers might have thought about it, they said not a word of criticism. Sheppy was too sensible to try to take the lead, and he joined the hounds many times and never got in their way.

Sheppy was never again shut up, so he had to make his own decision on hunting days. There was the care of the loveable but dull flock of sheep that nothing alarming had ever happened to yet, for the farm men were always around, or there was the exitement of the hunt and a much more interesting flock which would be travelling for some time on the road, where there was danger.

The hunt always won in the end and we would see Sheppy dashing away after his newer flock.

Above and below, a South Molton Staghounds head

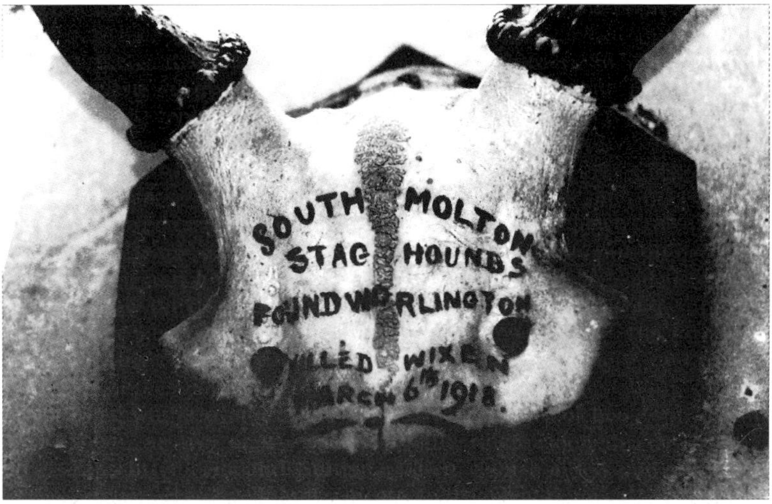

Running a pack of hounds is an expensive business and the mastership was nearly always taken on by a very wealthy man. The farmers who formed their new pack had a very vague idea of the cost. They all contributed according to their means and disposition to the expenses, but Mr Slader, being nominally Master, had to deal with the finances. His farm was small and not a rich one, and he was a generous man who had no love of money and saved little. So he was a poor man when he handed over the hounds to the four Yandle brothers who changed the name from South Molton to Tiverton Staghounds. They had given enormous pleasure and interest to their late owners and I doubt if any of them had any regrets. About the wives, I have wondered, but the only one I knew spent her last year with me and, though very poorly off, she never blamed the hounds but spoke happily of the great pleasure she and her husband and his friends had found in them.

§

Notes on Charlie Slader and his wife Ellen from Richard Stapledon's book *Exmoor Elegance and Rhythm.* Reproduced by kind permission of Richard's granddaughter Tina Snell.

In those distant days there were several notable characters in the South Molton area. I remember well George Rather, of the George Hotel; Sammy Coles, of the Unicorn; and Charlie Slader, of Hacche Farm. Rather hunted the South Molton Harriers and firmly believed in getting well primed before taking hounds off to draw. However, he was popular and showed good sport; or rather the hounds did, because they had to do nearly everything for themselves! Sammy Coles was a worthy publican; but Charlie Slader was the real character.

A typical thick-set Devon farmer, who always wore massive coats with huge pockets, the inside ones in particular were fully capable of accommodating a leg of mutton in addition to further delicacies. He it was who loaned to me my first pony – a delightful Exmoor named Rosebud. We soon became firm friends and I attended my first meet on her at eight-and-a-half at Bullaford Gate with the Dulverton Foxhounds – and my first staghounds meet, actually riding, at North Molton in 1911, when owing to the extremely dry and hot summer the meet was at 3 pm. Few, I suspect, can now recollect that occasion. Rosebud divulged many secrets to me about Charlie. One was that she always had great difficulty in carrying him home to Hacche in the evening after market days! She complained that she found him top heavy and very unbalanced when in the saddle. However, she worked out this plan. When Charlie slumped over unsteadily to the offside, she would quickly go with him right across the road and so prevent him falling off – likewise, when the fence had been reached, she would immediately have to reverse the procedure on the near side.

"Extremely undignified for a thoroughbred Exmoor," she commented. "But if Charlie had fallen off what then? I could have done very little about it!" All this I discovered when riding her, but of course, I never told Charlie.

On a very hot and dusty August day – and with no "tarmac" in those days the roads were dusty – hounds had crossed the railway line, and at ten years old I was returning from beyond Alswear with my father and several farmers, including Charlie. We stopped, of course, at the first pub.

"Have a drink, Charlie?" asked my father.

"Pint of cider, please sir," said Charlie.

It was duly delivered and went down in about ten seconds dead. "Now sir," said Charlie, "I'll have a drink!" And he was given the largest double whisky I have ever seen. Presumably the pint of cider was merely to clear the dust from his throat.

During the First World War Charlie collected together a mixed pack of harriers, foxhounds and staghounds with the intention of helping to keep down the number of deer. On one occasion, as the pack came up over North Molton Ridge some time behind their stag, and with more than half a mile between tail and leading hounds, there came to the road by three corner allotment Charlie, very red faced and hot with the thick coat he was wearing and riding his famous grey mare, named Mother Goose: he shouted, "Carry on, you vellers, I'll see thee all later on," and immediately veered left-handed to the Sportsman's Arms. True to his word, we heard him coming down the Barle Valley blowing his horn just in time to collect hounds two hours after we had seen him. Needless to say, the stag won.

Mrs Slader was the daughter of Arthur Heal, the famous Devon and Somerset Staghounds huntsman, a small frail woman with hunting in her blood, but extremely tough, like her father. She had every need to be to compete with Charlie! From a meet at North Molton with the Devon and Somerset Staghounds in April a three-year stag had been harboured in Hacche Wood. Mrs Slader was standing on the fence at the top of the covert listening to Sidney Tucker drawing with the tufters towards her. Sidney had a very nice voice, especially when drawing in covert. Suddenly the stag came along the ride towards her, shied on seeing her and, as he did so, both horns fell off. She jumped off the fence, picked up both horns, and started for home. She had three fields to cross; when crossing the second field she heard the tufters hit the line of the stag, but to her utter dismay, they came out over the fence, where she had been standing. She ran and ran as never before, absolutely terrified, arrived into the farmyard, hurled the horns away and rushed through the back door of the house just as the tufters, in full cry, appeared. She told me of her nerve-racking experience with an intensity and a sincerity, as I listened open-mouthed. I fully believed her at that time, as I still do now!

I can recollect no woman – except Mrs Slader, of Hacche – who was blessed with such keen sight or who possessed such a deep knowledge of wildlife and deer in particular. She used to regard hinds as her special prerogative. On hunting days she would leave the farm for her "throne" on Brewers Castle in the Barle Valley; and there she would sit, apparently engrossed with the sock she was knitting. But no hind coming either down or up the water could escape her eagle eye. When Ernest Bawden the Devon and Somerset huntsman was casting the water and on coming to "the Castle" he would pause momentarily to await her signal; if there was no response, he would immediately take hounds back again – so great was his trust in his sister!

Above: Charlie Slader and his wife Ellen with the South Molton Staghounds at Hacche Barton near South Molton 1915

Above: The South Molton Staghounds 1915. Left to Right: Charlie Slader (huntsman), Arthur Parker, Ellen Slader, Annie Stenner

§

Arthur Heal's Silver Hunting Horn

While researching the Tiverton Staghounds I had the chance to look at the silver hunting horn which was presented to Arthur Heal, one of the famous huntsmen of the Devon and Somerset Staghounds, by Connock Marshall in 1882.

I first heard about the horn from the late Arthur Parker of North Molton. He told me how he used to go over to Charlie Slader's at Hacche Barton as a lad. Charlie Slader's wife Ellen, as we know from earlier on, was one of Arthur Heal's daughters, and she would have inherited the horn when Arthur died in 1916. When Charlie Slader gave up the staghounds in 1919 to be succeeded by the Yandles, Arthur Parker told me that he drove Mrs Slader to a meet at Bealy Court to present the Yandles with the horn. As the Yandles were taking over she probably thought it would be nice for them to have it, as a good luck gesture perhaps. Having no children to hand it down to it would be the next best thing.

The inscription on the horn reads:

Presented to Arthur Heal by Connock Marshall esq at Cloutsham Aug 9th 1882. Prosperity to Staghunting.

I tried to find out from the local newspapers why it was presented to Arthur, but came up with nothing. It could have been in recognition of the number of years he had been with the hunt or the record number of deer he had killed.

On the bottom of the horn it reads:

Presented to the Yandles by Mrs Slader 1919.

This is an interesting story, and worthy of mention is the fact that the horn has connections with the Tiverton Staghounds – firstly Arthur Heal's daughter Ellen married Charlie Slader who hunted the hounds, and secondly it was presented to the Yandles at a meet of the Tiverton Staghounds.

Below, a photograph of the silver horn alongside some hunt trophies.

Hunting Trophies
Deer slot with clock presented to Percy Yandle from Captain Harry Amory. Found Haddon, killed Half Penny Bridge, 10 January 1914. Arthur Heal's Silver Hunting Horn and a slot presented to Tom Yandle by Harry Amory, 11 October 1905. Found Nethercott

17 November 1916
The Devon and Somerset Staghounds hunting in the Tiverton country

The meet of the above pack at Rackenford Cross with the new Master, accompanied by Tucker (the huntsman) and Bawden (the whip), duly arrived with their hunts and hounds looking in racing condition. A move was soon made for Rackenford Manor where the owner (Captain Boles) is a keen sportsman. He had given his Keeper (Kent) instructions to harbour a good stag for the occasion, which he did most successfully late the previous evening. Goss the recognised harbourer to the pack, was alert slotting early in the following morning, which he espied a fresh slot of a heavy deer, and following on was fortunate enough to spy a big stag, hind and calf in their lair. Hounds were kennelled, five couple drawn for "tufting" when soon the deer were afoot and went off together, but after bustling them about the stag was singled out. The tufters were stopped, and the pack unkennelled, then laid on when, away they swept through North Wood, as if making for Hares Down, but here he turned to the right and kept along under the road fence to the extreme higher corner of Rackenford Manor with the wind in his favour. From here he went to Spurway Mill, then to Ash Farm, and on to the Bampton district, where he turned and ran down by the Exe, and at Chain Bridge he was "set up" and captured. The heaviest stag killed during the whole season, and with all his "rights". A magnificent and noble looking animal, with a splendid head, fit to adorn any nobleman's or sportsman's hall.
James Merson

PS: One incident occurred worth recording as amusing when a young expert cyclist (hatless) was riding hard to see the stag, but failed to do so. I asked him if he had seen the stag, when he replied, "No. I only wish I had, as I have never seen a wild red deer." I told him to take the next turn to the right and push along for four miles or so as fast as he could go, "and thereabouts you may see not only a very large deer alive but killed at Chain Bridge". He hesitated, and said, "My father told me to return for dinner, I cannot, therefore, you see, go". Said I, "Please yourself, but before I was your age I should have left the dinner and tried to make it good at supper time." This reminded me of a barrister who had an extensive practice, and at busy times he found it most difficult to dine at the usual fixed hour. So on one occasion somebody wanted to see him on urgent business, and he, knowing the hour he usually dines, thought he would call on him an hour or so after and interview him when at leisure. On inquiring at the house "if at home?" "Yes, but he is having his dinner." "What! Dinner? I thought he dined so and so."

"Generally he does, but the master is exceptionally busy now, and it is most difficult for him to dine at the stated hour, he is now having his yesterday's dinner."
J.M.

§

2 April 1918
South Molton Staghounds

Perhaps some of your readers would like to hear of the doings of the above pack during the past few weeks. The weather with few exceptions has been favourable for hunting in the absence of "Jack Frost" and deep snow. Many lengthy runs have occurred with favourable results. The meets have been more numerously attended of late with a distribution of the fair sex. The following incidents I will narrate of interest.

On one occasion deer where found at Knowstone, but after running awhile the pack divided, Colonel Amory stuck to the greater portion, and ultimately set his deer up at Chain Bridge, while Charlie Slader with the lesser section decided to run another, which he also set up at Clayhanger, the latter being an exceptionally long run, with a journey of 25 miles back to the kennel. On the 6th inst., the meet was at Witheridge (twelve miles distance) where Dr. brown hospitably entertained those present. In due course a move was made for Affeton, where deer had been harboured, after tufting for an hour it proved blank, the deer having shifted, then a consultation was held, and another locality selected. Whilst en-route the Master (Charlie Slader) said he had previously found deer lying out in the adjoining moor on a fine day in the absence of stock at this time of the year. So it was decided to draw it, hounds soon threw their heads and sterns up, rushed off at a rapid speed without giving a whimper for a third of a mile and sprang upon five deer while in their lair. Then the "band began to play" with music that echoed far away, after the burst it was evident that the pack had divided, and owing to the scent being "breast high" the hounds were racing along, on and on continued each section until they eventually "set both deer up", where they were duly dispatched.

The point of great interest in their day's sport was the scenting power of the pack in winning those deer with the wind in their faces so far away, and then bolting like greyhounds running their game in view and mute, for not a whimper was heard until the end. Another instance showing the sagacity of hounds, was where the pack divided, one lot went off on their own account running out the scent when they retraced their steps. On this occasion the Master had taken his second horse and stabled him en route, so these hounds had actually returned to his stable, and there awaited their Master with the other hounds. The Master had had a long run, and killed his deer, so on his homeward journey he called for his second horse, where lay the missing hounds outside the stable guarding the horse within. He was told the hour they arrived, also that they would not allow any person near the stable, although the time was on the wing. I gather from this that the missing hounds not only had an attachment for the hunter but also for their Master. Hounds when running meet occasionally with accidents, and sometimes get caught in gins, so are unable to travel back to kennel that night, but on recovering or getting liberated in the morning they will find their way long distances alone until reaching kennel. Hunters have been known when turned out in the summer for a run to break away and return to their former stables, within sound of the hounds and voice of their Master.

During the season a fine stag was taken at Alswear, whose decapitated head with antlers weighed 24lbs 6ozs and he measured when outstretched 8ft 9ins.

§

22 January 1918
South Molton Staghounds

The meet was at Ash Mill on January 7th, when a herd of deer broke away, but ultimately, the pack got on the line of a single one, which gave a long run and was captured at Chain Bridge. On the 11th they again met at Gidley Arms, but the deer had shifted, so it ended on a blank day. At this time of writing (January 14th) the country looks very wintry, being enveloped in snow.

§

When Charlie Slader had the hounds from 1915 to 1919, the local paper stated in an article – below – that the Cheriton Otter Hounds were also kennelled alongside them at Hacche Barton near South Molton. One day Charlie wanted to see if his staghounds would hunt the otter.

14 July 1920
Staghounds Hunt the Otter
North Devon Sporting Incident in War Time

A pack of otter hounds is not made in a day and who is he that can safely determine the otter and its ways? Yet true it is that five couple of staghounds brand new to the game, did the trick by taking an otter on the North Molton Stream just prior to the Master of the Cheriton Otter Hounds being called up, in 1918, in which year the Cheriton were, for a time, disorganised. It came about in this way. At that time the Cheriton hounds were kennelled side by side with Mr C Slader's South Molton staghounds and this grand old sportsman made a sporting offer to lend five couple of his hounds to ascertain whether they would hunt the otter or not. They were to be hunted by the Cheriton huntsman, while he himself would act as whip. A meet was quietly arranged at South Molton Town Station, where the staghounds were joined by a couple-and-a-half of the Cheriton Otter Hounds. On being put to water to draw upstream, the three otter hounds hit the line almost at once, but strange to say, the staghounds kept to the bank. They would not take the water, but they acted as excellent whips. The otter hounds, being afraid to mix with them, kept to the water and worked it out beautifully, whilst the staghounds intently watched their every movement. They could not make out such strange adventures. Eventually, the otter hounds marked their otter and, on "Gayboy" striking off the key note, the staghounds dashed like mad towards the holt, but, although scent was hot enough to burn their noses, they acknowledged it not, and abruptly returned to land. Just then a sheepdog, evidently on a poaching expedition, appeared and commenced to hunt with the otter hounds in a most businesslike manner, but his services were not required. On the otter bolting, the staghounds again dashed to water, and, for a short distance, joined the Cheriton choir, and swam the otter most creditably. But when the otter did the "vanishing trick" they returned to land, and left the Cheriton to "work it on". These tactics were renewed every time the otter was viewed. Eventually the otter landed and the staghounds quickly took their otter. Meanwhile the three otter hounds had disappeared upstream. "They are hunting another otter somewhere," said the veteran Slader.

§

Chapter Four

Memories of the Yandles (1919–1945)

Richard Stapledon's book *Exmoor Elegance and Rhythm* contains a section on the Yandle brothers, who took over the hounds in 1919. It is reproduced below by kind permission of his granddaughter Tina Snell.

> After the war the Yandle brothers, Jack, Percy, Bert and Ernest, took over the hounds, which were then kennelled at Duvale. They were very popular and showed excellent sport. Percy and Bert used to hunt hounds on alternate days. This regime extended the country somewhat and meets were held as far south as Chulmleigh. The deer there had increased and formed a colony of their own. When found in the Cheldon Valley they no longer came back to the Stuckridge Valley and the Exe, but would make points even as far as St. Giles in the Wood, near Torrington. Personally, I always considered Bert to be the better huntsman of the two. They were altogether a charming family, sisters included! I knew their father, Tom, he was very knowledgeable in the hunting field.
>
> But on one never to be forgotten occasion we were standing not far from the cover side when Tom said, "I just see'd the back of 'un pass." With that he whistles and we "hollered" – up came Captain Amory. "Which way, Tom?" sez he. "There under the fence," sez Tom. As soon as the pack was let go, out came a Devon calf further down the fence. Tom bolted and we saw no more of him that day!
>
> To begin with Percy's sheepdog always ran with the pack – Percy farmed Duvale. And extremely useful this sheepdog was. During one hunt we crossed the main South Molton road where

some thoughtless rider had failed to shut a gate, with the result that a lot of sheep went out onto the main road. The pack was immediately held up, while the sheepdog came into his own, rounded up the sheep and brought them back into the field. The pack was then let go again. We were out on our bicycles with the Tiverton in the Exe Valley when an amazing incident occurred. On returning home my governess (now an extinct species) discovered she had lost her much treasured gold half hunter watch. Sorely distressed, she put a notice in the local paper. Within a week, to her delight, the watch arrived by post with a letter from Miller, the Harbourer. It appears that he was on his way home when at the bottom of Hangman's Hill, Oakford, his horse suddenly went lame in the near fore. Miller dismounted and, to his astonishment, found not a stone, but a gold half hunter watch wedged between the frog and outside of his hunter's hoof. Clearly the watch must have become detached from the clasp on my governess's coat and fallen onto the road. Later Miller and his horse came along and the horse unwittingly, but with exact precision, had put his hoof down exactly over the watch and so picked it up. The watch was quite undamaged!

Duvale, where the Yandle brothers helped their father, Tom, farm, was a very old house: the main room had one of those very big fire places with a small seat built into the side of the chimney on either side.

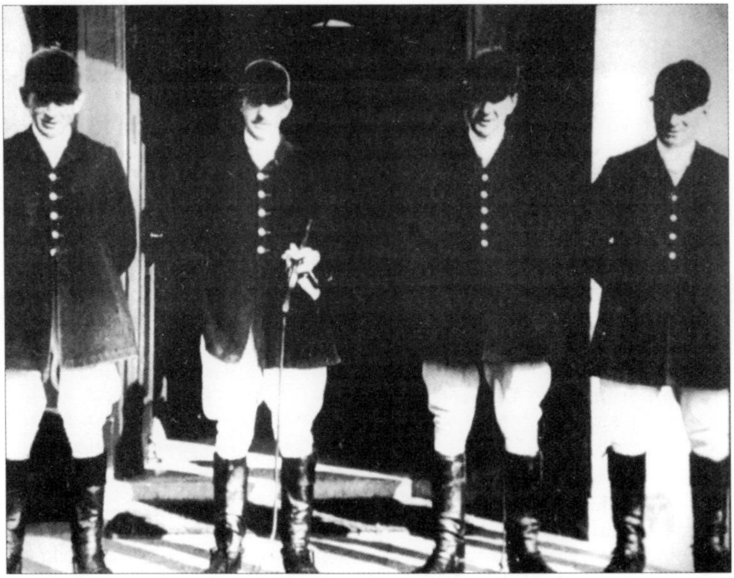

The Yandle brothers
Left to Right: Bert, Jack, Ernest and Percy

The brothers were all "maized" on hunting from an early age, but father Tom was somewhat of a martinet and kept his sons' noses to the grindstone. "Now then," he would say as he left on his bay pony for a day's hunting, "Get vore with thee work, else t'will be trouble, when I geets back."

The boys would rush their work in the morning and come in for as early a lunch as possible, and immediately go to the seats in the big open chimney. There they would sit, wait and listen in complete silence. The chimney was apparently quite remarkable for its acoustic powers and could pick up the sound of hounds running long before you could hear them when standing outside the farmhouse. It was Ernest who told me about this phenomenon and that hounds could be heard quite some distance up the Iron Mill stream. I have been to Duvale often, but unfortunately never on a hunting day to verify the authenticity of this tale!

These brothers had extremely powerful, penetrating voices which would carry considerable distances. They were capable of conveying information to each other quite easily when out hunting say from Hawkridge Ridge to the top of Slade Hill or from Haddon Hill to Storridge. And heavens, could they not holloa! One of many hunts that I had with them stands out so clearly and perhaps above all. A shield in my hall carries one of the biggest slots I have ever seen, and printed thereon is October 2nd 1925. The meet was at the Royal Oak, Gibbet, at that time a public house; Bert Yandle was hunting hounds. A big stag known to be frequenting the Hill Town coverts had been difficult to harbour; he had been continually on the move with several hinds since dawn.

The Hill Town coverts at that time were thick, rambling and spread over quite a large area, consequently there were many cosy secluded corners where deer could remain entirely unnoticed unless one happened to ride right in on top of them.

Tufting proved to be a very long and tedious task. However, Bert was possessed of unlimited patience and perseverance: he drew and drew, often on foot so as to omit no nook or bramble patch. But it was all in vain, the stag had apparently read the papers and vanished: clearly he must have left Hill Town.

It was now after 4.30 p.m., most of the riders and followers in cars were on the Tiverton–Rackenford road; all bore a somewhat depressed look and were preparing to return home after a blank day. Bert was coming across the fields towards the road with the tufters, when lower down the valley a single hound was heard running on his own. All talking ceased at once. What was it? Everyone instinctively asked the question. The hound could now be heard coming nearer and towards us. And then over a fence two fields in from the road came a hind. We were watching her cross the grass field when suddenly and unexpectedly over the same rack as the hind came the stag, not one hundred yards behind her and the hound in close attendance. And what a stag he was! But what a fickle spouse was she! Naturally the whole atmosphere immediately became electric: everything was bustle and hurry. The pack soon arrived and at 5 p.m. was laid on, where stag and hind had crossed the road. There was now a noticeable nip in the air and when let go, hounds fairly roared and raced.

Down the valley the usual way we went, but at Spurway Mill the stag and hind parted company; he went down the left side of the Iron Mill stream, the hind the right side, and consequently the pack split. However, the brothers were equal to the situation and after much shouting and cursing (those Tiverton hounds were devils to stop on a scent like this one) Percy and Ernest managed to stop and unite the errant couples with Bert at Stuckridge Bridge. The united pack then let go again, crossed the Exe to Wonham and fairly fled up the valley to cross the railway line near the Saw Mills, thence to Burston, Warmore and Pixie Copse, to drop to water by the Haddeo Bridge. There the stag ran down the water for a short way and we saw him leave for Weir with the last rays of the setting sun playing upon his antlers – their spread was huge.

Hounds took some time to come out of Pixie Copse, probably because the stag had been wandering in search of fresh deer; but in spite of Bert and his hunting horn they dwelt.

It was then up the water at a quickened pace to Hele Bridge and so into Exe Cleave. The whole valley resounded and echoed with the music the pack was now making in the gathering darkness.

As the leading hounds left the water short of Chilly Bridge to climb out left-handed across the lane and into Halscombe, I was alone with Percy and we were unable to see them clearly; it was as dimpsy as that! We made our way at the best pace possible up the lane to Broford, and all the while could hear hounds running on our left up the valley on the far side.

Clearly this meant Court Down and the Barle, and what then in the dark?

Right at the very top end of the covert all was silence for several minutes and not a hound spoke. Had they gone out? We were just about to set off when suddenly three or four couple bayed their stag.

There followed a terrific crash of branches and pandemonium. Obviously the stag had decided to return to the Exe, and as he turned down the valley he bumped into the main body of the pack, which was coming up!

It was now dark and as we both came down Broford Lane the sight that greeted us from the main road was both fascinating and fantastic.

Some fifty cars from Chilly Bridge downwards all had their headlights on and were placed diagonally across the road, so that the whole river was lighted up for quite quarter of a mile or more below the bridge.

The end came eventually just below Anthony's Weir at 8 p.m. – the hunters' moon was then resplendent and shining down upon us!

About 1920 I boxed two horses down in the special and had a great day. We drew White Hill, just south of the South Molton–Barnstaple road, and found about 12.30 p.m.

The stag crossed the main road where the pack was laid on. And now the line taken was Shallow Ford, up the Bray and under the viaduct, out left-handed by Brayley Barton, south of East and West Buckland, Gunn, Middle Dean and down the valley between Goodleigh and Stoke Rivers, up the water, swinging left to Loxhore, thence to the Arlington preserves. Miss Chichester's estate was sanctuary for deer and the few of us still left with hounds knew it: but the stag had somehow found his way through the boundary fence and hounds were now entering the very holy of holies – the gardens of Arlington Court itself!

The big wooden drive gate was chained and locked. Percy came to it first: when he was seen to be grinding his teeth one knew perfectly well that he was in one of his wild moods! He flung himself off his horse and attacked the gate: he could make no impression by charging it with his shoulder or by kicking it with his top boots. "Come on, you fellers," he shouted. "Us 'ave got to get drew yere." And with that four or five heavyweights set to work – the hinges gave way to the onslaught and the gate rolled over, held by the chain and lock alone.

"Now," said Percy, "us must all keep close together 'cos there's sure to be trouble."

We heard pandemonium a short way ahead – the worst had happened, hounds were baying the stag in the pond right in front of the very house itself! However, the clatter and noise of our arrival broke things up and we left the precincts and the stony stare of Miss Chichester herself as fast as we could. The end came half-a-mile further on and we then jogged back to Barnstaple, whither the special train had been summoned from South Molton. The point was 10 miles over an unusual line. We were well aware of how naughty we had all been and fully expected the solicitor's letter which arrived in due course.

Captain Amory, who had taken over duties as Secretary, was not at all pleased with us. However, it was not very long before he found his expressive grin again and said, "Well, I suppose boys will be boys; but no more of it!"

Left: Found Bycott, killed Lapford, 28 September 1907. Presented to Tom Yandle by Ian Amory

Ernest Yandle whipped in to his brothers, Percy and Bert, when they had the Tiverton Staghounds from 1919–1945 and also later carried the gun. I spoke with his son Tom, who is the Chairman of the Devon and Somerset Staghounds.

"My grandfather Tom Yandle was born at Washer's Farm, Wiveliscombe, in 1841 and came with his father to Hele Bridge, Dulverton in 1847. He was one of the farmers who started the Devon and Somerset Staghounds as we know them today, with the hounds being kennelled at Jury Lodge towards Pixton. A tenant farmer, he fell out with the Pixton agent and from there in 1880 he went to Duvale Barton near Bampton with his family. The four sons then spread out, leaving Uncle Percy and Bert at Duvale. Uncle Jack went down to Chevithorne Barton and Grandfather Tom came to Riphay near Exebridge in 1901 with my father Ernest. I still live there with my family today.

Before the foundation of the Tiverton Staghounds, the Devon and Somerset Staghounds would come down and spend a week now and then hunting the Tiverton country. I think they came down and stayed in a pub at Stoodleigh, hunting three or four days in the week. One year they had a bit too good an evening and got drunk. The following day the huntsman could not blow the horn and another fell off his horse. The Master said to my grandfather, 'Look, could you have them stay with you and keep an eye on them, seeing they don't get drunk, because it's a bloody nuisance if they can't hunt.'

My father and uncles had a meeting to decide who should go to war and because Bert was deaf they voted him to go to fight. He took his hunting horn and blew it at the front; he got gassed while he was out there but survived to come back.

When Harry and Bert came back on leave they would go hunting with Charlie Slader. Charlie used to send them a postcard (there were no telephones in those days) and a card came here saying the hounds were meeting at Ash Mill on Thursday, whatever the date was, for hind hunting. 'Be at Beaples Moor by 11 o'clock. If they're right let them run on.' So they went along and there was Harry Amory, my father, Percy and Bert. They waited and eventually the hounds came up on a small hind, so they stopped them, with Charlie Slader coming about 20 minutes later. He asked what it was and they told him it was a small hind. 'Oh that's no good, it won't cut up enough venison.' So he picked up the hounds and went back to Knowstone Wood. Capt. Harry said, 'You bloody old fool you won't catch a hind all the year'. So he went down for another hour and up he came with two strong hinds. Away they went and caught one at Washford Weir and the other at Holcombe Rogus. So Charlie Slader didn't do too badly that day. By the end of the war Charlie was an old man and did not want to continue.

At this time my Uncle Percy and Uncle Bert were at Duvale, my father had just come back from learning to be a draper, and Jack was at Chevithorne. So the four brothers got together and said, 'Why don't we take them on?' which they finally did. My grandfather was not pleased about this, he said financially it would be too much and having the hounds was a job for the gentry. It was all right to enjoy your hunting with them, but not to hunt the hounds. He would not let his boys wear top boots because the landlord would put the rent up. Getting hold of Charlie Slader, the brothers picked up the hounds at Bullaford Cross and took them back to Duvale, where Percy and Bert lived, and put up the kennels. They got some drafts in from other packs, harriers and all sorts; some were good, some not; a lot of the local foxhounds helped them, and that's how they got going. They got hold of a kennel huntsman as the Yandles knew all about the hunting but not about keeping hounds. Arthur Griffin was kennel huntsman for years, and his son Fred is still alive.

Percy and Bert took it in turns to hunt them, Jack was the Master. In due course Jack got married and put less time into it, later going to Fordlands, Hacche Barton where Charlie Slader was, and then on to Thelbridge Hall. I just remember Uncle Jack when I was about 12 years old. Percy was the wild man, he never married. Bert got wed in about 1928, and had Jim who we all remember riding his bicycle while following the hounds with a hunting crop, ready to be of assistance when hounds were in trouble. Bert married a keen foxhunting lady. He was a 'thinking huntsman', and would work it out and not get very excited; he was very good on the horn. Percy would ride roughshod over everyone and get so excited he could not speak.

There was an old boy from Switzerland who came to stay at the Carnarvon Arms. He didn't speak very good English and in the end became my godfather. He collected hunting sayings and hunting words, and there was one he had written down that he didn't know the meaning of. He heard them shouting it out and the word was 'UZURN'. Everyone looked and then asked who used this word. Apparently Percy used it, and Bert did a bit, but did Ern use it? No, he didn't. What it turned out to be was, 'Where's Ern?' My father never got very excited and when they wanted to shoot the deer my father would be trotting on behind with his gun and they would say 'Where's Ern?'

In the early 1930s the law came in about using a gun to dispatch the deer; my father was the first one for the Tiverton Staghounds to use it. It was a folding four ten.

Percy did most of the work being a bachelor and having Aunt Kate, Clare and Amy to look after him. None of the sisters got married. Clare never rode, but followed in a pony and trap, then a bicycle or car, and was latterly driven by friends. And so coming back to Percy, being a single man he could put all his time to his hunting and supervised the kennels and the horses etc.

They said that Percy never slept out of his own bed. Sometimes the hounds would go down to Cornwall, but he would not go down the night before.

By the time of the Second World War, the Yandles were all getting old. I suppose Uncle Percy would have been 62, and not many people want to carry on hunting at that age. They said they would continue anyway because nobody else would have done it.

They ran the hunt very cheaply. I have an idea the hunt income before the war was £600–£700, and they got a bit of dispensation, a little drop of petrol and things like that to allow them to carry on hunting the deer to control them. They got the ministry behind them a bit.

When Harry Amory came back from the First World War in 1920 he wanted to carry on hunting the staghounds, but of course my father and uncles had them by then. They asked him to be Secretary, which he did for several years. I think he was a bit of a nuisance to the Yandles because he was used to being in control when he was hunting them and he did not always agree with what they did. After the war he became Colonel Harry Amory.

Being brought up in farming, my father and uncles each knew what the others were going to say before they said it. They spoke broad dialect, so they could shout across the valley just a few words to say what was happening, which was very helpful – no need for CB radios then.

The Yandles would get invitation meets at the end of autumn staghunting and at the end of spring staghunting at Molland Moor Gate, but the Devon and Somerset Staghounds country where they regularly hunted was not all that good. Anyway, one year they met from here and found in Longstone Combe, and ran the length of Molland Moor. They headed towards Challacombe and met Stan Thorne on his horse, who then followed on with them. Going round a corner too fast, he came off and hurt his leg badly. I don't think he had broken it, but he had twisted it badly and of course he was in agony. Regardless, the Yandles said, 'We can't stop now, we don't know our way round here. You will have to help us. You can look after your leg tomorrow.' So they got him back on his horse and carried on. By that time thick fog was coming down and the hounds were running down The Bray. Eventually they killed the stag at Molland and Stan was still hobbling along a week later.

I told you my father carried a gun and he wouldn't get too excited, he was not one for shouting out in the field. He took everything as it happened, fairly laid back would be the modern expression. There was one famous day, down at Chulmleigh, when they found this big stag down at Gardener's End. They said it was like a bullock, it could hardly get through the bushes because his antlers were so big. They had been drawing all day and lots of people started going home. Then at four o'clock, in a little old corner piece, up he jumped. Uncle Percy, who had been on his feet all day, was so excited he couldn't get on his horse. He tried to blow the tufters on as he fumbled to open the gate. He went around the corner and this is the story he told, he said, 'There was Ern, and what do you think he was doing? Lighting up! I can't understand it.' So that was the difference in their characters.

By the time I was old enough to remember, the days of my family hunting the hounds were coming to a close. They hunted two days a fortnight in their own country and one day in the Devon and Somerset country by invitation, usually at Haddon, or a bit in the Barle Valley.

Between the wars staghunting was considered to be in its heyday, and the Yandles contributed to this in no small way. They were part of it, the Devon and Somerset were the senior hunt, supported by the Tiverton and the Quantock packs."

§

I spoke to Colin Yandle, of Barnes, London, son of Jack Yandle. Jack was Master of the Tiverton Staghounds from 1919 to 1934.

"My father, Jack, was the eldest of four farming brothers. In addition he had three sisters, Clare, Kate and Amy. Clare lived to be 108 in full possession of her faculties.

My father and his brothers all bought their farms during the depression in the late twenties/early thirties.

My father was 53 when he married in 1926, my mother being about 25 at the time. After I was born came my sister Cherry (who went on to marry the only son of Dick Stapledon), and another sister, Sally (who eventually married the son of the Mid Devon Master, Major Arden).

My uncles Bert and Ernest were also over 50 when they married, and each had a son: Jim and Tom. Uncle Percy never married and nor did his sisters. Aunty Kate lived with Uncle Percy at Duvale, and Aunty Clare and Aunty Amy lived at Fairfield opposite the Carnarvon Arms which my grandfather built for his retirement on Riphay ground.

During the war there was less formal hunting, hounds often being used to raise deer that were shot in the interests of agricultural production. My uncles often used to go to the meet in a couple of Austin Sevens with hounds on the back seat, or even in the passenger seat. During the war we had the nucleus of a pack of beagles which I hunted on Affeton Moor during the school holidays. It's all cultivated now. I believe my father and Uncle Bert farmed in partnership at one time. My understanding was that they both volunteered to join the army during the First World War, but they sent my father back to carry on farming as he was the eldest, being over 40 when the war started. Uncle Bert, I think, joined the West Somerset Yeomanry and I believe he was promoted to Captain in the field and took a lot of German prisoners.

My father was a tenant of the Amorys and for a short time he lived in a wing of Chevithorne Barton until an Amory son came home from the war. Then he moved to Fordlands where me and my two sisters were born. We have a picture of my father in a bowler hat winning the Tiverton Staghounds Members' race over banks, the course being over part of Fordlands ground.

We moved to Thelbridge Hall in about 1933. It was in fact the old rectory; they built a new one and renamed the old one. When my parents went to view it they asked a roadman digging the ditch where Thelbridge Hall was and he told them the only hall he knew was, 'Thicky tin place over there,' – the village hall – where I remember celebrating the Silver Jubilee and Coronation.

My father had semi-retired when he moved from Fordlands, and he had sold most of his farm equipment. We lived in some style then with a groom or handyman living in the stable yard and his wife working in the house doing the cooking, and a daily and a nanny or au pair to look after us children. The war altered all that and we had to plough the fields under the direction of the war Agriculturist Executive. My father used to carry a horn and I used to take it to the house from the stable yard after hunting, blowing all the time until one day I got a note out of it. I still have the horn and blew it in competitions, on one occasion beating the Mid Devon huntsman Tom Bunch who had to make do with a half bottle of whisky while I made off with a full bottle!

The day before Aunty Clare died I came down to see her and she greeted me with, 'Things aren't very good for the country'. So we had a bit of tea and sorted out the country, then she had supper in bed and was dead at half past five the next morning. I phoned up my wife and said to her I'd better not go hunting. I found out later that cousin Jim, Tom and everyone else were out with the staghounds by lunch-time but I don't expect Aunty Clare would have minded.

When cousin Jim died, Tom tried to make the funeral arrangements with the Bampton vicar. The vicar could manage Thursday or Saturday but not Friday. Tom said that was no good because they were hunting days, so in the end Jim was buried on Friday at Brushford, the bearers all being hunt staff.

I've lived away from Devon for so long that when I tell people that I am Jack Yandle's son they often say, 'I didn't know you existed'. I used to ride a pony out hunting on a leading rein with King, our groom, and as children he would take us out for rides. I think one year I beat Bertie Hill, the Olympic rider, as best child rider at Chulmleigh gymkhana.

I was also blessed with good heart, legs and lungs and I took to running cross-country at West Buckland School in North Devon. I went on to run for Cambridge University second team, came fifth in the Scottish Command in the army, won the Victor Ludorum at Seale Hayne Agricultural College, and ran for the Exeter Harriers. However, hunting became an increasing draw, and I took to following the Torrington Farmers on foot. Then I followed the South Herts Beagles and point-to-points, the Enfield Chase, Old Berkely, Surrey Union, Garth & South Berks, and Vale of Aylesbury. I still follow the latter three from London, where I have been since 1957, supplemented by periodic visits to Bampton and Dulverton to hunt around there, even though I am over 70 and have had a heart attack. A few seasons ago I went out with 15 different packs of hounds.

Cousin Jim, son of Uncle Bert, cycled everywhere, including on his hunting days. I don't know if he ever rode, but he had a tremendous knowledge of the deer. He used to cycle to Tiverton to do his shopping. He was a big man, over 6 feet tall, and about 16 stone. He liked to pump up his tyres really hard with a tractor pump. Onc hot day hc was coming back from Tiverton and bang! the heat burst his back tyre blowing his rear wheel to smithereens. One day when I was on the way back to London there he was cycling out to Taunton to watch the cricket. He was a bachelor and a good friend as well as being my cousin.

All in all I think our generation came of pretty good stock and have a lot to thank our fathers, uncles and aunts for, as well as our grandfather, Thomas Culverwell Yandle."

§

The death of Thomas Culverwell Yandle in 1927
(Mid Devon Gazette)

Mr Thomas Culverwell Yandle, a veteran sportsman, well known throughout the Devon and Somerset country has died at the age of 86. He was a successful agriculturist and was for many years, the tenant of Riphay Farm. In 1917 Mr Yandle retired, and went to reside with his daughter, Miss C Yandle of Fairfield. In recent years Mr Yandle suffered from failing sight and hearing. Nevertheless he continued to attend many of the meets, to which he was motored by his daughter. He listened intently to descriptions of the fields and the pursuit, and was invariably able accurately to forecast the probable course the deer would take. He was of the old school of sportsmen, kindly in thought and deed and possessed a keen sense of humour. His interest in staghunting was life long, he was singularly well versed in the lore of woodcraft and venery, and could always be relied on to find a stag for the Devon and Somerset or Tiverton Staghounds. Mr Yandle was born near Wiveliscombe and afterwards lived at Hele Bridge, Dulverton. He succeeded his father in that farm and then went to Duvale, Bampton. It was said that he was concerned at leaving the staghunting country for a farm on the river Exe where the Red Deer did not abound. He communicated this view to Mr Fenwick Bissett, the Master of the Devon and Somerset Staghounds, who laughingly said that the move would benefit both, for wherever Mr Yandle went the deer would follow. This was actually the case and deer multiplied in the fastnesses around the new home. For about 20 years Mr Yandle was at Duvale, after which he came back to the Dulverton district and took Riphay. He took little part in public life, but for a time was a useful member of Bampton urban district council. When Tiverton Staghounds started in 1896 he gave great assistance to Sir (then Mr) Ian Amory.

Thomas Culverwell Yandle

Talking with Robin Nelder from Cambridge about his memories of the Yandle brothers' era

"My great grandfather James Nelder and his wife Ann were the first licensees of the Carnarvon Arms Hotel near Dulverton when it was opened in 1876, Lord Carnarvon having built it as a small hotel in those days to service the market when the railway came through. It started taking visitors with people coming for the hunting. James died after three or four years and Ann ran it with my grandfather Charles William, who always said he was wise enough not to get married till his mother died because he didn't think two women in that place would have worked. He married Edith Gibson and they had six children, all born at the hotel. My father Reg was the second of those children.

The hunting stables were greatly expanded about the time the Tiverton Staghounds started. People came down to the West Country specifically to go hunting, and so the stables grew and they had 15 to 20 horses at the Carnarvon with another stable over at Exford. My grandfather was a great friend of old Tom Yandle who eventually retired to the house they built opposite the hotel, called Fairfield. He lived there with two of his daughters. Father was friendly with the four Yandle brothers who ran the Tiverton Staghounds, especially Bert, who was the youngest of the boys.

Father went out to Canada to farm and he didn't come back until 1923, taking over the hotel when his father and mother retired. He got very much involved with the staghounds, going to any meet within a reasonable distance of the Carnarvon, and being quite a part of the outfit as well as doing some harbouring nearby.

I started hunting with them in 1933 on my sixth birthday, meeting at the hotel. I rode with them whenever I could up until the war, so I got to know the outfit very well. Percy Yandle, one of the two huntsmen, used to have a curious collection of horses. He never had anything expensive but could manage them very well. My father had to buy horses for the stables at Exeter Horse Fair every year. These were to let out to visitors, so before he hired them out he had to ride them and see that they were well behaved and didn't have any bad habits. He once bought a black mare called Cinders and I remember him going out the first time and coming home very early, which was most surprising, because the horse had run away with him. Going out a second time he did the same thing and gave up the idea of letting it out to people. In the end Percy Yandle took her and everything went well until he took his cap off and held it out beside the horse's eye when the hounds were running and the deer was in view. He had a habit of doing this and every time Cinders would run away with him until he finally learnt not to do it. He had a number of 'not so good' horses, but he could manage them and got there in the end. He was an exciting and excitable chap to have hunting the hounds, for he would shout, holler and cuss. As a boy I preferred it when Percy was hunting the hounds because he would give you more excitement, but on a difficult day Bert was a very solid steady sort of chap working it out gently and he would be more successful.

I think Arthur Griffin, the kennel huntsman, probably played a bigger part than a lot of people realised. One of the things he always did when they killed was to paunch the deer (the Yandles never did that) and I think he also decided who got the slots and liver etc.

I remember one day we finished up somewhere near Hawkridge after a messy sort of day. On the way home up over the hill from Slade Bridge to Anstey Barrows a couple of hounds came in across the moor with a deer which had done a bit of work. We said,

'Go on Bert let 'em go,' but Nina his wife, who was always out riding, said,

'No, he's lit his pipe so he isn't going to let them go now.'

He was rather a dour sort of man but a very patient huntsman and beautiful on the horn. Ernest, another of the brothers, was much slower, and carried the gun. He was generally 'poking about', as my father used to say, but usually got to the right place when he was needed. It was quite interesting to see that the hounds knew whether Bert or Percy was hunting them. They would go straight up to whoever was wearing the huntsman's red coat and wouldn't take any notice of the other one, who would be wearing a bowler hat, a tweed jacket and still carrying a horn in case it was needed. They did the whipper-in's job but didn't do it wearing a red coat.

I remember riding back along the road in the dark with the sparks coming off the horse's shoes and no lights, but it didn't matter much in those days. I used to think when returning to the Carnarvon Arms as a small boy that I would be very glad to get home, and to think the hounds had another six or seven miles to go on the road. A long day.

There was one hound in particular that caused a bit of interest. He was called Racer, a white hound with two round patches on each side, one black and one tan, very unusually marked. He was the fastest hound in the pack being virtually unstoppable. He never became a tufter, they just couldn't stop him. There were also a couple of black and tans, which were highly regarded for their noses. I think they were brother and sister from the Dumfrieshire Foxhounds, called Paragon and Patience. I remember one day Percy said,

'Patience is down there working it out like a little brick.'

There were several others who were characters in their own way, including a white hound called Pilgrim who was usually leading. In those days they were probably breeding half their own puppies and were getting drafts from foxhound packs.

The Yandle sisters were very faithful followers in their Austin Sevens, Kate in one and Clare and Amy in the other.

Monsieur Simon, a rich man, was a regular rider at the Carnarvon. In the early days he would come over with his groom and horses, staying for the whole of the staghunting season. In my time he used to ride our horses and didn't bring any staff with him. He was very particular about everything being right and was very appreciative if things were done to his satisfaction, but he didn't mind saying if they weren't. He also used to bring his French hunting horn, and would go down in the garden in the evening to play it.

We used to have all sorts of interesting people that came down staghunting; there were two men from Cambridge, one being a senior tutor at Sidney Sussex College, and the other, called Davenport, who was the bursar there.

Until about 1941 I guess they were hunting more or less normally, and then it got more and more difficult with no petrol and so on. I remember down the valley between Cove and Bolham there were a lot of park deer in the wood. They took a few hounds and several people with guns, including my father, and killed most of them in a day.

I can certainly remember the people of the Carnarvon Arms stables and particularly the foreman for many years, Marshall. I don't think anyone knew what his other name was. He was very smartly turned out with a bowler hat, collar and tie, yellow waistcoat etc. and he was a proper autocrat with the people who worked under him like Frank Needs and Bertie Denscombe. At peak times we had four or five people in the stables looking after the horses, exercising etc.

I remember as a boy meeting with the Tiverton Staghounds at Haddon and we killed the deer the other side of Timberscombe, which is quite a long way. I don't know whether father got word or was looking out for me and another visitor who was out, but he came out in a car with the groom for both horses. That's the only time I can remember having a lift home. It would have been a long way to hack back from there, but generally speaking I used to ride home. I know father was quite impressed because it was a long hunt and in country I didn't know. He got down to Timberscombe below the village, saw the deer coming out of the woods with the hounds behind him, followed first by Percy Yandle who was hunting them, and then me. He thought I had done pretty well to be there at the end of a day like that.

I didn't always have a chance to go hunting because if we had visitors or children who wanted to go they got the pony and I didn't; it was family holdback. But I was very lucky there were two ponies one of which was an old chestnut called Rocket who got to the point where I had to really favour him uphill. It is amazing to think how tough ponies are compared with horses. I remember once in the Barle Valley father was on his second horse, and I had been keeping up with him on my pony. He said,

'Go on son, your pony will go on all day, go up around the corner and look for the deer.'

He thought mine would go better than the horse he was riding.

Very often when we were hacking home from the Dulverton side Percy would be in front with the hounds, and Arthur Griffin would be at the back with me beside him. I would be asking him the names of the hounds all the way home, until there came a time when I could pretty well name every hound in the pack. I remember the Yandles shouting to each other across the valley, 'Percy have 'ee seed ort?', 'No nort,' and they used to talk to each other across the valley, a feature they were known for.

At the station right beside the hotel there was a siding where they used to push the horseboxes in. On hunting days there would be six or eight horses loading, taking them up the valley to Molland and beyond.

When the war came a lot of horses were commandeered, and a couple of army officers came to look over the stables. They said they wanted to take six. Father particularly wanted to keep one, a big old bay horse called Squire, 16 hands, which he used to ride. Looking at them, he indicated which he preferred them to take, saying of one they especially liked, 'I wouldn't have that one, he looks sound but it's not much of a thing really.'

'Oh Mr Nelder you can't pull the wool over our eyes,' they replied.

Anyway they took it and left his horse, so then for a few years we only had one horse, my pony and a mare I think."

§

Talking with Steve Martin

"I have hunted with the Tiverton Staghounds for over 60 years and record here my memories of the first meet that I attended, on 6 November 1931, having arrived at Middle Garland from Canada on 5 November. The meet was at Garland Cross, a much different place than of today – I recall high beech hedges which gave some shelter, but these have since been removed.

The Tiverton Staghounds were kennelled at Duvale Barton, Bampton and comprised, to the best of my knowledge, 20 couple of hounds. The hunt was run by four brothers of the Yandle family, Percy and Bert acted as huntsmen alternately, and Jack and Ern acted as whipper-ins; when not hunting they were all kennelmen. Hounds met on Monday, Wednesday or Friday three times a fortnight. In order to reach the places furthest from kennels they were hacked to Gidley Arms, then a public house, the landlord being George Aplin, and were kennelled overnight in order to reach the meet, such as Garland Cross, the following day. There were no horseboxes in those days. All riders hacked to the meet and there were as many yeoman riders as there were landed gentry and gentlefolk.

I recall the meet at Garland Cross quite clearly, with the huntsmen in their splendid red coats and the hounds kept in order, responding to every command and obviously waiting for the 'off'. Every arrival was greeted with a cheery 'good morning' and hats were raised to one and all. Ladies rode side-saddle and had veils (not seen much today). I only knew my own family at that meet but soon came to hear the names that I still know today: Irwin, Govier, Boundy and Reed, as well as others who seemed to know all the ins and outs of the countryside. They seldom missed a hunt whatever the weather. In due course I acquired an Exmoor pony and it enjoyed hunting as much as I did.

I remember being on the road between Bycott Lane and Wixon, hounds were running up from Garland Cross when I heard the loudest holler ever. It proved to be Eddy Reed (Walter's father) and it was a holler I was to remember for the next decade.

Attending Chulmleigh School it was not uncommon to hear hounds running down the valley to Chulmleigh Bridge and at lunch-time if they were still around, one or two of us would take off down to Park Mill Lane or Egypt Lane in pursuit of the hunt, overstaying our leave and getting back to school late only to stay after school and write 100 lines, 'I will not hunt in school time'.

I always enjoyed watching hounds hunting to the line, absolutely devoted to the scent, noses down, and on and on. In those days there was no land that was out of bounds to the hunt or the field, although I do recall certain terms attached to Kings Nympton Park. To be able to run in any direction uninterrupted made a big difference to the job of huntsmen and the field. There were no motorbikes to break the silence and the first cars were frowned upon. I remember one old stalwart remarking, 'They can't hunt with one of they things'. Having ridden to hounds I feel now that I have joined the vehicle tribe; there is no better joy than to be mounted on a horse that understands as much about hunting as its master. Most places were readily accessible for riders and hunting gates were provided to get around the fields and not over them. The gates were placed conveniently and for the purpose of hunting, although I do recall that they were useful when cattle broke out between farms. When I left school Bert Yandle asked me to cut back the bushes and ensure all gates between Bycott Woods and the bottom of Horridge Moor would open and pull shut *from the saddle,* as I recall his emphasising. With these gates in operation it didn't take a rider very long to get from Waterloo to Chulmleigh Beacon – surprisingly the line that the deer ran in those days is much the same today. Sadly many of the copses and woods are now gone forever. When hounds met at Garland Cross we nearly always received a joint from the hunted deer; far superior I may add to that from the now domestic deer farm (or poacher)!

With the outbreak of war and my call to King and Country, I lost touch with the Tiverton. However, I recall joining in the hunt once again after the war and sharing my petrol coupons with an old school friend. I noted for the first time a new huntsman at the helm, the Yandle brothers having retired. We shall never see hunting in their calibre again."

§

Talking with Jack Broom of Bampton

"I've been riding ever since I can remember, having a little Exmoor pony. I wasn't tall enough to get on him and had to get in the hedge to mount. I would never ride downhill but would ride uphill like mad and go hell for leather on the level. As soon as I had to go downhill I had to get off, don't ask me why because I can't tell you.

I was brought up at a place called Nightcott near Dulverton, of course you can't hunt there. The Tiverton Staghounds have been through a time or two, the Devon and Somerset won't go anywhere near it. My father was a blacksmith and I learnt my trade with him. I had two sisters, and my uncle lived at home, him and father doing implements and so on.

One day the foreman of the Carnarvon Arms stables came along; there wasn't a lot doing at the time, and not enough work for all of us. He said 'I could do with you, one of my workmen has left suddenly. So I talked it over with my father and that same night I went down, and started work the next morning.

You started at the bottom and moved up as people left; there was only one chap between myself and the second-in-charge. The first year I was there the bloke above me left, I stepped up in his place and then there was another chap came under me. After I had been there a couple of years, foreman Marshall gave up and a bloke called Bert Denscombe took over from him, then I went up in Bert's place. Reg Nelder, the owner of the

Carnarvon Arms, had two horses hunting with the Tiverton Staghounds and whilst working my way up I eventually got to ride second horse to him. Our job was to go on to the meet with the horses and hounds. Frank Needs was the groom for Percy and Bert Yandle at Duvale; Frank Needs, along with Arthur Griffin, the kennelman and whip for the staghounds, would bring on their horses. I used to bring on the Carnarvon Arms horses down to Riphay the home of Ernest Yandle and meet George Stone his groom. Together we would go down to the Black Cat where the Yandles would come up with the hounds, and from there we took them on.

Meeting down the Chulmleigh end we would go down the day before. Very often there were three horses to go from the Carnarvon Arms as there was usually somebody riding besides the boss. We would kennel the hounds and horses at the Gidley Arms for the night, and the following day the Yandles would come and take them on from there to the meet. As there was only room for Frank Needs and Arthur Griffin at Gidley, George Stone and I would carry on down to the Red Lion in Chulmleigh and stay the night. We both had to sleep in the same bed. One evening the girls had fixed it and it collapsed as we got in. We let it stay for the night and didn't bother to pick it up. The girls had a good laugh the following morning when we had breakfast, but there was hell to pay with the housekeeper and me and Stoney got in trouble as well.

Coming down once we lost the hounds on Beaples Hill, which wasn't fenced at that time. We always used to go across there, but this time three hinds came up across the hedge and away went the hounds. It was a Sunday afternoon; George Stone, Frank Needs and I had three horses each, and Arthur Griffin had two, and we had a pack of hounds in the middle of us. You can ride with three horses but you can't go through gates, you have to go around. We eventually picked the hounds up at Ash Mill, and then we had to come back and go on again. We used to see some fun! You try stopping hounds with three horses that get excited when you crack your whip.

The hounds were hunted alternately by Percy Yandle and Bert. Our job was to go on to the meet with the hounds and then kennel the pack at a farm when they moved off and stay there with the second horses. If we met at the Carnarvon Arms or Bury the pack would be kennelled at Windwhistle – that's the top of Haddon. As soon as they blew for the pack Arthur

Griffin would come back, let them go and away we'd go. You would see some fun then, especially if a deer ran across; we lost them a time or two. When they found, we would start hacking back with the second horses. Generally we used to change horses at Gidley Arms when they met down the Chulmleigh end because nine times out of ten they nearly always came back to Chain Bridge. There weren't the cars or motor bikes to turn the deer like there are now, they had it all clear going. By the time we got home with the first horse they would usually have killed at Chain Bridge or somewhere down there.

When we went out to Exford we would stop at the White Horse and lodge at Alfred Lantell's parents' place. He used to be kennelman for the Devon and Somerset Staghounds. Once when I took three horses over everybody was going to a dance. Ken Crook, who was grooming at Exford at the time, and his wife also worked there. We all went to the dance which finished at two o'clock and then I went back to the White Horse and stayed talking before going to bed back at the lodgings. I hadn't been there but half an hour when Mr Lantell called me to get up and do my horses. Afterwards I went back and had my breakfast and then went on with the hounds. I think they met at Shallowford. I hunted all day, went back to Exford and fed, left there at 10 o'clock and rode up to Comers Gate and across to Mounsey Hill Gate. I was dead tired so I put all the reins in one hand, lay over on the saddle and went to sleep whilst travelling back across Winsford Hill. Where do you think I woke up? Coming into Lady Street in Dulverton! I never found out where those horses came down, Higher Combe Drive or Marsh Hill. Bloody daft wasn't it, supposing anything had frightened them? Mind the horses were tired as well because they had been hunting all day. A horse will always take you home; if you're lost and you let the horse go he will take you home. It was half-past twelve or one o'clock by the time I got to Lady Street. It used to be a narrow road and the clattering of three horses' hooves woke me up with a start.

Back then the hounds could find their way home as well as the horses, but now they go by lorry and they don't know the way back. The only time they would get boxed was when we went up to the Quantocks and they would go on the train from Dulverton Station up to Wiveliscombe and then hack from Wiveliscombe to the Quantocks. Those train boxes were nice things, all padded and you had a compartment for yourself. It was only from Dulverton Station to Wiveliscombe then you had to get out again, but it was several miles if the horses had to hack. Once the Yandles met at Haddon and killed at Treyborough (on the way to Bridgwater) in the dark, with a hurricane lantern. We hacked from there back to the Carnarvon Arms after 7 o'clock at night. It was ridiculous, but we used to enjoy ourselves a sight better than they do today. That night there was Frank Needs, George Stone, me, Winkle Potter from the Lion Stables at Dulverton and two or three others, and we hacked all the way back behind the hounds. I had three horses that day.

The work used to be all right, but long old hours. It wasn't what you would call heavy work, and we used to enjoy it and enjoy the money. You would think nothing of picking up four or five quid a day in tips. Back then that was the equivalent of 20 quid in tips today, so that wasn't bad. A packet of Woodbines was 4*d* for ten, a packet of 20 Players was a shilling and a pint of beer was 6*d*. I didn't have a bad job, I used to get 39 shillings a week and get a Sunday off every third week; the first Sunday you would work all day, the next Sunday you would work until dinner time and have the afternoon off, and the next Sunday you would have the whole day off. You worked seven days a week and there was no such thing as overtime. I've started at 6 o'clock in the morning and still been there at 12 o'clock at night, but we didn't used to mind.

There used to be a French man come to the Carnarvon Arms each year who would hunt six days a week. He would arrive in July and go back at the beginning of November. He was very fussy. When you gave him his horse if it was raining you had to cover the saddle with waterproof, if you let a spot of rain get on his saddle he would show you up in front of the crowd. Everyone knew him and when you came home with his horse at night he would come out and blow his french horn and that would get the horses going. He would never give you a ha'penny while he was there but always left a good tip when he went. It was worth picking up, and always in an envelope.

I carried on with the Yandles till I was called up in the army. I had to register with the war police for six months in the 1920s. I was called up in the June and supposed to do until the Christmas, but they didn't say which Christmas, so I finished up doing near enough seven years. When I came out of the army I took on my father's business with about £100. In the end I worked for the Council driving a steam roller."

The four Yandle brothers when they were young men with their father Thomas Culverwell Yandle, taken at Riphay near Exebridge.
Left to Right: Bert, Ernest, Tom, Percy, Jack

Chapter Five

More memories of the Yandles, including the days of Ken Webber, Percy Pennington and Aubrey Besley

Talking with Denzil Shapland of Thurle Farm, Chulmleigh

"I was born at Thurle Farm, Chulmleigh in 1919. In 1895 my grandfather came here from Uppacott, Mariansleigh. He used to like a fair bit to drink, and rented under the Fortescue Estate. I take it that one night the agent out there got Granfer well and truly drunk. He had already bought Thurle Farm, and that evening the agent got him to sign the lease on Hansford Barton which the Fortescue also owned. So in 1895 Granfer had to go there to live and Thurle stayed empty till 1910 when Father's brother, Uncle John, got married. Then Granfer and Granny and Father came up here, but by that time it had got in a terrible state. Father got married on 6 November 1918 and I was born on 4 November 1919. When we were nippers there were 40 acres of ground two fields from the yard which Bill Crocombe has got now, that was all covert, and there was 140 acres of Colleton also covert.

This was an ideal place for deer, foxes, badgers, everything. You would see the deer lying there all summer, out in the middle of the day and they didn't take a bit of notice of you, being used to everyone on the farm, and that went on all my life. When the war started they became pests; there were 26 deer in the 40 acres of one sort and another and they had to be got rid of. Percy Yandle came down with three couple of hounds and put out six or seven of us with guns around here and we shot seven of those deer. I expect it was the spring of 1940 and of course there was no hunting right through the war. That's what Percy used to do during that period, shooting up one or two when they got a bit thick.

I remember one time out spring stag hunting, they took a very unusual route. Generally crossing this farm they would head for King's Nympton Park. You could not always go in there depending on the mood of Squire Tanner and they would try and head them off. Anyway this time he crossed near to Chulmleigh and didn't cross Thurle but made for Colleton Mill going across the Taw, on to Handsford, up to Ashreigney – absolutely different country to what we've been used to – and then on to Winkleigh. We had got an Austin Ten and Father used to sit on the front seat with the sliding roof back. He said, 'There goes the deer, look he's only about a field in front.' The two Miss Yandles, they were ahead of us with their Austin Seven and they stopped the hounds, with the riders being a long way back. They were holding the hounds when Percy came up. 'Cor blimey you silly b...s, why did you stop them for? We shan't do any more today,' and those hounds never spoke afterwards. Holding them for ten minutes meant the scent had gone and they never picked up the line again. It could have been a master hunt if they hadn't done that. Although it was strange country Percy said we would have got there.

We took back several deer in the back of the Austin Ten. When they had the opening meet down this end it was generally at Chulmleigh, and the kennel huntsman, Arthur Griffin, would hack the hounds down from Duvale the day before and kennel them overnight at Percy Pennington's. That was always a big day, practically all the Chulmleigh folks would come along and see these hounds in the night time. I suppose it was just a red letter day. For years Father harboured the deer on the farm so we always had some here and Percy Yandle would come down and say, 'What have you got for us then Charles?' The pack would be kennelled on the farm then.

I served in the Home Guard in Chulmleigh during the war and there was no mistake about it, we had seven or eight chaps who were damn good rifle shots, winning several competitions. After the war was over we kept on the 303 rifle club and used to shoot on the range. We had been down there one Saturday – I wasn't doing any hunting then, shooting that was my sport, the twelve bore or the rifle. When we packed up in the afternoon this deer came up to where we were and went in the brimble bush and laid down. Any rate, we packed up our gear and walked back to Park Mill and Ken Webber and Percy Pennington who had taken over the hunting from the Yandles were there with the hounds and they said 'We've lost the deer.'

'I know where he's too,' I said, 'in a brimble bush up by the rifle range.'

Course they didn't believe me. I said, 'He might not be there now, but when we left he was.'

We had to walk back a quarter of a mile from the range to Park Mill and I said to two or three of the chaps, 'I hope he's still there when they go back.' Anyway he was and I think that was the first deer Percy and Ken killed just after the war was finished. One of the chaps on the rifle range wanted to shoot the deer at the time and I said, 'Not bloody likely, don't you do that, leave him, it's nothing to do with us.' The funny thing about that was, hunting wasn't really my sport, the gun was.

On the farm Father and I used to trap and kill 2,000 rabbits a year, we were shooting when I was about 12. Father reckoned that to be any good at this, when a rabbit comes out of a hole you've got to kill it within four foot. He was a master twelve bore shot and used to say, and he wouldn't be far wrong, that for every 25 shots you should pick up 22 rabbits. Mind you, he didn't kill them all.

After the war was over the Tiverton Staghounds became a subscription pack, in fact it was a subscription pack before the Yandles finished. Then my uncle Percy Pennington and Ken Webber took on, they had a lot of things to learn. It wasn't easy to do what the Yandles did.

When Mr Besley took them on that's when my son Chris started hunting. My mother started him off because after Father died Mother went into Chulmleigh and lived on her own beside the church. She was a master hunter, going with Reg Hannaford and Charley Western. That was the three that would go every time they went out; Reg had got an old Austin Twelve, I believe it was.

I remember the time when I had a stag down by the bullocks. He had got two atop. Any rate he was there all summer and the next year he was three atop and still hung about. That winter

Chris picked up one of his horns, he had just shed it the spring before, and the workman on the farm picked up the other one and Chris has got that pair of three atop horns on a board. One of them is a bit lighter than the other because it lay in the ground a bit. The following year he was four atop and Aubrey Besley came down here and said, 'I'm meeting at Chulmleigh tomorrow, I want to hunt your stag.'

'Not likely mister,' I said, 'he's a beautiful one. I've been mixing with deer all my life and I haven't seen a better one.'

'Where's he to?'

I said, 'I've seen him this morning. He's either in Farmer Down's or Lakehead Moor.'

'Well,' he said, 'I'm going to hunt it tomorrow.'

Course that was it and I said fair enough. Any rate they couldn't find the deer and in the night he said, 'Where's that stag?'

'Well, I've got him in the barn, he's shut up!'

I never made out why they never found him. Anyway I didn't see him the next day but the day after he was back again. They didn't bother come looking to hunt him again, and I was just as well pleased. Any rate, he shed his horns and nobody picked up his four atop antlers. One day he was in his velvets and I got fairly tight to him because I suppose he was used to seeing me, I wasn't a stranger. I saw he had five atop – five beauties all his rights and I thought to myself what a smasher. I saw him regular and one day, come harvest, he had been found in a 12-acre oat field at Colleton. There he was, my stag, five atop and all his rights and the poachers had put a bullet in him and he went in there to die. They talk about cruelty and the funny thing about it is there hasn't been a deer that has stayed on the farm since. They might go across here but they never lie here.

Lord Fortescue had a son called Denzil. Course most of the tenants when they had boys as an honour called their sons Denzil. When I went to school there were four Denzils in one class, myself, Denzil Mortimer, Denzil Mock and Denzil Prettyjohns. Poor old George Jennings the Headmaster, would call us Denzil one, two, three and four and I'm the only one of those four left."

§

Talking with Stafford Babbage of Winsford

"I was born in 1927 in Chulmleigh where my father ran a corn merchants business. One of my first recollections was seeing my father's hunter go by the window as they returned from hunting with the staghounds. Father was never a foxhunter, and he told me he had hunted with Sir John Amory. My grandfather was a keen staghunter also, and died in 1900 aged 41 after a rusty nail caused blood poisoning.

I was brought up in Chulmleigh in an era when there were no support systems for the farmers – no grants, no subsidies – and times were very hard. Children ran about with no shoes or socks on their feet, tuberculosis was rife, and youngsters died very young. Those were sad times. Farmers could not pay my father for anything he sold them. Every year they would come in for a feast. Once a farmer came up to my father and said, 'Sorry governor, I can't pay you, but I've got a rick of hay you can have.' My father replied, 'I don't want your hay, I want your money.' That was typical of the times.

I rode a little pony belonging to Nick Prettyjohns, and Billy Pennington whose father, Percy, hunted the Tiverton Staghounds for a few seasons, rode a little grey pony. We never did any serious hunting, but when we did come across the hounds we would follow on. Living in East Street we saw the hounds coming up of a Friday, and they would hack up all the way from Duvale Barton. At that stage the Yandle brothers were hunting them. There were no lorries then and only wealthy landowners had transporters, but there was nothing like that in our area. You would see the hunt staff come up and stay overnight at Chulmleigh town with Percy Pennington who had a dairy/poultry business in the high street with shippens in the back. Having hacked about 20 miles from the kennels, they were tired and ready to get their horses and hounds to Percy's place. The next day they would meet in Chulmleigh Square and hunt all day, probably killing at Umberleigh or Portsmouth Arms. Times I've heard the Yandles say to their staff, 'You better get on back'. There weren't many cars about, but somehow the Yandle brothers got back to Duvale. Sometimes after a late finish, perhaps when it was hind hunting and it was dark, they would only get as far as Gidley Arms, so they stabled there and got back the next morning. It was a really hard life. Hounds would cover tremendous distances, and there is no comparison to what happens today when people box to the meets and then home afterwards, but perhaps that's for the good.

Before the war I was watching hounds one day and there were a lot of deer about. Coming out of Wixon we counted 30 hinds and I will always remember that they were all in a line. Tom Cullis was with me at the time, one of my young friends that I went to school with. Later, during the war, there were literally no deer in Wixon, they were all shot. It was very sad but that was part of the war effort when meat was rationed and whatever.

When I was very young, I went to school near Turners, close to the playing fields in Chulmleigh, behind the rectory. If the hounds were about running down from Chawleigh Barton, the teacher, Mr Jennings, would let us go down the lane and see them killing at Chulmleigh bridge. That is quite a thought really, but that was the way we were brought up you see.

I remember one day in 1945 Charlie Western the postman told my father that he had slotted a hind and a calf at Stone Mill. I passed Stone Mill the other day going to the Cheriton Hunt Dinner and Annual General Meeting, and the same deer rack was still being used. In 1945 when Charlie Western came back and said he had slotted a hind and calf it was quite an event because there were only 12 deer in the area. I remember seeing 12 come out of duck ponds at Affeton and those deer were either there or at Kings Nympton Park. That was a refuge for them because everyone was after them what with meat being rationed. Then the war ended, meat came off ration, and hunting started seriously again. The number of deer increased with deer filtering off Exmoor crossing at the Jubilee Inn into the Rackenford/Stoodleigh area.

At the time the Yandles gave up hunting and a few hounds that were left were kennelled alongside the Eggesford foxhounds at Wembworthy. This was when Ernest Ellicott of Chenson Farm took over as Master, with Percy Pennington and Ken Webber hunting the hounds. The Quantock Staghounds came down and took some of the best hounds, but I remember there were four or five couple left and they started up the Tiverton Staghounds again. We would go in the evening to see Percy Pennington skin the deer, and then we would go home and have a bath and read our comics, *Tip Top* and *Jingles*, I remember they were the ones at the time. All this is quite clear, as if it happened yesterday, although it was several years ago.

After a while there was talk of purchasing a cottage at Chulmleigh Bridge for the purpose of having kennels there, but things were not organised, and when funds were not forthcoming, the purchase did not go ahead. Then Ken Webber took the hounds on at Hilltown, Mariansleigh, as joint master. He started breeding a few hounds and the situation gradually improved. At the time I recall he had a job to find deer; Rackenford side there were only four that we knew of. I was out one day watching from Cove side and they had drawn from Swineham Hill right through Rackenford Moor, right down through what we called the chicken houses. Eventually, about 4 o'clock, hounds found a hind and calf and ran across the fields towards Chain Bridge, where they were stopped. I think Mr Ellicott at Chenson was the Master, and Ken Webber took over soon after that. Once or twice we ran up hinds and I particularly recall one occasion near Eggesford Station. The hind was up a stream near Southcott and Mr Ellicott went up with his gun. In the end they decided not to shoot her in order to let the deer numbers build up, which I thought was very sporting.

Back in those pre-war days and up to a point after the war, the deer would regularly cross out from Eggesford and right out to Bondleigh Moor towards the Halwell Junction, Okehampton area. After the war Ken Webber took hounds down there, as did Aubrey Besley and Robin Venner when he was Master. They would kill some lovely stags, meeting at Halwell Junction, Folly Gate, Brandis Corner. I remember we killed at Boyton Bridge, which was just north of the Launceston/Lifton area. Sadly the Forestry Commission would not let the staghounds down there. It was a pity because it's an area that could have been developed.

Living in Cornwall for a while, I went out with the Bolventor Harriers and saw 14 deer on Bodmin Moor. It's an area that could have sustained a pack of staghounds had they been properly run like the Devon and Somerset, Tiverton, and Quantock. Perhaps that wasn't to be, and I understand the Forestry Commission let the St Hubert Club in there shooting the deer as they do elsewhere, for example Thetford Forest in East Anglia. When I was up in Norfolk from 1970 to 1974 I saw some deer terribly injured with shotgun wounds. That's another subject. If you shoot deer you will get casualties.

I remember when Ken Webber was hunting in 1951 that hounds were scarce. Being in Kent at the time, I would bring down any hounds I could from the local packs. They were often hounds belonging to the South Down Foxhound kennels which had started rioting on roe deer. Mr Dagety was the Master with kennels at Ringmer near Lewis, Sussex. The hounds travelled in the back of my car on a Friday night (a company car I might add) to my parents' place in Exeter, where they stayed in a garage overnight before going on the next day. My mother would complain about the mess they made, but I cleaned it up afterwards.

I had the odd day mounted with the Tiverton Staghounds from 1952 onwards and met my dear wife in 1951. Pre-war we would meet in the Affeton Castle area, Rackleigh and the deer would regularly run right away and very often kill at Chain Bridge by Duvale Barton. The Yandles would bring out their puppies just to join in the finish of the hunt.

From my days on the gun was used, but my uncle was turned against staghunting when they used to rope them and cut their throats in front of the baying hounds. Of course it was an era when pigs were killed on the farm with a knife in their throat, and cattle were poleaxed. We used to watch in the abattoir at Chulmleigh and it was a way of life you were brought up to.

When I was very young I went badger digging. It was 1935 or 1936 and I went with a friend of mine called Richard Brady, whose mother used to keep what was an Inn right by the village pump at Chulmleigh. We were catching tiddlers one day and along came the Cheriton Otterhounds. We finished up under Park Mill, Chawleigh Barton and got home at 8 o'clock. I chased my mother upstairs with an otter pad. I never found out where it went.

Buying Mouseberry Farm for the Tiverton Staghounds when Robin Venner and Sid Gillbard took on the Mastership was a very good move because it was right in the middle of the country. Although it was a stopgap for different people like Ken Webber and Aubrey Besley etc. to take them, we will always be grateful they did, but one cannot beat a hunt having its own kennels as they do now.

All this I found most interesting to recollect. The Tiverton Staghounds have been a great source of interest to me during my lifetime and I hope to get out with them more regularly."

Talking with Mr Victor Mock of Burrington

"I was brought up at Sheepsbyre Farm near Chulmleigh. When the staghounds were about my father used to collect us kids together and take us to certain viewing points. If they were drawing around the Cheldon Valley, he would say, 'Right then you lot, the hounds are coming,' and he would take us off down to what they called 'Little Field' where the racks were, where the deer came through, keeping his eye above the hedge and he would say, 'Right keep quiet'. Once the deer had come through he would say, 'Stay still, the hounds will soon be here'. We would see them going up through Wixon, Bycott, watching the top of Horridge Moor and when they disappeared out of there, Father would say, 'They're making for Head Bridge, we won't see them again today.' And that was your hunting. That was your entertainment back in those days, except for a bit of rabbiting in the winter. There were no telephones, so the only way to find out whether they had killed that day was to go to the blacksmith's shop, perhaps for an ounce of tobacco or shoeing. That was how the information filtered back. I used to have a cob which I rode a bit but never actually went hunting with it myself. The sport grew on us, and the longer it went on, the more we did it.

Just before I left school the hounds were in the area, they had come in from King's Nympton I think. It was a very hot September day and we were digging spuds. Father was in hospital and two or three of us and Mother had got the horse plough spinning out the potatoes. By 4 o'clock everyone was crawling around too tired to move and Mother said, 'Right, we'll load up what we've got and go home.' Unknown to us the hounds had come into Wixon and gone through the bottom of Sheepsbyre. They had been drawing for an hour-and-a-half when suddenly they found and came right into the field where we were. I ran from the yard to Benley Cross and Arch Routcliffe, who farmed at Bealy Court, arrived there with his Ford 8 car. He was the first chap I rode with hunting in a vehicle. 'Come on,' he said, 'jump in here with me.' I had run all the way there and was covered in mud and dust.

Away we went to Cheldon, just below the village where we saw one of the Miss Yandles. Arch Routcliffe knew her well as he did the harbouring around our area together with Eddy Reed. Miss Yandle said they had killed the deer down by the bridge, and after exchanging a few words, she went off. Arch took me down as I had never been there at the end of the day and then the hounds were hacked back to Duvale.

He dropped me back to Cheldon Cross and I walked back to the yard to unload the spuds off the cart. I will always remember Mother saying, 'I thought you were tired when we finished this afternoon.'

'Oh I soon got over that,' I replied. Hunting became more and more of a bug as the time went on.

I was only 13 or 14 years old when I officially left school in 1936 or 1937. We went to school at Week and in the dinner hour between one and two rather than be in the playground when the bell went, more often than not we were over at Week or the top of East Week, South Week, Muddy Gate. If the hounds were around when we heard the bell go we would come running back and Miss Wadgers the teacher would say, 'You're late again boys, you've been hunting haven't you?', and we would skulk down under the desk and carry on with our work. This is how our hunting started, and from there it developed into going whenever we could. I didn't have much chance really, but that just made me more keen and I took more notice of where the deer were. Later I got into harbouring.

The pony that Eddy Reed used for hunting he also used for his harbouring down through Bycott, Wixon, Sheepsbyre, and looking around the various places along the Cheldon Valley. The hunt would drop him a card relying on him to find the deer. One day we were out taking in the cows from the moor when he came up on his pony and spoke to us. 'Have you seen any deer around here?' he asked.

'Oh no Mr Reed.'

'Well there's nothing around here, I'm off to the Cheldon Valley.'

Two days later the hounds came to Benley Cross, and after the meet they found the deer in Sheepsbyre quarry – that fouled us. When we saw Eddy again he said, 'Ha, you didn't know he was there did you?' It turned out to be a three-atop stag!

When the hounds were taken to Ken Webber's farm at Hill Town I helped to build the kennels. I got married and went to work there the same year as the hounds in 1948, taking a cottage on the edge of Mariansleigh village. After the war there was no way of getting into a farm anywhere, and my wife and I worked for Mr and Mrs Webber for three-and-a-half years. I was there to do the farm work really but I used to get involved in picking up carcasses and doing bit of skinning etc., getting more than ever into the hunting. Jack Sing and I used to go off evenings in the autumn when it was nearly dark. I remember once we went with this Fordson tractor and trailer to Spittle to pick up a dead horse in the middle of a field. Of course it was dark being October, so we called into the farm and Mr Down wasn't too pleased. I was supposed to have collectd the horse two days previously when it had died. He cracked right into me.

'This is a fine time of night to come, you should have been here two days ago,' he said.

'Well I'm sorry Mr Down but we've been sent now, can we borrow a light to see the horse?'

Lighting the tilly lantern, one of the lads came up with us and we used a digger and a wire rope to load the carcass onto the trailer which had no side boards. Fortunately the horse fell onto the trailer. Then we realised there was no jack on the trailer, so we had to lift up the draw bar, prop it up on something and back onto it. Then we set off towards Hill Town.

Between Beara Cross and Garland we met a policeman on his bike. 'Good night', Jack Sing said. We had no rear lights, only two headlights on his tractor. Jack kept looking back over his shoulder to see if the policeman was coming. Anyway we got back home and Bet said, 'Where have you been?' Luckily we had a good excuse for being late, otherwise she might have divorced me! We hadn't been to the pub anyway.

I got involved in the kennels a bit from time to time, getting to know the hounds. Very occasionally I would ride a bicycle exercising in the late summer, but I never did very much with the horses.

Eventually we had a farm at Stoodleigh and saw the hunting when they came that way. The memories of the Yandle family to me were always a bit special. They were professional people really, and when I moved to Stoodleigh I got friendly with Jim Yandle, Bert's son. We used to get on very well together; he used to come with me harbouring, asking 40 questions, doubting what you knew. If you said you had seen a deer or you saw a slot, he would say, 'How old do you think he would be?' or, 'Are you sure it was a stag?' and, 'Do you think it would be huntable.' I would say, 'You better go and look yourself.' A terrific chap for harbouring the deer, I missed him a lot when he died.

One of the Yandle brothers would drive more than he rode. Down our end, if they went into Sheepsbyre or in Muddy Gate to come to Week, Bycott, the one that drove the car would go to Bycott Lane and if he saw the deer cross there he wouldn't stop, but would shout at the top of his voice. The brothers all had terrific voices, you could hear them the other side of the parish. They were sure to be heard wherever they were. Then Mr Yandle would be off to see them come into the butter factory or somewhere like that. Invariably four or five of the best hounds would be down there long before the rest, and then the Yandles shouted again. Often they were short hunts. If scent was good and there was nothing in their way, no barbed wire etc., and if everyone opened the gates, they went right on. They were very successful with their hunting, and they would ride well too, often flying along with the reins resting on the horse's neck. 'No good holding the reins,' they would say, 'the horse wants help coming through'. But they were a real team, there's no doubt about that.

The deer originally drifted down this way from the Stoodleigh area. Very often more than half of them would go back that way, out through Gidley and on. You used to hear, a couple of days later, that they had killed at Chain Bridge. However, as time went on and the deer started breeding down here, they didn't go back to Stoodleigh so much. We would find in the Cheldon Valley and hunt around there being down at Kings Nympton Park in no time.

They were wonderful days with the Yandles and I'm glad I lived through it. The thing that disappoints me now is all this fuss about hunting, but what really concerns me is the fact that the deer will disappear if they stop hunting. I'm pretty sure they will. They can bring in all the legislation they like, but a lot of the farmers that don't hunt and have never hunted, accept the deer and accept the hunters. When they have gone they will say, 'The poachers are having their share, why shouldn't I?' I think the deer around this area will be very thin on the ground, but we shall have to wait and see."

§

The Tiverton Staghounds buy some hounds at Exeter
(*Tiverton Gazette*, 19 May 1921)

Sale of Hounds

Master of hounds and other interested parties from all parts of the West attended the first annual hounds sale held by Messrs. J A Collings and Sons, at their Repository, Exeter. Although there is a general shortage of hounds throughout the country, the catalogue included about 40 couple of foxhounds and harriers, drafts being sent from the East Cornwall, South Devon, Dulverton, East Devon, Lamerton, and Tetcott Foxhounds, and Seavington and Fowey Harriers' kennels. The majority of the lots were sold, the highest price realised being 40 guineas for one-and-a-half couple of the Dulverton Hounds, the property of Lord Poltimore. Among the hunts that purchased hounds were the Taunton Vale and Tetcott Foxhounds, Devon and Somerset and Tiverton Staghounds, Culmstock and Cheriton Otter Hounds.

§

Wednesday, 12 December 1928
Historic hunt from Bealey Cross

Followers of these hounds who attended this fixture had a long and strenuous day, when one of the toughest of all the tough deer for which this part of our country is famous, led hounds a merry dance from a quick find until daylight failed close to Barnstaple town, and beat hounds in the end. This good hind was found at once by the tufters in the Huntacott Coverts, and after running a big circle in the valley below, returned to Huntacott, where the pack was laid on. Scent was good throughout the day, and hounds screamed away to the valley of the little Dart, and came to water a little above Chulmleigh Bridge. Here a long check ensued, but at last, towards noon, the deer was fresh found in a small plantation above Stone Mill. Hounds then ran fast past Cheldon Rectory and Duckworthy to Winsood Moor, and down the valley past the keeper's house to Round Wood on the opposite side of the little Dart, then up through the woods which fringe that side of the valley, across the river just below West Worlington, and up to Affeton Moor. From here the line lay by Muddy Gateway to the Week Valley, and up to Odan Moor, where a left-handed turn took us along the high ground to the Meshaw–King's Nympton road at the crossway where it is joined by the road from Romansleigh. The chase then continued over the moors below Highridge and up to the road near Jose's Cross, and down to the River Mole near King's Nympton Park. Our hind then turned upstream, left the water on the further bank and continued her course past Chittlehamholt to the River Taw at Kingford Bridge. Here the deer was viewed in the water, and it seemed as if the end were fast approaching, but after going down stream for nearly a mile she left the water on the right-hand side of the valley, and without touching the big water again kept in under Warkleigh and opposite Umberleigh until reaching Hall. This straight-necked hind still held on her course and climbed to the top of Coddon Hill, which she crossed, and came down to the stream between Bishops Tawton and Landkey. Even now our quarry was not beaten but gaily climbed the next hill, overlooking Barnstaple where, as darkness was coming on, hounds were stopped shortly before 8 o'clock, and a real good hind which was never far ahead of hounds lives to run another day. So ended a fine hunt, hounds being about 28 miles from kennel. The point from Worlington to the spot where hounds were stopped measures a good 17 miles straight across the map, and hounds must have run double that distance.

During this run a young motorcyclist from King's Nympton gave a lift to another young man, and together followed the devious route led by the stout-hearted hind. When near Chapelton Station, the shades of evening commenced to fall, and the mechanically mounted sportsmen decided to return home. The driver asked his friend on the pillion to assist in starting the engine with his feet, hobby horse fashion, in order to improve on this method, the passenger slipped off and pushed the machine until away it reared "on top". When near Umberleigh our young motorist stopped to speak to an acquaintance to whom he described the run which he and his friend had enjoyed. On being asked where his friend was, he replied, "Up behind me," but looking around, he stared at the empty pillion and added, "He isn't though! He must have fallen off. I must go back and look for him." Turning quickly he clanked down the road for a mile or so and found his friend studying a timetable as he trudged towards Umberleigh Station!

§

Friday, 27 April 1934
Hunt on Bodmin Moor

On Friday April 27th Tiverton Staghounds met at Pinsla Park Lodge, Glynn, near Bodmin. No distance is too far for the Yandle Bros who brought 14 1/2 couple to the meet which is over 80 miles from the Tiverton kennels. All difficulties occasioned by the long distance from home were got over by the kindly co-operation and generous help of the Master of the North Cornwall Foxhounds, Captain Hall, who arranged for the transport of hounds, horses and the hunt staff and provided additional horses and accommodation at St. Breward. It must be many a long year since the hills and valleys of Bodmin resounded with the notes of the staghunter's horn, but at one time red deer seem to have been fairly plentiful in Cornwall. History relates that in the reign of King Henry III a certain Lady Athtone incurred the displeasure of that monarch, and was fined six hundred pounds for having killed six stags at different times near Looe, and salted them down for her servants' use. Subsequently the deer in the duchy ceased to exist, and the nucleus of the present herd of some eight or ten deer no doubt came originally from Exmoor, from which the deer have spread Southwards through the country now hunted by the Tiverton Staghounds. It has been well said that the love of staghunting and the desire to see the stag is engrained in the nature of the Westcountry man and certainly the men, women and children of Cornwall, augmented by visitors from Devon, Somerset and Dorset, showed themselves no exception to the rule, for the riders present at the meet and during the day could be numbered by hundreds. In addition to the large number of people in cars and on foot. The pack having been kennelled, quite near the meet, tufters were drawn, and operations began in the wooded valley, semicircular in shape, which runs from Cardinham to the Fowey Valley at Bodmin Road railway station. Here the harbourers reported deer to be lying, and the whole of the tufting could be watched from Cardinham Moor. It was not long before two stags were on foot, but scent in the covert appeared to be almost non-existent, and it was not until about half past one that an opportunity occurred of laying the pack on the line of one of the deer. The stag was at first unwilling to leave his stronghold, but finding hounds unpleasantly close, he rose to Cardingham Moor, in full view of the large number of foot people and others who were waiting there. After crossing the moor and keeping above Pinsla Park, hounds hunted over some enclosed country and through various large woods, and came down to the River Fowey. A long cast down stream to Glynn led to no result, but on trying upwards in the direction of Liskeard, the line was recovered, and the chase continued through the grounds of Lewarne away to the St Neot River and into the Fowey valley again under Doublebors House. Here the stag was reported to be well over an hour ahead, but hounds were able to hunt for a considerable distance up the valley, until another long check occurred. At length a cast back led to a fresh find, and hounds now at close quarters with their quarry, streamed away over the neighbouring moors on the west of the River Fowey, then came down to the river, which they crossed and climbed the opposite side past Carkett for Siblyback Moor. Here the stag lay up in a bog, down to Siblyback, eight miles from Launceston where he was taken shortly after 6 o'clock, near a mine shaft before he could reach the stream below. Thus ended an enjoyable hunt, in the course of which a great deal of country was covered, the furthest points being over ten miles apart on the map.

§

Tuesday, 5 September 1934

The season began in accordance with the usual custom with a meet at Swineham Hill on Wednesday September 5th. We were especially pleased to see the Master of the Quantocks, Mrs Winbush, with Mr Winbush, who with their usual keenest stayed until the finish. To the universal regret Mr Jack Yandle who held the mastership for 15 years with such marked success retired at the end of last season, and his place has been taken by his brothers Messrs P. Yandle, E. Yandle and A. Yandle as Joint Masters. The late Master was out on this occasion and will, it is hoped, find it possible to continue to hunt regularly with his old pack.

§

Friday, 25 January 1935 Hele Bridge
Fitting Prelude to Master's Wedding

The meet was fixed for the day previous to Mr Ernest Yandle's wedding, and was largely attended by the relatives and friends of his charming North Country bride, as well as by the regular followers of these hounds. An enjoyable hunt was a fitting prelude to the subsequent festivities, and all join in wishing the bride and bridegroom the best of luck, and continued prosperity to the pack which the Yandle family have hunted so successfully ever since the war.

§

Left: Percy Pennington, huntsman of the Tiverton Staghounds at Chulmleigh 1946

Below: Percy Pennington, huntsman of the Tiverton Staghounds in 1946 coming down to Leigh Cross, Chulmleigh

In conversation with Aubrey Besley

I spoke to Mr Aubrey Besley who was Joint Master and huntsman of the Tiverton Staghounds from 1958 to 1969. He talked of the four Yandles who hunted hounds from 1919 to 1945 and for whom he had a lot of admiration.

"Percy and Bert Yandle hunted on alternate days, Ernest carried the gun, being a first class shot. Jack was older again but I did not know him so well. When the hounds met down the Chulmleigh end they would bring them the day before to Bourne Farm behind the Gidley Arms and stop the evening. In the early days of the Yandles hunting, the deer would run back from Chulmleigh, but as the deer decided to live down there the younger ones who were born in that area did not come back and so they hunted further down as far as Portsmouth Arms.

Percy did not get married, neither did his three sisters Clare, Kate and Amy, Clare living to be 108. The Yandles were real craftsmen at their hunting and had terrific voices, if they shouted you could nearly hear them in Tiverton. Bert was the clever one with the hounds, Percy bought the horses and was impetuous, he had to rush everywhere. If that was the quickest way he would take that route, always scraping himself and getting his face covered with blood. When changing their horses they would jump across and the second horseman had to come on quickly. The brothers had the knack of the job, Percy would keep George Snell galloping up beside him for a long time before changing over. Just when you thought they were going to jump across and George took his feet out of the stirrups to get off, Percy kept going. You don't see that now, that was all part of it I thought.

Mr Aubrey Besley on horse (Joint Master) with his father standing beside him on the right. Standing to the left, Mr Aubrey Hosegood (Joint Master)

Percy Yandle told me he never had to stop for fog down at

the Chulmleigh end, but up at Stoodleigh it would prevent him from hunting. He said, if you have a frost and want to test if you can hunt then you must go out in the middle of the field and if you can stick your finger in the ground its alright to go hunting, but if you can't then it's no good.

The Yandles told me the story about General Livingstone-Learmont who lived at Stuckeridge House; he used to ride with the Tiverton Staghounds and Foxhounds. One day one of his horses caught its toe in the stable yard and went down cutting its knees. The General made Wilson the groom take the horse down to Duvale for the Yandles to be given to the hounds. Wilson rode a horse and lead the injured one. When he got there he said to Mr Yandle,'The General has sent this horse to be destroyed.'

'Oh,' said Percy Yandle, 'you can't have him put down like that.'

'Well that's his orders.'

'You go back and ask him if I can buy the horse.'

So Wilson rode back to Stuckeridge and gave the message to the General who said, 'You ask Yandle how much he's going to give me.'

On the return journey Percy said, 'Six pounds.'

Off Wilson went again, and the final word was yes, Percy could have him. They kept that horse, and got him right, riding it 13 seasons with the pack. It's absolutely true, Bert and Percy have both told me that story. When you were out with them they would tell you all these things, I appreciated it and enjoyed listening to them.

1956 Tiverton Staghounds in Chulmleigh.
Left to Right: Jim Cole, (whipper-in), Ken Webber (huntsman), Daisy Webber

I said to Bert Yandle about the record number of deer they caught, but they didn't like to hear that. They felt that it was the sport they provided that mattered, never mind how many deer were caught, but they did say they were out on 48 days once and caught 52 deer.

When the deer was at bay Bert Yandle always took his cap off, saying it was a sign of respect, he has given you a good run now you should take your hat off.

At Duvale Percy Yandle had half a door that hung on top of the galvanised roof and he pulled a cord to let the door go bang if the hounds started to fight. It stopped them just long enough for him to get out there.

The Devon and Somerset Staghounds used to have a week's staghunting in the Stoodleigh area staying at Duvale. I think they brought some horses and also hired some to give their lame ones back at the kennels a rest. Back in those days there were more livery stables around, including two or three at Dulverton. Bert told me that as boys, when the Devon and Somerset were staying at Duvale and hunting in the Iron Mill Valley, they could hear the sound of the hounds when the wind was right coming down the chimney at their home.

When the hunt staff came home from a day's hunting from Chulmleigh their route was Gidley, Creacombe, Swineham Hill, and back the coach road at Stuckeridge. At this point they would start blowing the horn to warn them at Duvale to be out ready to take the horses in.

The Yandles taught me all about harbouring and I started in 1950. The postman in the Oakford area would help me, he was a most knowledgeable man. He used to ride a pony. I made it my business to see him. Going around with the post he would watch the hedges to see where the deer had been crossing and give me the information I needed. It saved me miles, he was naturally born to look.

Bill Ellicott would do a bit of harbouring for me when I was hunting the hounds. One day when we met at Chawleigh, Bill came up to the meet and said, 'The deer's gone out, he's crossed just above Stone Mill and into East Leigh.' I told Ivan, my whip, to go up to East Leigh where they cross on the top. 'If it's a huntable deer you let the hounds go, don't stop them.'

The hounds get to know your habits, they know you as well as you know yourself. I decided not to get off my horse, and I said, 'That's it you fellows,' and they jumped in over the hedge, drawing the cover on their own. It was two hours since the deer had crossed and to start with the hounds did not speak, bearing around to the right as they spread out. Then I heard Traveller speak, he would speak to a stag but not to a hind. I waited, for what seemed a long time, to see which way he would go. Then Ivan shouted on the hill and off we went, never touching hounds till we bayed the deer. I always thought everything went right for me that day. We went up the Cheldon Valley, Muddy Gate, Oldham Moor down towards Romansleigh and swung back; of course he wouldn't have got turned back in those days by cars. We killed the stag in the middle of Horridge Moor.

Meet at Rackenford, 1956. Right to Left: Jim Cole (whip), Cyril Manning, Ken Webber (huntsman)

I used to get into trouble because I wouldn't let anyone shoot the deer before the hounds got there. Mr Yandle said, 'Don't you ever let them do that, you'll never make a pack of hounds.' I remember I could have let them shoot the stag under Cheldon once, from there he went by the milk factory under Taw Green and we lost him. I was criticised for that but it didn't deter me one slightest bit, I did what the brothers had taught me and they were right, dear old boys.

When I took over the hunting, Mr Whitmore arranged for me to have six couple of unentered hounds from Sir Watkin Williams Wynns' pack in Shropshire. They came down by train in horseboxes to Tiverton station, where I collected them. One of those hounds won the first prize in their puppy show, but they didn't value them unless they did their job. Sir Watkin Williams Wynns bred more hounds than they ever wanted. Mrs Matson, who was keen on this pack, came down and looked at them. She said, 'I see you have still got that first prize hound.'

'Yes, I don't know how I came by that one madam.'

Well she wasn't going to elaborate, not to me anyway.

Three or four of those hounds turned out very well, but that hound wasn't any good; he was there for his looks.

Meeting the train with the horseboxes you daren't let the side down, because all the hounds would be gone. Somebody had to climb in to the groom's side through a little latch and catch the hounds, passing them out to Jim Cole, the whip, one at a time. I then had to put collars on and couple them up and lift them into the Landrover.

Bert Yandle told me to take all the hounds I could get from any pack, never mind if they were any good, but to buy plenty of cartridges. He also said to take any skirters I could get. Fred Tucker, kennel huntsman of the Silverton, let me have a Welsh long-haired skirter from his pack. The Master, Captain Knight-Bruce, hunted the hounds and I think he had four or five couple of these Welsh hounds. However, the next Master, Michael Austen, didn't like the look of them and was going to put them down, so Fred Tucker let me have one of these hounds called Morgan and told me he was a good hound to hunt. I took him and that got us on our feet, that hound together with some hounds of Mrs Smyth's bitches, a bitch that she let me have, and a bitch that the Tiverton Foxhounds gave me unentered. After two seasons I could see Morgan was hunting well, taking to deer hunting, he would hunt the road through 20 or 30 cars.

Aubrey Besley Joint Master and huntsman 1958–1969

Bert Yandle would come every year to see what hounds I was going to breed from and said, 'What are you going to use this year then?'

'I don't know Mr Yandle.'

'Have you got any hounds you like?' I took out Morgan and he said, 'I've seen him hunting a bit.'

I can see the old man now, lighting his pipe at the same time he was talking to you and burning his finger. I thought he would turn Morgan down flat, being Welsh.

'When he comes to a hedge Mr Yandle,' I said, 'he stands back and takes off like a racehorse, pitching off on the other side.'

'Do you like that hound?'

And I said yes.

'You've got to use him then.' And that decided me.

'Well you would never use a rough-haired hound like that, would you Mr Yandle?'

'Never mind what he looks like,' he said, 'you don't employ a man for his looks do you, but what he can do.'

It's true, and he gave me the best advice. He didn't want to build the pack up to show, but to do the work. He gave me the ideas and I implemented them. I spent a lot of time on the breeding, watching what hound was doing what; if I didn't I shouldn't have done anything. When I gave up the hounds, I left 95% of Morgan's bloodline there.

I kept him 12 months longer than I should have. He got old and couldn't hunt very much. I might take him out to Stoodleigh and if he wanted to go home he could, but I kept him to use him again.

Mr Yandle said, 'You've got to hit right and breed from the right line that will produce 75% workers.' Once I hit that line he said, 'Now you keep to it.' Of course the old man was right, wasn't he? I did everything he told me to the letter, and that's the only way I got on.

People today want nice looking hounds to show, but that doesn't catch deer. It's alright if you can afford it, like the Duke of Beaufort etc., who have the staff and the money. You can't afford to do that down here, you've got to sacrifice one thing or the other and I wasn't going to sacrifice the work for the showing. One of the things the Yandles told me was you've got to breed your own hounds, you won't do anything if you don't, and you must watch what you breed from. They taught me what I should look for; if it wasn't for them I wouldn't have known what to look for.

Ken Webber, who hunted the hounds before me, knew deer. If he was going along slotting he knew when he was on the right one. Ken had a hard job I reckon – if he had the facilities available today he would have been the star man in my estimation, but the money wasn't about. He was running the kennels for about £600–£700 and couldn't afford to expand what with his farming and one thing and another, but he did extremely well under the circumstances. I had some good hunts with him, he found deer where a lot of people would never think of looking; he seemed to have that sound knowledge. Ken was an unassuming chap and wouldn't fall out with anyone. If you didn't keep him in sight when going through a cover he would be gone; if I lost him down the Chulmleigh end I would have to start tracking him.

When I became Master and huntsman, Ernest Mortimer was the secretary. One day he took up a load of poultry to Smithfield Market in his brother Bill's van. I went up with him and he said at the same time we could go to Moss Bros to look at some red coats. I suppose I would normally have gone to Windsor's in Exeter to buy one, but it was all new to me. There were second-hand ones there which had been well maintained; I should imagine they came from the best hunts where they would have a new coat every year. We brought back three red coats, the other, which didn't look like it had been worn much, was for Jim Cole the whip.

Ernest was a good secretary. Everything had to be right, being a Wing Commander in the Air Force. He kept me on my toes, which was a good thing. Geoffrey Sellick was also a good secretary and Jack Adams a good Chairman.

I remember I was on the Gidley road at 10 o'clock one night looking for a lost hound when this car came along, slowing down behind me. When I looked around I thought it was Sir Dennis Stuckley's vehicle. Earlier the hounds had run into his pheasants at Affeton and I knew I should have stopped them. I thought I was going to be in trouble so before he said anything I apologised for going in there.

'Oh that's all right,' he replied. 'What sort of day have you had?'

So that occasion didn't turn out so bad after all. When you think you're in trouble, sometimes it works out all right, and when everything seems OK that's when the phone will start ringing.

When I had the hounds there was an old man of nearly 90 called Bert Heal who was a great uncle to Arthur Heal who hunted the Devon and Somerset Staghounds. He farmed Stanterton Farm at Washfield and when he retired he had a little cottage in the village. He would say to me, 'Don't you ever pass here unless you blow your horn.' I used to blow well before I came to his cottage, he just liked to open the window and ask what we had done and that sort of thing. By doing that it made his day. In the summer when we did the exercising and got the hounds fit we would always go down to his cottage, and he would bring us out a drink; he was one of the real old stalwarts.

Mary, my late wife, remembered the time when she was at Wonham Barton, not far from Duvale, and she had a visit from Jon Pertwee who later became famous as Dr Who. He used to come down from Highleigh and go into the larder and pinch some cakes if he could. One day she caught him and threw a bucket of water over him! He ran off and she didn't see him again. Mary had a photograph of Jon's mother on a horse while riding out with the Tiverton Staghounds.

We met at Knowstone Moor one day, drawing thc tuftcrs down under the sheep dip by Kidland Castle where we found an autumn stag. It was the middle of October and this one didn't want to run. He lay down beside a wood rick in the middle of the cover and didn't move. Cantering up with the pack I layed on the hounds but the stag didn't get up until the very last minute, the hounds almost surrounding him. Suddenly my horse put the brakes on and I went straight over the top of him. They reckon I landed where the deer had been lying – the stag got up for me to lie down.

An artist's impression of Mr Besley coming off his horse in direct line of the stag

At one time I had four grey horses and Ivan Webber, my whip, said, 'For God's sake don't buy another one they're too much to look after.' When buying a horse it had to be sound. It may not be pretty to look at, but it had to have four good feet. As it happened the horses I saw were usually bays or dark bays which I didn't like, greys seemed to suit me better. I understood why Ivan had a job looking after them, and poor old Mary would always be washing the beggers. I couldn't have hunted the Tiverton Staghounds without Mary's help.

I remember Jack Sing used to come out and bring his horses in a made up trailer with a steep ramp, pulled by a Fordson Major tractor. I wish I had a photograph of it.

When the three packs of staghounds came to Crowcombe House on the Quantocks in 1970, Alfie Giles the Quantock Staghound huntsman hunted them. By that time I had given up hunting, but it was still in me. I knew all the hounds, they were a little bit different from when I gave up. There were 6 1/2 couple from each pack and I was interested to see how the hounds were hunting. When they brought the stag to bay I watched them and there were five couple of Tiverton Staghounds, one couple of Quantocks, and one Devon and Somerset hound; all the rest were way back. I thought that showed the calibre of the Tiverton hounds.

When Squire Tanner had Kings Nympton Park times were difficult, just like today. Sometimes you could go in there and others not at all. When he died his widow wanted to see me. I was ushered into this great big sitting-room with a big fireplace. It was a bitterly cold February afternoon and a tiny fire was burning in the grate. The old lady was sitting in the armchair with shawls wrapped around her to keep warm. She said, 'I want to help you. I will let you come into the park but don't stay too long.' This would have been contrary to her husband's wishes, but she was originally from Warwickshire and had her own hunter, previously having hunted with the Warwickshire foxhounds. The squire would never let her hunt with the hounds down here, although he did. I think he might have ridden in Sir Ian Amory's time. She said, 'I miss my hunting but there, I really do want to help you.'

Mrs Wingfield was the lady who kept me well informed about the Park – you've got to have inside people, haven't you. Dr Wingfield would shoot and fish on the estate and was well in with the squire who would open up his heart to a fellow like that. Of course he would come back and tell his wife and she would let me know if I was going to be in trouble; she was so good to me. When Mrs Tanner died the King's Nympton Park Estate went to the niece and I had to go and see her. She said, 'I'm quite willing to let you carry on the same as Mrs Tanner agreed.' After the business we would talk about something that she liked – fishing and shooting. If ever I was hunting down there and she was fishing I would leave the hounds and ride down and speak to her for a minute; it was time well spent. Jim Medland, the bailiff on the estate, was very good to me as well."

Meet at Chawleigh in 1965.
Left to Right: Cyril Manning, Aubrey Besley (Master and huntsman), Ivan Webber (whip), Robert Ayre

Mrs Wingfield who kept Mr Besley informed on King's Nympton Park

§

Extracts from Ivan Webber's diary while he was riding second horse and later whipping-in to Mr Besley

"We were exercising hounds along the main road on foot one day when this big Mercedes car came along beside us. The car stopped and the gentleman got out. He was wearing plus fours and a bow tie and his wife wore a nice flowery dress. The gentleman was talking to Mr Besley and he said, 'I think it is a wonderful pack, I really do'. Just as Famous was going to do his little job over his leg I shouted, 'Famous', and the gentleman said, 'I'm sure they must be'! It didn't matter where Famous was, he would cock his leg over people; we stopped taking him to the shows for that reason. He would pinch the ice-cream from the children and lick all the chips he could find, and would never ever go around the ring with us.

Another time we were exercising the puppies with Mr and Mrs Besley and Jim Cole. I was riding one horse and leading the other. Mr Besley was on in front when an Austin car came around the corner with Mr and Mrs Smith from Rackenford in it. Mrs Smith was driving and the car was loaded with eggs and chickens going to Tiverton Market. When they came around the corner and met us, Mrs Smith panicked and drove over the hedge, tipping the car on its side. All our horses bolted one way and another, with hounds going in every direction. By the time the Master got the hounds back Mrs Smith was just climbing out of the window saying, 'I'm all right'. There were eggs and chickens everywhere. She looked in the window and said, 'Come on Tom, get out'. He was throwing the chickens in the back seat as he climbed out. We uprighted the car and they saved what they could and went off to market. We never heard anything from them – not a court case like you would today. In those days a court case would have ruined us so we were grateful to Mr and Mrs Smith for not claiming any damages against us."

Ivan Webber (whipper-in) 1964–1969, displaying the biggest head taken above Cove Quarry during Aubrey Besley's Mastership

§

Talking with John Lake of King's Nympton

"My father was born at Lake's the butcher's shop at King's Nympton, one of a family of nine, six brothers and three sisters, all eventually riding hunting. They used to have the Hunt Ball there for the Tiverton Staghounds in the slaughterhouse. One of Father's brothers would play the violin and another sister would play the piano. They would have a fair session at these Balls and there would be another gang in the house playing cards, and that was how it went for several years.

Father eventually came to Howards Mill to live and that is where I was born. I can remember the Yandles hunting an autumn deer just up the valley towards Huxford and father went down and brought the carcass out with a horse and butt (a short tipping cart in other words), and I walked behind that one with the riders coming out behind me. I wasn't very big then. I remember when Percy Pennington and Ken Webber were hunting the hounds. They would hunt on alternate days and on the days they weren't hunting they would be whipping-in to each other. Percy was only there for a season or two and later on Charley and John Ellicott shared the whipping-in for Ken Webber. One would go one week and the other the next.

When Percy and Ken took on hunting from the Yandles, rationing was still in place and the gear people wore was anyone's guess; it was what anyone could get hold of, for example there were no riding boots as such and everything was on coupons, including the coats right up to 1948–49. I remember Percy Pennington wearing a swallowtail dinner jacket like the undertakers wore, he couldn't get a red coat at the time because of the rationing. It was two or three years before anyone could get very much.

I hunted on Walter Reed's pony a few times and one day from Spying Copse we started a big stag. Percy Pennington was hunting them and he cursed me for getting in the way. We went right up to Colleton Mill, into the Manor, coming back the road at Bridge Reeve, up across and finished the other side of Merton. No one had any fit horses and there were no second horses back in those days, they just ran out of horse power. Percy Pennington turned around to me and said, 'You little bugger, you're still here in spite of everything.' We stopped at the Eggesford Foxhound kennels on the way home and had a cup of tea with Bert Wills the huntsman. In the end we hacked all the way home. The next time they were out they did virtually the same route and finished up at Jacobstowe, and that was on one horse; no changing horses or anything.

I bought a hunting horn for Walter Reed once at Yendells in Barnstaple for £2. I wanted to repay him for letting me ride his ponies. He took it but gave me the money back and that horn has been legendary in North Devon, and he has been blowing it ever since at sheep fairs for the hunt and anywhere and everywhere. He has also fooled several people on non-hunting days by blowing it.

There was no gun as such on the hunt horses for two or three seasons because you couldn't get them; they used to land up going into the nearest farm.

When I left school you could do virtually all the hunting for the season from the Chulmleigh end. I went right through a season and they never went up the other end at all."

§

Talking with Ken Blackford from Rackenford

"I was born at Malson Farm, Rackenford, and Father used to hunt with the Yandles. They always had their opening meet the first Wednesday in September, at Swineham Hill. That was a regular occurrence, I've heard them say. I've heard the story told when Father used to ride and one day they found a stag in Little Rackenford Brake and he went right away to Gidley and on to Chulmleigh, and they killed at North Tawton. When it was time to come home, I suppose it was dark, and they came back to Lapford and a chap called Henry Bedell said, 'We shall never see Rackenford again'. They stopped there and went in the pub and stabled the horses and then rode home in the moonlight. They got home about half past two in the morning.

My memory when I first started hunting was of Ken Webber. My uncle, Alf Pincombe, had a garage in Rackenford; he used to like a bit of hunting and we used to hire a car from him for the day – he didn't charge a lot. Trouble was, they liked to stop at every other pub and have a drink.

It was very rare for a deer to come across to Rackenford because no deer lived here, as such they were very scarce. I remember I was ten years old and I was home from school one day; Father was making a hedge just up the top of the lane and I was up there tinkering around when a stag came in across the field with two couple of hounds after him. All the vehicles started going up the road, I say all the vehicles but there weren't many in those days. In any case, we heard the horses galloping up across the road toward Rackenford and we got up the top of the road and had a lift with somebody, and they killed that stag at the bottom of Worthy Farm. That deer had come all down the Chulmleigh end onto Kennerleigh Wood and had come right across Puddington and that way in and, like I said, it was very rare for a deer to come this way back in those days.

Then we got into the days when Lord Eldon was up at Rackenford Manor. The first deer that I can really remember stopping here was one day when the foxhounds met up at the Manor and four deer came down under Wilson's fields. I walked out there the Sunday morning and I saw these four deer and they stayed around here for quite a while. That was the first time really that I can remember having deer in our valley to stay. About ten years ago over Wilson Lane, Linda my daughter and I saw about 21 stags in a little three acre field. They ranged from big autumn stags right down to prickets. Since then they've gradually become more established here. We've had more deer I suppose in the last two years in our valley than we ever had; it's nothing to see 20 or 30 deer here regularly. We never used to see them like that years ago. You could say there are probably 30 deer down at Bradford, another 60 or 70 up around Rackenford Manor, and another 20 at Moortown. I suppose today hunting is a totally different style because to a certain extent it relies on the vehicles' information, but years ago if hounds couldn't hunt it, or the huntsman slot it, I would say many deer were lost.

For four or five seasons now I have been helping out Stuart Kelland the Joint Master, together with Michael Snell and Brian Palfrey. Taking the burden away from Stuart a little we all help by arranging meets and seeing the farmers and doing a bit of PR work. Covering Bradford, Ashmoor, Creacombe, Moortown, Witheridge and Templeton areas, we have no set boundaries. I enjoy doing it but sometimes it can be a bit frustrating when hounds split up on fresh deer as our country is not that easy to get across, incurring a lot of road work. I must say the farmers are most helpful and tolerant and it is particularly pleasing to be able to hunt regularly around the manor area thanks to the Paxton family."

§

Talking with Betty Palfrey from Bullaford Farm, near South Molton

"I started hunting with the Tiverton Staghounds when Mr Besley was hunting the hounds, he was a good Master and a great hound man and was respected by everyone who was lucky enough to have hunted then. I was fortunate to be able to mix business with pleasure. In the summer Mr Besley would buy many of his hunt horses from me, so that he had enough horses ready for the coming season. I think I am right in saying that one of the first horses he bought from me was for his late wife, Mary. It was a very attractive grey mare about 15.2 hands and Mary enjoyed hunting her for many seasons.

That was when I lived at Lodfin Farm, Bampton, with my uncles Edward and Robert, who enjoyed the horse activities. Then we moved to Bullaford and carried on selling good horses. I had a lovely lady, Mrs Wimpenny, who kept horses here at livery. She came from a great hunting family in Yorkshire. When she came to the West Country she hunted three days a week with different packs, but she really did enjoy her days with the Tiverton Staghounds. She put me to shame the first day we were going to hunt with this pack. I had tacked the horses when she drove in the yard, looked at them and said, 'Well off come the nose bands. I have read about this farmers' pack, and the tradition is no nose bands.' From then on we never used them.

Time went on, Mr Besley retired from the mastership and Mr Robin Venner and Mr Sid Gillbard were acting Masters, with Walter Ash as huntsman. Good sport continued. I remember a meet at Swineham Hill when we killed at Cullompton. During that day Mrs Wimpenny was chased by an anti-hunt person with a broom and my horse jumped in the River Exe by Bickleigh. We were among the few people at the kill and were so proud to be given a slot.

I remember hunting at Chittlehamholt. We were riding single file down through a wood. Walter was standing at the bottom of the path having lost his hunting horn. Someone said, 'What are you waiting for Walter?'

He said, 'I have lost my hunting horn, and I'm waiting for Betty Palfrey to find it.'

They laughed and said, 'She is blind as a bat.'

He said, 'She can't see very well and will be looking down, so there is a chance she may find it.'

Sure enough, I was looking down in order to avoid the overhanging branches and to protect my contact lenses, and I found it, picked it up, and handed it to him.

Another day's hunting at Chittlehampton, when we were riding through a wood a man approached with a shotgun, hurling abuse. I thought, what do I do now? So I put my arms up and said, 'I surrender'. He put the gun away in amazement and we quickly got out onto the road.

I would go on telling of memorable days but I will close by saying how lucky I feel to have hunted in that era when the hunting was good, there was very little hassle and we worked hard and played hard. Those were the days."

§

Talking with Brian Seward from Bampton

"My grandfather bought the bakery in Newton Square, Bampton, in 1908. Today I continue to bake in the traditional way and also enjoy finishing my wedding cakes in another traditional way, with royal icing fine piping, which is also a craft seldom seen today. My wife, Caroline, together with our eldest son, Roger, and his wife, Dawn, run the shop which has become a modern and busy convenience store under the Spar sign, employing several local people during our long opening hours.

As a schoolboy I began hunting with the Tiverton Staghounds and continued for a number of years, until my last horse was too old. A notable character, Jon Pertwee (Dr Who), met us at the theatre one evening when our sons were still riding ponies at local gymkhanas. While chatting with him, Bampton was mentioned and Jon said, 'I don't suppose you know how I started hunting with an old farmer's pack of hounds, called the Tiverton Staghounds?' He went on to tell us how he bought his first pony for five bob at Bampton Fair and lived at Highleigh, near Bampton where he was brought up on our home-made bread which was delivered to the door.

When I used to ride regularly with the Tiverton Staghounds there was a young lad who always rode some wild pony that his parents took a liking to in their dealer business. I found him more than once, sat on the ground miles from anywhere, asking, 'Have you seen my pony?' I knew that he was a gutsy lad who could go far with horses if he stuck with it, and he did. He was Luke Harvey. As most people know, he became a National Hunt jockey who progressed to television as a presenter on the Racing Channel. Very good he is at the job too.

When I left Blundell's School in Tiverton in 1957 I went to Plymouth for two years to learn my baking trade. I used to skive off on some Mondays or come home early on a Friday to go hunting. I used to say I had to go and see my uncle. On my last day as I left Plymouth my headmaster asked, 'Well Brian, we knew you cleared off on some days but where did you go and who was your uncle?' I explained that although technically not a blood relative, Uncle Aubrey Besley was a close family friend and known as Uncle to me, and of course he hunted the Tiverton Staghounds as well as being Master. My headmaster laughed!

The hounds used to hunt a lot on a Monday and a Saturday, so I still learnt my trade with a little pleasure thrown in at the same time.

In 1959 Caroline came to live in Bampton from Westward Ho! She loved riding horses, so for a long time she used to keep my horse exercised during the week, and groom it before and after my day's hunting, without us ever meeting. She reckons that nothing has changed and I 'had it made from day one'!"

§

Talking with Sally Luxton whose brother John Lucas is Joint Master of the Tiverton Staghounds

"Born at Lakehead Farm, Chulmleigh, I remember being very friendly with Captain Coombe's daughter. He was Master of the Eggesford Foxhounds at the time and I used to go up to the kennels quite a lot. Anyway, one day I decided I would ride hunting and they met in Chulmleigh and we hadn't left the meet but half an hour and I couldn't stop my pony. Captain Coombe told me to go home and I think Father wasn't very happy at the time because they used to come over our land. For quite a while I didn't go hunting, and one day the Tiverton Staghounds ran through our ground so I thought I would go with them. I know I went up to Pyne Meadow Cross and went down towards Spittle and again my pony ran away with me, overtaking everybody, going up to Lightleigh Cross. When I got up beside Aubrey Besley, the Joint Master, I think I was nearly in tears and he said, 'Where have you come from my dear?' I thought here goes I'm going to be sent home again and I didn't say anything. He said, 'Well where are you going?'

I said, 'Well I can't stop.'

He looked at me and he said 'Never mind, you ride with me all day and you'll be all right,' and that's what I did, and they killed just below Watertown.

I remember once I fell off when my pony had hitched his toe in a molehill in the Cheldon Valley. Mr Besley stopped the hounds, and all the field had to stop while they caught the pony and then we all went on again. He would never go on and leave anyone. I used to ride with Maureen Ayre and Jean Gillbard and back then we used to ride from Howards Mill to Lenton. From there we always used to race and see who could get to Head Bridge first out of the three of us. Jean wasn't quite so brave, but Maureen and I used to be neck and neck, there wasn't much between our ponies and we used to ride right down the middle of the main road.

From my Hunt Diary

Spring 1965

The hounds met at Labbots Cross, the blacksmith came and put a new set of shoes on my pony the same morning.

Mr Snell couldn't get to the meet so I waited for him and then we rode along together.

When we got to Chawleigh we saw some cars going towards Lapford Wood so we rode along the road in the same direction. We were nearly in Lapford Wood when we saw two stags going along in the field by the road, so we told Mr Besley who then put the pack of hounds into the field where we'd seen the stags. The hounds went very fast and soon we were all galloping across the fields and jumping small jumps, trying to keep up with the hounds.

The stags soon parted and the hounds went after a nice spring stag which took us to East Leigh. The hounds checked in the valley but soon went on again and then we went on to Romansleigh. The hounds checked again but soon got going across the fields and I was lost until I came to the road near Bishopsnympton.

We rode along the road to Bish Mill where the hounds had checked again, but they went on and killed the stag near Molland, but not many people got there as it was a long way from the road. This was a really hard day for horses and hounds.

On 30 April 1965 the staghounds had their last meet of the season at Benley Cross. Mr Snell and I met at 10 o'clock and rode to the meet together.

The hounds found at Wixon and ran into the Cheldon Valley where we got left behind a bit, but we took a short cut and got into the lead again.

We crossed Bishopsleigh where our point-to-point course is and then we galloped for miles until we were nearly in Sandford. The hounds checked near Sandford, but we eventually saw the stag go out over a nearby hill, so we rode on and then came to the Exeter/Barnstaple main road which the stag crossed at Priestcombe Farm.

After crossing the main road we rode towards Yeoford and here the stag stopped in a little stream where we thought he was going to be shot, but just as they went to shoot him he galloped off as fresh as he was in the morning, so everyone set off at a gallop once more. We went on and the stag was killed at Tedburn St Mary and the hunt Master gave me a slot which I was very pleased about."

§

The Tiverton Staghounds at the Fox and Hounds, Eggesford, 1960. Far Left, Aubrey Besley (Joint Master and huntsman), Middle by hounds, Ernest Mortimer (Sec.), Jim Cole (whip), Cecil Turner, and Far Right, Edward Batting

Chapter Six

Walter Ash, Ray Giles, Ray Burrow and Ray Dart

Talking with Walter Ash who was huntsman for the Tiverton Staghounds 1969–1975.

"I was born at Sandford near Crediton in 1928 and left school at 14. I took on a bread round in the village with a pony and trap and delivered to 100 houses. The trap lights were candles, and on rough days when they all blew out I used to go home with no lights. The old pony would trot along, taking me on the road, and I couldn't see a thing in front of me.

After that I went into gardening at the girls' high school in Crediton, where I stayed for about 12 months. Then Mr Pincombe at Broaden Hayes, Sandford said, 'Why don't you take a job with horses somewhere, because you're mad keen.' He said, 'I've looked in the *Horse and Hound* and there's a job at Withycombe near Dunster. If you're interested I'll take you up there.'

So we went in his 1936 car with running boards, and that was a fair old journey from Sandford in those days. We got up there and met Major Worthington who was Master of the West Somerset Foxhounds. He said, 'I want someone to do a bit of gardening and look after my horses in the winter.' I got the job and stayed there for 12 months. Then he said, 'They could do with you at the kennels.'

There was an old chap, called Sid Lockyear I think, and Bill Langdon. Anyway, they eventually left and Mrs Lavington came as Master and she asked if I would stay and be the groom and ride second horse to the huntsman.

I said, 'What about clothes?' because I hadn't got very much then.

She said, 'I will buy you a sports jacket and a pair of boots.'

I shall never forget it, she bought me a pair of brown boots with American Canvas tops, a nice pair of breeches and a tie.

Then Dick Carter, the huntsman, left and Ben Wilkinson came from the South Durham and he said, 'I want you to be second whip to me.' I had five seasons with Ben, then he left and Cuthbert Thomas was Master and huntsman, along with Cyril his brother. They both came to me and said, 'Would you like to be our kennel huntsman?' and I had 11 seasons with them.

After that, Mr Phillips came as Master and he wanted to bring Tony Collins as his whip with him, and he said he was ever so sorry he had to let me go.

Then I heard about this job as huntsman of the Tiverton Staghounds and I phoned up Geoff Sellick and he said, 'We've been looking for somebody, if you want the job come and see us. I will get the committee together and meet you somewhere.' I told them I would meet them half way at a place called Cross Keys, just outside Taunton. I met them all there in the pub and had a chat.

Walter Ash (huntsman) at the kennels, 1972

When I retired from hunt service in 1994, Robin Venner told people at my farewell party about when I met the committee at Taunton. He said, 'Walter jumped out of his car with a horse's head on the front and he'd got on a lovely pair of slacks and sports jacket and a red waistcoat, and he walked up to me and Sid Gillbard shaking our hands, and I didn't think he was the ruddy huntsman, I thought he was the bloody Master.' Those were the very words he used.

When I came to Tiverton Staghounds in 1969 they were just moving into new kennels at the run down Mouseberry Farm near Worlington. It was a mud pit to start off with, no concrete down and the mud used to run right through the kennels. We started by having 100 tons of shillets put down, making what we could of the situation. It's a king now to what it was. The farmers around lent the money for the hunt to buy Mouseberry. At the time they could have had the electric put in, but it was going to cost them £4,000 and they didn't have it. The kennels are still powered by a generator, and now if they want the electric put in it's going to cost about £32,000.

I think it was three years before they built a bungalow just down the road for my whip Ray Giles. Before that he was living in a council house at Rose Ash. I think we made those kennels. We worked every Sunday and lots of volunteers came along to help concrete the place and it was wonderful how they all worked together.

The hunt bought three horses off Mr Besley, the previous Master and huntsman, and Moore's transport of South Molton brought all the pack from his kennels at Leigh Barton near Loxbeare to Mouseberry. I said to him, 'Don't you go running away because I want you to come out for at least a week or a fortnight,' and he walked in front with me behind learning the hounds' names. Mr Besley is a wonderful gentleman and the nicest man I've met as a Master. He was highly delighted when I asked him and he said he never thought any huntsman would ask him to do that.

After a week or so he came in for a cup of coffee and said, 'Those hounds love you now Walter, and they love me, but now I must go away from them.'

I wanted all of the people to help me – it's like a football team, I was only the centre forward and if you haven't got the rest of the team feeding you, you're not going to do it on your own. Unless you've got a team outside left and right and behind you

Walter Ash (huntsman, 1969–1975) with his daughter Carol giving him a hand

coming on, you score the goals for them, or try to, and if they don't feed you it's no good.

To start off I used to load up three horses and go to George Beer's at Nomansland for the shoeing. Half a day would be gone. Now the blacksmith comes to the kennels. For transport we had a Land Rover and trailer and we would travel with five couple of hounds in the Land Rover and another lot in the box, and two horses up behind. Later we had Moore's transport of South Molton and also Henry Webber of Rose Ash came along with his lorry. With a bit more money coming in, they bought their own lorry.

In the second season we decided to buy a black mare bred by Tom Miller of High Bickington, my tufting pony, then we went and bought Chester from Betty Palfrey.

I was looking for a lost hound called Drummer one evening, and left the car by Beaples Fence and walked in one big field where the link road is now. I blew and blew but all I heard were Moorland engines all over Molland and Yeo Mill, all chuffing away on that moonlit evening. I blew again and ten minutes after that a car came up the road. I stepped back out of the field into the road and said to this woman, 'You haven't seen a hound anywhere have you?'

'Oh yes,' she said, 'I have just come over Molland Common, and there was one coming along.'

Anyway I stayed there blowing and he must have come to what is the link road now and started howling. I blew again and he came straight over the fence to meet me. The sound of my horn must have been travelling right across Exmoor and that hound picked it up. It was a lovely clear night, you could nearly see the deer on the moor. Another time I had been hunting all day, killed the deer, done all my work, and got in about 10 o'clock. I had my meal, sat there until 11 o'clock and then the phone went to say there was a hound at the Black Cat. I had a Rover 2000 then, and I didn't take the Land Rover because it was too slow. When I got there I touched the horn twice and that hound came up the road and jumped in the back of the car. I said, 'Where have you been all bloody day?' He licked me all over. It must have been half past one when I got back.

When I went into King's Nympton Park I used to have a chat with Miss Stoddard and would say, 'What are you doing madam, it's lovely to see you, we've had a fair day and now we've lost the deer and have come in with you.' I always had a yarn and wouldn't worry about the hounds, and that's how I got on."

Walter Ash (huntsman) at the end of the day, 1972

Talking with Ray Giles who spent 11 seasons with the Tiverton Staghounds ending up as huntsman.

"I was born in Plymouth in 1942, left school at 15 and started working in a Navy outfitter. After three years, I got fed up with that and decided to earn a bit more money by working on a building site for a few years. We had a bad winter one year and most of the sites were laid off, so I went to Torr Point where I worked as a stoker on the gas board for a while. That closed down and I moved back into Plymouth getting a job delivering bread for Mother's Pride. I stuck with that for a while, but decided it wasn't for me. I then went into the Royal Navy dockyard for a couple of years, fitting out the ships.

I suppose I started to get into horse riding as a hobby and used to go out on Dartmoor just hiring horses and riding them. Then I started taking them hunting on a Saturday and got more interested in horses. The dockyard wasn't doing so well, so I went as an insurance agent for a couple of years, but I wasn't too happy with that so I decided to look for something else.

We moved to the Hatherleigh area and I got a job lorry driving because I wanted to do something with horses. Where I used to go horse riding, the owner of the riding stables, who was at one time Master and huntsman for the Lamerton at Lewdown, said they needed a whipper-in at the Tiverton Staghounds. I rang Sid Gillbard the Joint Master and arranged to go for an interview. The job had already been taken, but the whipper-in had started for a day and didn't like the skinning. I struck lucky by making an enquiry at the right time and they took me on.

I settled into the kennel side of it very quickly. Walter Ash, the huntsman, and I got on extremely well, he was never the bossy sort and never the sort to moan or shout, which was ideal. If you did something right he would praise you up for it, which helped me a lot.

I spent six years whipping-in to Walter and it was quite a happy time. The hunting was good then and you could go over most places without any trouble. There wasn't that much fuss made even if you did happen to run through the few odd places. You might get an occasional phone call. The League Against Cruel Sports were very low profile then; what ground they had they never looked after very well. If you happened to run through it there was never anyone there and nobody was any the wiser. We had some good hunts and good times. I think deer ran a bit further and a bit straighter, there wasn't quite as much turning and I think you got better hunting through that and better hound work.

When I started with Walter there weren't a great deal of cars, you would get more staghunting time. But for hind hunting in that first year, if there were 15 cars out, that was about it and there were only two motorbikes to start off with. The drivers were very helpful and would take a message to get the pack lorry, and things seemed to work very well. I think the hounds were allowed to hunt a lot more because there weren't the people around to see the deer so much, so really the hounds had to do a lot more work.

We were very lucky because Mr Besley left us with some Welsh hounds which were really invaluable to start off. There was Leaper, Grocer, Gallway and Guardsman. For staghunting they were absolutely brilliant, especially on the water; we used to catch a lot of deer with them. These Welsh hounds were devils to stop, you could stand in front of them and crack the whip and shout, but they would just keep coming, going underneath your horse and piling through like you weren't there. It took a while for them to be stopped. Eventually I learned to stop them, but then I couldn't move because as soon as I moved my horse they were gone again. I took a tip off Mr Besley who used to tell me the only way to stop them was to get off your horse, grab the first hound, give him a little smack and get back on your horse again. Then they would follow you. I used to do this and it worked.

Grocer got the idea that if you stopped him he would stay back about 30 yards, look at you, then suddenly disappear. You thought he had gone back towards Walter with the other hounds but in actual fact he used to make a wide circle around Walter and the next thing we knew we used to hear him behind us speaking to a line. I think he had more brains than were good for him.

The Welsh hounds were good on stags but didn't like the hinds as much. I know when we were hindhunting once someone phoned up at midnight to say that a hound was baying this stag in the river. We hadn't seen the hound all day, it just decided hinds weren't good enough and that was that. Once the Welsh hounds were on the right deer they would never leave it.

Walter had a hound called Drummer, I beleive he was from the Weston and Banwell Harriers. He turned out to be a brilliant dog on the water which you needed in the staghounds because a lot of the deer could be lost in the rivers and waters. As I said, in those days people didn't see the deer so much and you had to use hounds to cast the rivers and they used to prove their weight in gold. A lot of the older hounds were good Welsh crossbreeds. Luckily, when I took over as huntsman Walter had just bred a puppy called Marksman, he was only a puppy when Walter left so I hunted him on and he was probably the best hound I have ever seen on the water, extremely good whether he was on the water or not. I saw him one day when we had come from the Stoodleigh end. We ran a stag into Wixon, going through there and coming out at the bridge under Brooklands where we lost it in the river. I walked down and looked around and the first thing I noticed was that Marksman was missing. Someone had seen him going back the stream, so I walked until we got up to Week. He had gone on a long time ahead of us hunting the stream right up through, coming out in the road and back into the lane again higher up, then dropping into the stream. He hunted right up under Wixon then turned around and came down the stream again. By the time we got there he was baying the stag in the bottom of Wixon in the stream, all on his own. Marksman put me right a lot of the time on the rivers, you could trust that dog 100 per cent.

Another day we were up at Rackenford Manor and dropped into Moortown, in the stream. Off Marksman went, straight down to Waterloo. Everybody said he was taking the drag down, but I disagreed because you could see the old dog was going down the stream but he wasn't speaking to the water, he was sniffing the leaves and speaking. He took the line right down to Waterloo, under the road and straight down through and he bayed the stag at Creacombe Farm. He knew what he was doing as long as you didn't mess him about, he could work it out all on his own.

When Walter was hunting them we met at South Molton one year and we found a big stag in White Chapel which we killed in the Punch Bowl, out near Winsford. That was a marvellous day's hunting, the hounds hunted it all on their own all the way.

The best hunt I had was with a pricket that I found under Chulmleigh Woods and caught at Tedburn St Mary. We looked it up on the map afterwards and it was a 19 mile point. It was a bit worrying in places – I never did figure it out how the hounds got into the middle of Crediton. I picked them up in part of a field in amongst all the houses, and I never knew how they got there. They picked up the line and went on and that was the only time we caught forward to them from Morchard Wood. They sort of got away from us and we couldn't get nearer than about three fields away from them, they were really pushing on. Once we got beyond Morchard Wood it was all fresh country to us and it was hard going in places.

Just before Tedburn St Mary there was a set of fields with paddocks in and a little goyle. They sort of checked in the road and I cast them down the goyle. Up jumped the stag and I went running up across the field because someone had my horse. When I got to the top of the field and jumped out into the road, an old lady from the nearby bungalow said to me, 'You will have to get a move on.'

I said, 'Why's that?'

And she said, 'The motorway's just over the hill.'

I ran up the road and there was the Exeter–Okehampton dual carriageway, and there were the hounds and deer going across it between two lots of traffic. My heart nearly stopped, but they made it across all right.

I learnt one lesson early on, when Walter was hunting the hounds and they split. He was on the hunted hind and I went back on about three couple that were running a fresh hind from Chittlehamholt. We couldn't stop them and ended up hunting in the Filleigh Estate; it was only my second season. I had never hunted hounds before, and knew very little. They ran around the Filleigh Estate and they lost it once or twice. I was fairly confident, so, with no one to look over my shoulder, I cast them a few times and by pure luck they seemed to hit off the line. They stuck to the hind extremely well, eventually crossing the road to Bremridge where they lost it.

I was going along the field by the viaduct wondering what to do next when suddenly, out of the field at Bremridge, came this hind, running right across in front of me into the stream. I put the hounds on and they disappeared out to Charles Bottom. Coming up in the stream, I walked with them and they lost it again. There was a little bridge with ivy on it, and I decided I would go as far as the bridge. The hounds disappeared under the ivy and went quiet. I started shouting to them thinking I better go back and all of a sudden, out from the bridge came

At the Butchers Arms,
15 April 1976.
Left to right:
Ray Giles (huntsman)
Sid Gillbard (Joint Master)
Ray Burrow (whipper-in)

Holding the pack at Snydles Marsh. Left to Right: John Lucas (Joint Master), Michael Snell

Honiton Hound Show 1979. Far side, Dennis Boyles, huntsman of the Devon and Somerset Staghounds, with his son Kevin holding the hounds. Near side, Ray Giles, huntsman of the Tiverton Staghounds, with Ray Dart, whipper-in, holding Mindful and Delta. © Philip Lashbrook

Former whippers-in David Ford and Dennis Boyles

Above: Left to Right: Ray Dart on Chester, Ray Burrow (huntsman),
John Lucas (Joint Master), at Chawleigh 1991 © Baths Photographic

Below: Walter Ash on Chester with the Tiverton Staghounds at Swineham Hill 1972

The wedding of Jenny and Fred Hayes, 13 May 1978 alongside the Tiverton Staghounds hunt staff. Left to Right: John Lucas (Joint Master), Robin Venner (Joint Master), Fred, Jenny, Ray Burrow (whip)

Tim Laman,
Hon. Secretary

Guy Loosemoor (whip)

The pack at the end of the day near Landkey

Hounds at Ash Cross

Dunster Show 1980. Whipper-in Ray Dart holding the hounds, together with huntsman Ray Burrow. Hounds Left to Right: Monarch, Moorland, Merlin
© Oliver Harvey

Taken between 1975 and 1979 at The Green, Chettiscombe. Left to Right: Ray Giles, huntsman and Robin Venner, Joint Master. © Philip Lashbrook

Above: Taken between 1975 and 1979 at The Green, Chettiscombe. Left: Ray Burrow (whipper-in). Right: Ray Giles (huntsman), with Dudley Down walking towards him © Philip Lashbrook

Below: Taken between 1975 and 1978 at Horseford Farm, Worlington. Left to Right on horses: Ray Burrow (whipper-in), Sid Gillbard (Joint Master), Ray Giles (huntsman) Standiing in foreground is Garfield Cole

Above: Guy Loosemoor (whipper-in), Filleigh Sawmills meet, Boxing Day 1999. On this day he hunted the hounds as John Norrish had flu

Below: Presentation by Robin Venner (right) to Joint Master John Colthorpe, standing down in 1988. Pictured here at Lakehead Farm, Chulmleigh

Putting on the Pack

Blowing for hounds near Spurway Mill

Tiverton Staghounds' New Year's Day 1992. The Globe, Chulmleigh. Walter Reed standing, Tony 'Bones' Allibone (whipper-in), John Pearce, (Joint Master and huntsman), and his wife Jane (Joint Master)

Jack and Elsie Sing's Diamond Wedding meet at Woodhills, Ash Mill in 1992. Left to Right on horses: John Pearce, Sharon Mogford, Tony Allibone (whipper-in), Ivan Webber

Jack and Elsie Sing's Diamond Wedding meet at Woodhills, Ash Mill in 1992, with John Pearce (Master, huntsman, 1988–1995)

An apple a day keeps the doctor away.
Whipper-in, Guy Loosemoor

John Norrish (huntsman), with son Peter (whipper-in) at the Exeter Inn, Bampton, 1997

John Norrish (huntsman), talking with the harbourer, the late Cyril Partridge

Left: John Norrish (huntsman) at Honiton Show, 1998 © Ginny Brind

Below: David Ridge (whipper-in 1995–1996) at Witheridge

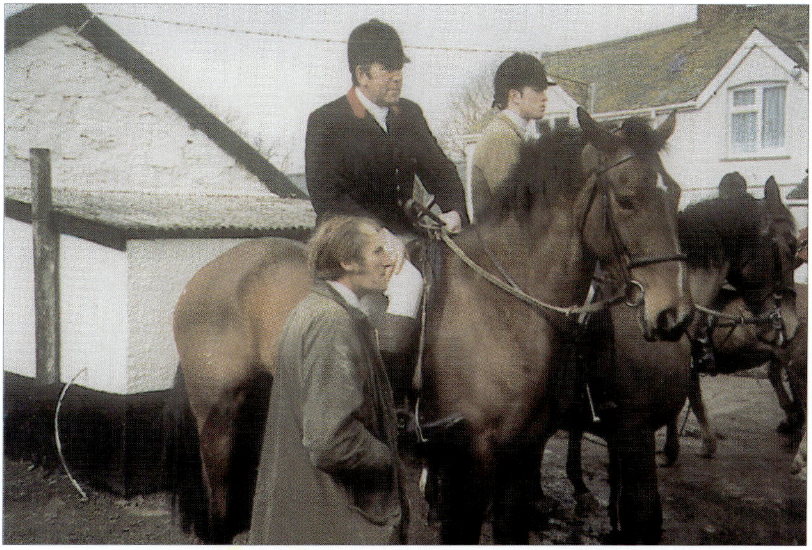

Left to Right: Stafford Blake (standing), father and son Stuart and Stephen Kelland, David Ridge (whipper-in) at the kennels meet, 1995

John Norrish (huntsman (red coat) and Richard Down (Quantock Staghounds huntsman)

Left to Right: John Lake, Norman Brend, John Lucas (Joint Master), David Ridge (whipper-in, 1995–1996)

Ivan Webber, Joint Master, 1995–1996

the hind with three couple of hounds behind her, coming to bay beside me. I thought, there's only me here, I will go in and catch her. She ups with her front legs and knocked me flying, so I learnt another lesson that day!

Luckily some of the others came back by then. I think Haurice Hopper had a gun and shot her. So that was my first experience of hunting hounds.

I think you've got more confidence when you don't know much, and I think the more you think you know the more you realise you don't really know at all. That's when you start to get a bit hesitant, whereas when you're young, you're confident and you sort of dive right in there with no thought that you may be wrong. I think confidence really gives you the edge.

When we met at South Molton and went out to the Punch Bowl at Winsford, Walter was riding an old mare called Roseanne that never liked the smell of blood. After gutting the stag he walked back to the mare with a bit of blood on his hands. She took one sniff of it and took off and I had to go off and catch her. He used to love that mare, but she couldn't stand the smell of blood.

I used to have a horse at the same time called Turner's Mare because Cecil Turner used to own her. I loved that mare the same as Walter loved his. I always remember one day Walter was hunting and found himself the wrong side of the boundary hedge. The hounds were going along so I suggested we swap horses, and I jumped over the hedge and took his and he took mine. He went on and I went on with his mare and when I caught him up again I said, 'Thank God I caught you up because I've never ridden a more uncomfortable horse.'

He said, 'I was just going to say the same thing about yours.'

It's funny, we both loved our horses, but we couldn't ride each other's. It must have been their different stride. I know Walter's Roseanne would shift on and she used to dish a lot. I think that's what I used to find uncomfortable, she would throw her legs out all the time and was a bit on the lumpy side.

One thing I liked about Turner's Mare was that she could jump. When I was whipping-in we crossed Cheldon one day going across the meadow into the cover and there was a five-bar gate in front of me. I jumped it, followed by Celia Young as she was then. That was one thing about Turner's Mare, she would never refuse a jump – even if she didn't make it she would have a crack at it. I never knew a horse with the staghounds that would jump like it. As far as we knew she had never done any jumping before, but she was just a natural and would actually take off and jump within about three or four strides, you didn't have to gallop hard.

We had a mare through Walter's acquaintance, Nelson Burdon, from the Quantocks. It was a little Arab and she was a whipper-in's horse. I used to ride a horse called Shevaughn. She was a little devil, we only had her when she was four or five years old. The first season she didn't last too well because she didn't have the stamina. What amused me was every time I jumped on her she would buck like anything. We had her a bit later than Chester. I started hunting her and I used her as a second horse. Whenever I took her out of the lorry and put the pack on she always used to let go with four or five fly bucks. One day we were at Chain Bridge and they told me that they were bringing the pack and my second horse to me. They said that Mr Manning of Fire Beacon was riding Shevaughn. Coming along with the hounds I thought, Oh my God almighty, she will put him off for a pastime. But the funny part was he turned up and she hadn't put a foot wrong, she was as good as gold which I couldn't understand. As soon as I got on her she decided to give a few bucks again.

Another horse we had was a black horse called Jack which took two-and-a-half years to get right. After that we had one good season out of him and then he was struck by lightning. That horse was unpredictable. I think the hunt bought him from Cornwall. I used to exercise him behind the hounds and coming back the road to the kennels one day I could feel this horse beginning to bunch up. Suddenly he started galloping on the spot and took off. I couldn't stop him going straight through the hounds, past Walter at full gallop all the way to the kennels, where he came to a screaming halt in front of the stable.

Walter said, 'When you went past that horse had got his eyes closed!'

This used to happen every morning, I just couldn't make it out. I took Jack the first morning hunting at Affeton Moor Cross to show the hounds some deer. It wasn't a proper day's hunting. Going through the path, he suddenly dropped his back, took off and went galloping through the cover. No matter what I did I couldn't stop him. We went out over the hedge the other side, up over the field and smacked into the hedge full speed – that's the only thing that stopped him.

I think I rode him about eight times hunting, going two days a week, and Jack used to do the same every time. He would close his eyes and bolt, hitting anything on the way. He then went and chipped a bone in his knee in the stables, and was put out to grass until the spring. We had him back in again and he sort of changed, he didn't seem to bolt but turned into the nappiest horse I ever came across. Whether it was because he lost a bit of weight being out to grass during the wintertime I don't know. Out hunting he would suddenly decide not to go through a gateway and he would stop and back back as fast as he went forward. We eventually cured him of that and he went back to bolting again.

One day I was at the saddlers and I was telling him about this horse and he said, 'Why don't you put a rubber bit in his mouth?' which we did and never looked back. After that we could ride him with two fingers. However, the following summer he was struck by lightning, which was a great shame.

We had some funny horses. One we called Jake the Peg because you never knew which leg he was going on. If you put him over a tree in the cover, even if it was six inches off the ground, he would trip over it. I remember one day we had a nice hunt and we were going down across the river at Bickleigh. By then he was down to a walk because he was shattered – I don't know how I got over the bank the other side – and coming up to the path in front was a set of rails about four feet high. I was barely into a trot and people beside me said, 'Your horse is never going to go over that,' but he went over it with the cleanest jump. When he was tired he would jump anything, yet he couldn't do it when he was fit.

When I left the staghounds I went to the Cottesmore for 12 months as kennelman, which was enjoyable. It gave me a different aspect, being foxhunting and also hunting in a slightly different way up there. At the end of the 12 months I got a job as kennel huntsman with the West Somerset Foxhounds, moving to Carhampton and I was there for 17 seasons. I'm now out of hunt service and living a very happy life, having a few days hunting as a follower of the Tiverton Staghounds."

§

Talking with Ray Burrow who spent 12 years with the Tiverton Staghounds firstly as whipper-in and ending up as huntsman

"I came to Tiverton Staghounds in 1975 having previously worked for the Duke of Beaufort's hunt as second horseman to Major Gundry. I spent four years with Ray Giles as whipper-in, then I had 12 months with the Stevenstone Foxhounds and returned to the Tiverton Staghounds in 1980 as huntsman until 1988.

I was born at Wilson Farm, Worlington, but we moved to Knowstone after my father's death when I was two. We often used to see Ken Webber with the Tiverton Staghounds and he would hack from Mariansleigh out to Swineham Hill, where we would see him going across the moor. One particular day they appeared and Mother took us up to Hares Down Cross. We saw Ken Webber and Mr Loval, who was a keen hunter. Mr Loval's horse had lost a shoe and I picked it up, thinking I had the world. We later heard that they had killed the deer down at Chain Bridge. Little did I know that one day I would be killing deer there myself – it's funny really.

When I was growing up and the hounds were around I would hardly go to school; I would go up to meet the bus, hide behind a gorse bush, wait until it had gone and then go hunting.

When I left school I went to work for Walter Barber at Bullaford Farm near Yeo Mill, and used to get paid £2 a week. He had point-to-pointers. Walter found a hunting horn on Pauls Moor one day with a Sir John Amory's staghounds inscription on it and it was the first hunting horn I ever learnt to blow in my life.

I remember Walter had two Dulverton East hound puppies. In the bad winter of 1963 I used to go out with them to see if I could find a fox. The worst part was that one day the puppies went into my bedroom and tore up my wages which I used to put by my bed. I could have cried. Managing to sellotape them together, there was one note that I couldn't find the serial number to. Nevertheless I took the rest into South Molton and they gave me some new ones. I told this story when I was judging at the Dulverton East Foxhound puppy show and said they owed me a pound!

When I was hunting the Tiverton Staghounds I lost a doghound called Magic. I went out that Saturday night looking for him and on Sunday I walked every inch of that day's hunting in case he was hung up in the wire somewhere, but there was no sign. I just couldn't make it out. Anyway time went on and one night Bob Street, huntsman of the Tiverton Foxhounds, phoned me up. He said,

'Are you a hound short?'

'Well,' I said, 'not really, but I have been missing a doghound for a long time.'

'I've got one in here, but it's a bitch,' he replied.

I said to Bob I'd come over anyway. I don't know why I went but when I got there I had a look and said, 'No it's not mine.'

We then walked up through the kennels and suddenly a hound jumped up beside me and I said, 'Good God, you've got my Magic.' The hound knew my voice and was so pleased to see me. He was mud all over from marking a fox.

Bob said, 'I don't know how long I've had him, but he's been hunting, look.'

If I hadn't gone over there that night, I don't think I would ever have found him, it was like it was ordained.

When Ray Dart was whipping-in to me I had a telephone call at half past one in the morning. These people in Bampton said,

'We've got a hound here and have rung around to the different hunts but it's not theirs.'

I thought that it was a bit fishy and it could be a set up, so I got Ray Dart out of bed. We got into Bampton and I said to Darty, 'This doesn't look like a hound at all,' and he agreed with me. I think at that stage we were both half asleep. I said to the people, 'It's not ours, but we will take it home and at least it will be in a kennel.'

On the way we had the hound in front with us in the pick-up. I said to Ray, 'This looks more like a pointer.'

When we got back I put it in a lodge on its own and the next morning I let the hound in the flesh house to have some grub. In the meantime the phone rang and it was the people from Bampton. They said, 'Please, please, whatever you do don't let that hound escape because it's not a hound it's next door's pointer.'

Anyway, I came out and the bitch had jumped up at the latch of the flesh door, opened it with her nose and was gone.

It was not long before I had a phone call from Eileen Elstone down at Lutworthy. She said, 'Have you lost a hound?'

'Yes I have,' I said. 'But it's not really one, but don't worry. Whatever you do don't let it go.' Of course then I had to take it all the way back to Bampton.

It's marvellous how some hounds have a homing instinct. We had two from the Taunton Vale Harriers because they hunted deer and they were fell hounds (light-framed). I don't think I hunted them but twice; one of them was called Traveller and he was a cracking hound. We went over Molland Common coming back through on fresh deer one day. I don't know where we had met but there were hounds everywhere. Mr Basset of West Anstey had a couple shut in and that evening, after feeding the rest of the hounds and putting them away, I went to get these two hounds. When I got to Mouseberry Cross, just turning right to go to Burrow Cross, this Traveller dog was coming back the road. He had only been in our kennels a matter of a fortnight and found his way home in that short time. He hadn't been round there exercising and didn't know anything yet he was coming back the road – I couldn't believe it.

Jim Yandle helped me a lot when I was huntsman. He wouldn't say very much but he would put you right and wouldn't make a big thing about it. I used to listen and take notice, at the end of the day he wasn't far wrong. My first day hunting the hounds we met at Cudmore Cross and they ran across the A361 to the Shillingford main road; brow tray two he was and I lost him in Raddington. It was a very warm day and coming down the path I met Jim. Very quietly he said, 'Ray go down the path and you will see my push-bike layed down. Let the hounds go in there.' So I did. There was a fair bit of gorse and I only went in so far. Up the stag jumped. We later killed him at Haddon under the reservoir.

I know it's difficult at times, but when it comes to it I always reckon you've got to trust your hounds, they don't tell lies. I remember meeting at Witheridge Moor once. We found a stag which was brow tray two and took him through Morchard Mill right down to Bickleigh. I shall never forget that day. He came down the little side stream by the bridge and everyone said the stag hadn't gone down. We had a little bitch called Goldfinch; she went across the little stream just under the bridge and there was a manure bag hanging over the side, she just sniffed it and went 'booh'. I thought that's good enough for me. Casting down the river, Tim Laman and Ivan Webber both came along and said 'You're wrong Ray,' and I said, 'I don't think so.' I trust my hounds. If I had to cast the hounds from there to Exeter I would have done, but that bitch was outstanding and I was convinced she was right. Anyway the stag was on the river bank and I was casting down. He came up towards me going right into the grounds of the fisherman's cottage. He finally stood at bay at Ashley Tip. As I was going up the main road I saw all these posh cars coming down. I asked Mr Venner what was on and he said it was the wedding of Suzy Hancock and Nigel Dunn. They'd just got married at St Paul's Church, Tiverton and were on their way to Southwood Farm for the reception. I got up to Ashely Tip and the stag broke bay coming down the side of the cover with me riding along the main road parallel to him. Suddenly he swung up over and I had to go up the drive where all these wedding guests were going. This chap came running down with a swallow tail coat on and he said 'You're not to shoot the stag Ray.' When I got up there it was stood right beside the marquee with hounds all round him, honest to God. John Roffe-Silvester, who was later killed in a car crash with his wife, came out and said, 'Look Ray, take the hounds away, we don't want any trouble.' So I did.

It's funny really, when my daughter Katrina got married she had this woman's book and in it were things that could go wrong at a wedding, and one of them was hounds baying a stag at a wedding reception. You wouldn't credit it would you? The incident caught the local and national papers, with some of the headlines being 'Oh deer! Hunt turns wedding into a stag night', 'Finds sanctuary in marquee, hunted stag gate crashes wedding', and 'Stag saved from hounds by wedding guests, top-hat men foil hunters'.

In the end the stag was pushed out and went across the field into the cover. While we were waiting for the lorry I said to Mr Venner, 'Couldn't we just go and lay onto the stag?' but he said no, so that was that. Looking back it was the right thing to do, but when you're hunting the hounds all you think about is getting a tally, then your job's fulfilled. I know it sounds stupid, but to me it was my job done. Now I look at it completely different. At that time I was killing a spring stag each time I went out, I couldn't believe my luck. It was just like it was so easy, that's confidence I suppose. Technically, to be honest, I count that one.

In my book I had two outstanding hounds when I was with the Tiverton Staghounds. One of them was Merlin. A kid could hunt that pack of hounds with him, if you hit the water you just sat on your horse and watched him and he would do it all for you, there was no question about that, he had a sixth sense. We also had a bitch called Goldfinch. She was a mismatch to be honest; her mother came from the Torrington Farmers' hunt and they couldn't keep her in because she jumped the walls. We had her up at the Tiverton Staghounds and when she was in season she jumped over the wall while we were out on exercise. We had a dog called Forger that would never go out on exercise, but on a hunting day he was right up there. If you took him on exercise he would be gone, so we didn't bother with him. This bitch (called Gamble or Gaity, Gamble I think) got out and of course mated with Forger and that was how Goldfinch came about. It was never meant to be at all, but that was one of the best hounds I ever had, Goldfinch was literally mustard. Some of Goldfinch's puppies went to the Devon and Somerset who were short on puppies at that time. I took out two-and-a-half couple to Dennis Boyles, some of them were Goldfinch's breeding, some of them were Mistic's breeding. Mistic was Merlin's side, if you know what I mean, brilliant hunting line, no question about it. When it was time to hunt they turned out good hunters and the Devon and Somerset bred from all of them.

When I went out to the Devon and Somerset Staghounds as first whipper-in to Dennis Boyles after I left the Tiverton Staghounds, they had a lot of Goldfinch's line there because Dennis bred from it and kept it going and this is where Godfrey came from, the same old line. Tiverton Staghounds have him now. I think he came in John Norrish's second season. Dudley Downs' daughter Betty walked Merlin. A lot of people walk puppies, and the puppies don't take any notice of their owners later on, but Merlin knew Dudley.

One day we were coming back from hound exercise on our push-bikes and Dudley and a friend were getting out of a car in the distance. Merlin heard his voice; I told him to hold up but he wouldn't and he went racing over to him. I took Merlin out to the Devon and Somerset because they wanted to use him; he was a way from home and wouldn't work or do any hunting.

They wanted to get some bitches in whelp but he wasn't interested so I had him back. After that I remember meeting at Chawleigh, spring staghunting. We put on the pack later and Merlin was there but they ran so fast, killing at Eggesford Station, that poor old Merlin was done for. Being out with the Devon and Somerset he hadn't done a lot of work and never really recuperated. He was old mind, and he went down hill. I think he exerted himself and did too much. I let him run free and he used to sleep in the barn and do what he wanted.

Dudley Down came over one morning before we went out hunting and I said, 'Go and see Merlin because I don't think he's going to be with us much longer.' He went and sat down beside him like a child. This particular morning I loaded the hounds in the lorry and then I came in to change. I will never forget it – out of the barn came old Merlin, down across the yard, his old head swinging and he walked to the bottom of the ramp and looked into the lorry to the other hounds, turned away and went up into the barn. When I came home he was dead. It was like he was saying goodbye to them, and it touched me a little bit. He was a marvellous hound, just like his father, Marksman.

I remember Cyril Manning was a wonderful shot. He used to ride a little racing pony, Easter Bonnet, and he would slip off and shoot a deer just like nothing. I once saw him shoot a stag down at Cove right across the River Exe. He was brilliant in his day and so was Geoffrey Sellick who was also a cracking shot.

I remember meeting at Swineham Hill, Aubrey Besley and Kipper Heywood had harboured a stag in Rackenford Moor and they thought it was brow tray two. We found him quite quickly in Withy Beds and had a remarkable hunt. We killed him right in Wellington behind the factory and I never lifted those hounds a yard. I know the first check was Ashbrittle; I changed horses at Chain Bridge onto Springside, a chestnut horse who was shod the day before. We were nearly into Wellington and Merlin was taking them down the water, going 'booh wooh'. Mr Venner was shouting across to stop them but I decided to let them go a bit further. They went on across the field and there was Wellington straight in front of me. The stag was in the water right under the factory when they shot him. I know I went to the Quantock point-to-point the next day and Dick Lloyd said, 'I hear you had a wonderful hunt yesterday Ray. I've been looking on the map and I worked out it was a 17½ mile point!'

We met at Venhayes, Bampton once, Geoff White's. Now that was a fair hunt. Getting out to Withleigh it came in to snow and there was a bit of a check. When we got out onto the road it was beginning to get white with snow. I thought the hind had run the road; the hounds were feathering the road hedge and I cast them along the road until I saw this Tesco bag. I said to Ray Dart, 'I bet the hind won't pass that bag, I reckon she will go left or right.' We got nearly up to it and the hounds got up over the hedge and flew away. We killed her at Morchard Mill.

When I was second horseman to Major Gundry he said to think like a fox. Very often when I was hunting I used to think of his words. When you have a check, look around and see what could have turned your deer; it might be a sheet of galvanised in a hedge or shiny paper blowing or anything really, it's just those simple little things. When you have a check you hear people behind you saying where they think he's gone, but they're guessing; anyone can guess. If you keep your eyes on the hounds all the time and never take them off they will give you the clues even though they can't speak to you. Sometimes it's just seeing their sterns going, especially hounds you really know like Merlin, Magic, Goldfinch and Dewdrop.

I can remember when the Quantock Staghounds came down by invitation in the Tiverton country and Alfie Giles was hunting them. They killed at Huntsham, behind the post office, and Alfie asked if he could have the head. They said yes, but he wasn't going to take any chances, so he took out his knife and cut the head clean off there and then.

I never forget when we were living up at Knowstone, if I saw a red coat coming up the road I would run and open the gate for him and I tell you what, he would say, 'Thank you young man,' and you thought you were somebody, do you know what I mean? You looked up to them when you were a kid. Mr Whitmore came along one day with the Dulverton East because we had lost some fowls and I remember his shining, leather boots and studs around the bottom – I thought that was marvellous. I was so fascinated to see it and thought it was something really special, the cry of those hounds and the sound of the horn, there's nothing like it."

§

Talking with Ray Dart
whipper-in to the Tiverton Staghounds
1980–1985

"I was born at Broadmead Farm near Rackenford and never went hunting as such but always watched the Tiverton Staghounds from the fields if they came by. Mr Besley was hunting them at the time when we were kids and he was the man we used to look up to. He would always stop and have a tale, even if the hounds had gone on, having time to speak to everyone. When we got a bit older we used to ride our push-bikes, me and my brother, with Geoff Boundy, after the Tiverton Foxhounds. I never rode a horse until I was 15 because I always thought I was going to be a farmer. I went to Bicton College to learn farming, but it wasn't like father taught us and I didn't stick it very long down there.

I got interested in hunting when I used to go and help Mr Scott at the Tiverton Foxhound kennels. Later he got me a job with the Devon and Somerset Staghounds, riding second horse. I learnt kennel management from Dennis Boyles, the huntsman there, and he had very high standards. After two seasons I went to the Monmouthshire Foxhounds, becoming the youngest whip in the country.

I had never jumped a fence, so before I went to Wales Mrs Harding, the Joint Master of the Devon and Somerset Staghounds, rang up Mr Barnard, the Secretary, to give me some lessons in jumping over his hunter trial course.

The Monmouthshire was a run down pack and the hounds were always killing sheep and hunting bullocks, it was terrible. It frightened me to death. With a fresh huntsman it took us three seasons to get the pack right. In the first season we only killed two brace, they were still killing sheep for a pastime and one day the Master ordered us home, telling us to put all the hounds down immediately that day. It was a grim task, but it was the only way. Then we got in some fresh hounds from other packs. There weren't a lot of foxes up there, and by the third season we had killed 15 brace.

One day I had a phone call from Mr Venner, Joint Master of the Tiverton Staghounds, to say that the whipper-in, Ray Burrow, was leaving and there was a chance for me to come home. That would have been the 1979–80 season. I took the job and I remember the first morning we hunted from Affeton

Moor Cross going into Homer to draw. There were several young stags in there and I saw this monster of a stag get up and then drop down again, so I told Ray Giles, the huntsman. The stag was there by this holly tree and Ray cast his hounds along, and up jumped this two atop stag. They all laughed and said I didn't know what a big stag was, not yet. We brought the hounds back, trying again at the exact spot and up he jumped, a big four and five atop stag. We killed him down at Cheldon eventually. John Lucas, the Joint Master, gave me one of the slots and he said, 'You will always remember that one.'

In Ray Giles' last season in 1980, Jack Sing told the Tiverton Staghounds about a horse which was coming up to the Exeter horse sale. He was called Marchy and came from the Blackmore and Sparkford Vale country. He had a big knee, but he was guaranteed all right and was a puller; they gave £250 for him. We took him on hound exercise and he went proper, he was strong and a puller. The first day I whipped-in with him we were going down Harpson Lane and there were people in front of me. Jack Ashton didn't see me coming and shut the gate on me. The horse's head came up and I went straight over the gate landing on some concrete. That horse was as hard as nails. For parting out deer he would gallop after them and race them. He would hardly stumble and never had a day's lameness. I had some wonderful days on him and I think if he had been younger he would have been another Chester. They eventually sold him for £550 to a man at Dolton who rode him hunting for several years.

John Ackland and Donald Moore helped us a lot when we lost our deer. We were hunting a stag from Cheldon one day and went across to Burridge and onto Chenson and lost it. For some reason Donald came back saying he had seen him cross the road nearly down to Bridge Reeve. We put the hounds on where he had said and went miles hunting this line before we lost it again. Donald came back again and said he was under this hedge out at Stafford Moor, miles away from where we were. Laying the hounds on, the stag jumped up, going right back to the Cheldon Valley where we lost him again. That was the day Donald kept us going, poking away on his motorbike.

Rob Venner was at a party at Bondleigh when he heard about a horse. Some woman said it had been to six breakers and she had heard the Tiverton Staghound chaps could ride anything. Anyway, Ray Burrow and myself brought this horse back and we called in at the Portsmouth Inn, Chawleigh where we saw Clifford Bridgeman and Dudley Middleton. By the time we got back it was way past midnight and Ray was boozed up a bit. He said, 'This horse is bugging me, he is too quiet. Let's go in and get the bridle and saddle and see what he's like.'

We got the bridle on and went to put the saddle on. Of course he bucked the saddle off before we got the girth up and Ray said, 'We can't leave it now.' It took us ages but eventually we got a stick and pulled the girth over so we could do it up. At half past one in the morning we finally got the girth done up and Ray said, 'If I hold his head, you jump on him,' and that's what we did. He held him up tight and I put my foot in the stirrup and managed to get on him. Ray led me around the stable and then said, 'We can go to bed now we know we can ride him.' It was two o'clock before we eventually got to sleep. The next day he bucked me off, but we managed to break him in the end.

In 1984, after a meet at the Black Cock, Molland, I came off my horse and injured my back badly. I tried to turn the deer from going out to West Molland. Usually they turn away from you but this one came right into me and took the front legs right away from the horse. I went down, straight into the ground and the horse came over the top of me. I was out of action for a while and I got back whipping-in with a struggle. The one person I was indebted to for getting me through the season was Janette Govier, now Janette Lake. She used to ride on and stop hounds. I was getting to the stage when I couldn't do this, she was good to me. I was only meant to take four painkillers a day, but the pain was so bad that I was eating them like smarties, getting through 12 or 13. Coming home at night my back would be red hot and in a couple of days a bruise would come out. One day I came home and said, 'That's it, I'm finishing.'

I went to see Mr Venner and told him and he said, 'I've been expecting it, I know you can't cope.'

I said, 'I think it's time to get out while I'm at the top.'

It's a funny thing really because he looked across the table and he said, 'Well is that what you think?'

I said, 'Yes, all these jockeys get out when they're at the top.'

'Perhaps I ought to do the same,' he said, and about a fortnight later he went and gave his notice in as well.

It was quite a turn of events really at the time. We finished the season at the Black Cock and they all said, 'You've got to come in for a drink.'

I remember saying to people, 'Anyone want my boots and my coat now I've finished?'

Mr Venner said, 'I wouldn't be so fast, you hang on to them, you just might need them in a year or two. You're a young chap, with rest you could get it right.'

After I finished I had two months where I didn't do anything and had three or four days' treatment a week. Liz and I went up to Rose Ash to live and Bruce Ayre, over at Munson, said, 'If you can work stood up straight I will teach you how to milk a herd of cows, there are enough farms around here that would put you on to relief milking.' So that's what I did. In the middle of the day I could rest and that's how I got through the first 12 months.

For more than 12 months I never sat on a horse. Then I went down to Roger Veale, the blacksmith at Swincombe, Rose Ash. Liz used to keep her horses down there and he said to me, 'You want to go for a ride on my wife's horse, he's nice and quiet.' So I jumped on her horse and that's what started it off again. Then I got to help the Dulverton West and I whipped-in to Terry Beeney later taking his job as huntsman. So Mr Venner was right about keeping my boots and all that.

The year after my accident I remember we ran close to Torrington and the stag ended up on an island in the River Torridge. This was the day of the opening meet of the Torrington Farmer's hunt and during the day the stag came close by, with most of their followers joining in, leaving the Master, Henry Morrish, on his own. He wasn't a happy chappy, but that's all forgotten now. We were close to John Prouse's that day and we went back to his house where he fried up some of the liver. We got home some time after midnight.

On 1 May 2000 I gave up the job of huntsman of the Dulverton West Foxhounds and have now come out of hunt service."

§

An account of a run by Tiverton Staghounds on Friday, 16 March 1984, meeting at Swineham Hill and killing at Wellington, recorded by Philip Lashbrook

"History was made from the meet at Swineham Hill on 16 March 1984, the tufters were taken to Rackenford Withybeds on a bright sunny morning with a cold east wind, where there were quickly several deer afoot. A suitable spring stag jumped out into the road and shook himself and headed down the valley to Westcott. The pack were laid on at 11.30 outside the Withybed, with interference from other deer at Spurway Mill they crossed high up to Pinkworthy Farm to come in above the scramble field. Then to run the length of the Iron Mill stream to Stuckeridge, Chain Bridge, Duvale Wood, Holmingham Quarry to cross the Exe into Jim Yandle's, up through Shute to Bampton down to run the north side of Huntsham to Cudmore Cross on dusty ground. We slotted the deer through mud in a gap in the hedge at Thorn Cross and by now an hour in front of hounds. We were joined by a local lady being a Tiverton supporter (then quite young) who had not time to dress for the occasion nor put a saddle on her horse, but cursed Ray for riding on without her. Now across Heniton Hill to Pool Farm, Ashbrittle to run up the River Tone, a crash of music told us the pack had fresh found at Hagley Bridge near Waterrow, probably the first time the deer had known he was being hunted, now going on to Bathealton to Kittisford Farm to Higher Wellisford, Thorne St Margaret through Holywell Lake following the River Tone to bay at Tonemills Wellington at 3.50. Brow, tray, and two each side. Master Robin Venner, huntsman Ray Burrow, whip Ray Dart (not out due to injury) 16 mile point – 24 miles as hounds ran, a hunt to remember – proper job!"

§

Telling the tale as Jan Stewer would have told it, with Evelyn Waldron at Kings Nympton

In the late 1980s early 1990s, when John and Janc Pcarce were Joint Masters, a social evening and meal was held in King's Nympton Village Hall. Evelyn Waldron came along and talked, in Devonshire dialect, about her days out with the Tiverton Staghounds. All of the stories are true.

"Good evening to e all, yer us ave had a good dinner, you knows Bill Slee e knows what e was about when he hanged up ees hat to Sally Squires and put ees feet under her table. I'm not goin to tell e who I am goin to mention tonight, in case a few of e take to yer heels and rins.

Well us be yer tonight to a staghounds dinner, you knows they hounds they've got to have a good nose about um, to find they stags. More difficult if scent's not good and by gad they stags be crafty. What about that Norman Ellis, e's never ome, I've yerd of a grass wider, poor old Joan er must be a hunt wider. I thought Rob Venner was goin to be yer tonight, they tell me e's gone playing bingo, never heard tell of a varmer playing silly games like that afore, I suppose any excuse is better en none.

Ounds met one day at Jim Haye's to Molland, huntsman put the ounds in the cover opposite the farm, they couldn't finden, e was more clever than they thought. Mother and me us was parked in the big layby on the old A361 looking across, and do e knows after a time out comes the ole stag and e was a big un, bin around a bit e had. He rinned halfways across the field which had been ploughed, rubbed ees nose good and proper in the earth and rinned back in cover again. Ounds couldn't hunt im, and do e knows they tell me e was out in the field in the evening eating away as if nort ad appened. Well you know you git good entertainment out unting, even if you haven't got a horse. I remember a few years agone, when these yer cameras come een what's got these yer things they calls zoom lenses on them what takes things that's appening two or dree fields away. Well us was down John Lake's stonches one day, 'ounds was in the fir plantation down under, Mother er looked across the field and seed a bloke way a contraption sticked up, well er thought to erself, that's one of they anti everything blokes, so er thought er had better see to een. I don't know if er thought e needed a knock on the ead, anyway er made er way over to him and I'm darned it twadn that there Richard Lethbridge. I tell e I reckon ees got a few rare snaps. I'm blowed if you know where e's turning up to next, e's bin and gone way with the evidence before you've realised it, over the yers us ave seen some of ees films.

Well, Mother, you know her goes out hunting way her sister Shirley Grant sometimes, poor old Rodney e can't go cause e's got to stay home and shoe the 'osses for them that do go, you know I think er goes as much for the fun as the unting. Stupid lot some of them when them out unting you know, fore and back like they was on a race track, think nort of blocking the roads, mind you they don't vor long if Shirley is around, her soon moves em on, they jolly well move when er shouts, they don't git a second chance or er move their cars erself. Soon as they see er out with er rid bag they goes in higher gear and they is off, but er catches up to em.

I remember once ounds met Sampson Cross, so they put the ounds in Padely Wood, wasn't long afore they heard the horn blowin down under Yawtown. So Terry Irwin e was stopped up Hele Cross, e got jumping about, 'Stag's gone out,' e said, 'jump in boys.' E'd got ees own boy and Andrew Tucker, couple of likely lads, course they wasn't so fast, and Granfer e was already in the Land Rover. I don't think e gits out much caus e's afraid that sometime or other Terry would go and leave en behind. Terry said Chittlehamholt, so off they goes speeding right drew Chittleholt to the cross way just before you gits to Ian Tucker's place, looked back and pon me soul they couldn't hear nort or see nort. Well all e could do was turn round and go back, cause e'd took off so fast e didn't wait to yer whether the horn was blowing for gone out, staying where they'm too or going ome. Do e know ole Terry was furious cause when come too it was poor old Walt Reed down under Yawtown practising a few notes on ees horn. Course just as they turned round and came back ounds had gone out and was up Orange Moor.

Talking of Walter Reed, once you know they found a stag at Filleigh and e give em a good rin all the way down Bishops Tawton to Hall, there they lost un for a couple of hours, couldn't find en nowhere. When all of a sudden a couple of fields away they heard John Pincombe shouting, deer had gone out down ees place, so Walter e was standing in the hedge beside us up tother side, and e's got a pretty good voice, so e started shouting. Norman Ellis was standing there too and e said, 'What be shouting for Walter, stag hasn't gone out yet.' Well e said somebody down there was shouting so e thought e might as well, I wonder who the poor ole huntsman takes notice of.

Another time ounds met Kissing Gate Cross, who should be there but Denzil Mock and Dougie Ridd, well I tell e both of them can stretch it a bit, what you might call economical way the truth. Well ole Mock e was winding Dougie up a bit, you know neither one of them knowed whether other was telling the truth, course Terry e had to come along and put en ees say, well when twas getting hot I thought twas time to leave, anyway hounds started tonguing then so subject was closed.

Talking of Denzil Mock, seed Walter Ash tother day and e reckoned when e was hunting ounds, best scent ever was once when e let the pack go Beara Cross and ounds went away top speed. Walter went full pelt to East Cheldon, time e got there ees tongue was anging out so e stopped for a rest. Along came Denzil Mock and e said ounds be out to Lapford, well e didn't know whether to believe en or no cause Mock's tales sometimes is like the fishermen's, they grow a foot a minute. Walter realised Mock was telling truth and took off again. E didn't catch up way the ounds before e got down ambrosia.

Yer what about the ferret racing, pon me soul there isn't a spare drainpipe left in the parish now they've started that ole caper. When they had it down here twas on the night of a hunting day. Stafford Blake wanted to come so e had to leave the ounds to go home and have ees tea and change into ees best clothes to come down yer. Well on the way down e was passing Hapenny Bridge when somebody told en stag was in the water across the field. Well he couldn't leave en there so e went in to investigate all in ees best shoes. Course when e looked up and down the river wadn't nothing there. Somebody had'n on you know, e must be a good boy scout always prepared way ees gun. He came to the ferret race all plastered in mud. I wonder what ees wife said to im when e got ome.

Betty Courtis you knaw her's mazed about ole ferret racing, I bet Dougie ee'll have to sell the cow and get er a ferret now. Can e remember the time when they killed a nott stag over to Essebere Witheridge. Well the ounds met Sletchcott Cross in hind unting season, Stuart reckoned e'd got a good hind over Padely, so they found this yer deer put ounds in and in no time they was off and add a good run when they caught en to Essebere, well I reckon a stag looks like a hind when e haven't got no orns.

Yer, don't some of them go a speed way their vehicles when they'm unting. Poor ole Arold Chugg he went just as fast one day going backwards, went right up over the edge and tipped over, poor ole boy what was riding in the back got pitched out on top of his head. Others ad to be pulled out upside down out through the window. Good job nobody was urt but I bet tho boy had a eadache next day. Yer it all appens out unting.

Had a good day up to the opening meet, strange country to Mother and me, but Shirley er knows where er was goin. Anyway Stafford Blake had got the biggest stag ever was seed harboured up there so off us went well tanked up way whiskey and sherry and all that grub. Ole Stafford knows what ee was about when e picked ees wife, you can't beat marrying a good cook. Anyway us took off, Shirley knows where was a good spot us could see everything, and darn me when us got to where you turned off ole Terry was there stopping everybody, us ad to go along bottom road to stop deer going into enemy territory. Shirley wasn't very pleased but done what er was told. Well us ad a good spot right below the cover where they was drawing, us yerd the orn blowing up and yerd the ounds speaking en and out, mind you twas a proper thick wood in there, they could only walk around. The stag e was crafty, e wouldn't budge.

Course there was plenty of advice out in the road for the huntsman. Some thought e ought to put the pack een to get n out. Somebody said nosy parkers was there in the morning and turned im out, anyway after a while things went quiet so us all drifted away and went to another place, all us seen was riders going across the fields to another place so us moved again. My dear soul where us went to us ad to open and shut umpteen gates, the track us went on was a bit steepy and Mother er took fright in case us tipped over. Anyway us seed some sport, hind and calf and yearling came out and got everybody excited, and stag rinned across the fields to the back of us, but e was a spring stag, bit too fast for this time of year. Then us seed huntsman and ounds pulling out and going back to where us started in the morning.

They'd had the message the big stag was still in the cover, so us went back and parked same spot as us was in the morning, wasn't long afore us yerd ounds speaking well, folks hollering and shouting and then us all sat up and took notice, because we yerd the bushes rattling in the cover and was expecting stag to break, but turned out to be a bloke all excited. E reckoned e had nearly stepped on the stag, e was lying in a bushment, e supposed e frightened en and when tho stag jumped up e went right down again, e could have caught en by ees horns. I wonder why e didn't. Anyway tho chap was quite breathless, I wonder who'd been scared most.

Not long ago ounds met Affeton Moor Cross. Well, twas our King's Nympton hunt ball on the Friday night and as twas the point-to-point on the Saturday they ad to ave the meet on Thursday. Well, Mother was in a bit of a fix, er had a big haunch of venison to cook vor the hunt ball and wanted to go hunting as well. Well er thought to erself put meat on low oven as it would take several ours to cook. Time ounds ad rinned about Affeton and found they would sure to make for King's Nympton Park. They would be ome middle afternoon, but it wasn't like that. Ounds took off, went all up about Lapford, Morchard Bishop, New Buildings and back to Worlington. Course Mother er was riding way er sister Shirley Grant and they was just passing Thornham Chapel when Mother remembered meat in oven. Well er didn know what to do because ounds was speaking well and going on and us was miles away from ome and if er said anything to Shirley she would tiss a bit to have to leave them. Anyway er did say to Shirley, 'Us must go ome and see to the meat in oven.' My dear soul Shirley let off steam having to leave ounds and who should be passing but thickey young Evans boy, milkman from South Molton and heard it all. Course e's Mother's milkman and e drove it for ages. 'Hope you meats all right in oven missus.' Er nearly chucked the bottle of milk back at him time or two. Anyway turned out right in end. Shirley took Mother ome, meat was done to a turn and Shirley met ounds again Bera Cross coming back to Park. So er turned around and instead of being last on scene er was first.

Well thank ee for listening to me old stories and forgive me if I've insulted e but I wish e all goodnight, a safe journey ome and good unting."

§

Talking with Jane and John Pearce, Joint Masters of the Tiverton Staghounds, 1988–1995

"On 1 May 1988 we took over from the committee and acting Masters, John Lucas and John Colthorpe. We employed Anthony Allibones, always called Bones, as our whip and he was with us for five years. We could not have had anyone better in the flesh house and he was good with the farmers too.

Our first summer was spent getting to know the farmers and the country. Sharon Mogford arrived to help with the horses and stayed for the seven years duration, eventually being our whipper-in – very good she was too.

Our very first meet was at Cudmore and it was a short day as we had to stop hounds because of Huntsham Shoot. The opening meet was at Uplowman Court, we found at Rifle Range and killed at Court Wood, all his rights 3 and 4. At the kill, John could not paunch the deer as he had stabbed his wrist while clipping a horse and had stitches. This was the only time he didn't paunch his own deer. The stag went back to Mrs Middleton's that night. We decided we should have this, our first head, mounted, but unfortunately the head had already been taken off and the stag skinned. However, Mr Rose the taxidermist did an excellent job replacing the skin, and you cannot tell where the join is. Unfortunately the walls on the bungalow at the kennels were not strong enough to hold this head, so it was at Alan Mogford's for six years.

Our first day hind hunting was at Crowdhole Cross. We found Monkey Moor on to Bradford Woods, Prison Farm, Kennels, Week, Waterloo, Horridge Moor, Huntacott, Stone Mill, Chawleigh, Cobley and finished in the dark going towards Worlington.

Our first Christmas Eve we met at Terry Hamlin's at Worth Park, Washfield; we found at Hatherleigh Wood and killed at Black Cat. We had worn out the new shoes on two of the horses and had to have the blacksmith, Gerald Green, to shoe them on Christmas Day so they could go again on Boxing Day. That was the day when John's horse came down on the road at Thornham Chapel, going round the bend, and was concussed, but still hunted on from Watersplash.

Accounts of days, 1989–1990

We had a nice autumn stag hunt from Cudmore Cross, found at Priestlands, laid on the pack, going onto Zeal Ball, Hayne Moor, over the main road, Skilgate Wood, Union Jack (before Paul McCartney bought it), over the reservoir, across Goviers Down to the reservoir, back up the goyle to kill on Maurice Scott's farm at a 1.45 pm. All his rights 5 and 2.

A good hind hunt from Cove saw us finishing in the dark near the M5.

We had a meet at John's parents' place at Great Bradley, Withypool in February, finding at Bradley Bog, Knaplock, Barle Valley out and round the Punchbowl, allotments, Ashwayside, Slade, Tarr Steps, Westwater, Lords, Willingford Bridge, Combewood Goyle, Cuzzicombe Post, Twitchen, and finished at Marsh Bridge at 6 pm. They were very fast on the common.

1990–1991

27 October: met Portsmouth Arms, Burrington. Found Northcote Manor, then onto Upcott. Did a circuit to Hacknell, laid pack on at Hansford Bridge, through Hansford, Deer Park Copse, High Town to Horridge, stopping the hounds when the stag went into the centre of the deer farm and was between the fences. The deer have a habit of going to other deer, even farmed ones.

January: we met at Spurway Moor Gate, found Waspley, Plushetts, Wind Whistle, Champles, Chain Bridge, Duvale out towards Morebath. The Devon and Somerset, not realising it was our hind, laid their hounds on in front of ours and we hunted up to them so we had two lots of tufters hunting together. Eventually we lost our deer.

1991–1992

January: met Cobbacombe Cross, found Allen's Down, Coombe, Chevithorn, Pitts, Waterworks, Lakes Down, Croydon, Upton Fishponds, Bickleigh Wood, Newbridge, Cove, Bolham, Bickleigh Wood, Newbridge, Sommerclose, Stoneton, Washfield Wood up the goyle to Courtenay Cottages where she was taken in the porch of the cottage now lived in by Les Greenslade.

1992–1993

Spring Staghunting: met at the kennels, found Cuddenhay, Gardners End, Homer, Longwood, Cobley, Eastleigh, Two Bridges, Stonemill, Mounticombe, Stone Plantation, Sydham, Parsonage, Horridge Moor, Bycott, Garland, Highridge, Little Silver, Alswear, Tidlake, Mariansleigh Wood, Uppacott and killed under Milltown at 3.15 pm. The stag did about 18 miles in two hours.

Bones (the whipper-in) left at the end of the season to go to the Dulverton East as whipper-in, and he now hunts them.

1993–1994

Martin Blackmore came as whipper-in for a short period and then Sharon took on the whipping-in with Andrew Sexon helping in the kennels. He also did some whipping-in.

Spring stag hunting: we met at East Kidland, laid on from Muckford, towards Luckett, Wadham, Luckett, Jubilee, Shapscott Barton, Swineham Hill, Ford Valley, Western, Graces Bridge, Pickes, Westcott, two gates parallel with the link road to Rifton, up to Batesworthy Road, Rifton, Diptford, Ennerleigh Valley to Cotley, killed the deer in stream under the link road.

1994–1995

Met Joces cross, found well-harboured hind in Meethe Wood, went Pedley, Helewood, King's Nympton Park, around once, Helewood, Pedley top of Meethe cover, bottom of Caplecombe, crossing the river between Parsonage and George Nympton, and onto Habbots Lane towards South Molton, stopped all but one couple with the hind going around South Molton and back up under Blastridge, Alswear, Bish Mill, Newton gorse by link road. Fresh found in gorse, Bishops Nympton, Rodsworthy down stream and out over Quince Cross, Yardewood, Catkill, Nethercott Moor, back to Catkill and killed at 5 pm. This was approximately 25 miles as hounds ran. We had her head mounted as she was so game.

A week later we had another hunt of 25 miles from Chulmleigh Beacon. Drew and found Bycott, Horridge Moor, Chulmleigh Beacon, Colleton Manor, over the road, railway line and river. Handsford Moors under Burrington towards radar station, over the main road by radar, swinging right and up towards the top of Vauterhill Stud, down under High Bickington village, around Atherington to Umberleigh. Fresh finding at Four White Gates, down opposite Greendown, past Broden Hill, over the road below Hilltown, back through Broden Hill, down to Clapworthy Mill, over iron railings and into the river, out over the top and killed in goyle below Parsonage Farm, George Nympton. A very good hunt.

Our last meet was at Oakwell, Kings Nympton, and it poured with rain. Drew and found Magpiery and went Parsonage George Nympton, out to the main road, Frenchstone, Woodhouse, on to Broomham, Littlewood, Yealmacott, Womford, Meethe Wood, Parsonage, Narracott, around Limes Lane, back of George Nympton, Womford Bridge, up across Joces Cross with the pack on, into Venn, Howards Mill, down the water to Meethe, Helewood, down the water into Kings Nympton Park. We took hounds in and drew for one-and-a-half hours before finding him and killing under the weir.

During the time we were at kennels, BSE came along. This caused the renders to put up the charges in excess of £100 per bin. In the bins was the stuff the hounds could not eat so we were forced to make charges for collecting dead stock. We had meetings with other hunts and we all agreed on what to charge. It was a very expensive time and changed a system that had worked well for ages. We also had the League Against Cruel Sports following us a lot of the time, with up to five vehicles. I don't know what they expected to achieve by making films and taking pictures all the time. We certainly had nothing to hide, but it was annoying always being watched even when hounds had been loaded in the lorry.

We were lucky in that we had been breeding horses for years and we ended up having nearly all the hunt horses home-bred, which was nice and also rare in any sort of hunting.

We had seven very enjoyable years and were sorry to have to leave. During the summer we were usually successful when we showed the hounds at Dunster and Honiton Hound Shows. We won the cups at Honiton for several years. We introduced a puppy show as well as an open day so that the puppy-walkers, who were numerous and brilliant, could be looked after."

§

Chapter Seven

John Norrish

Talking with John Norrish, the present huntsman of the Tiverton Staghounds

"When I was a baby my mother would take me out in my pram with the Tiverton Foxhounds. Then as I got older she transferred me to the pillion seat of her bicycle.

My passion for hunting grew, and after spending seven years as a bricklayer learning the trade, I was not happy. By that time I was married to Angela and I stopped working on a building site and for 12 months took on a milk round. Then I went part time into the Tiverton Foxhound kennels as kennelman, going out with the hounds each day. From here I went up onto the moor and became second whipper-in at the Dulverton West Foxhounds for Joint Masters Mr Bertie Hill and Mr Smyth, learning the style and ways of operating in the field.

One day we were hunting on Jack Witheridge's land and the hounds went down the valley towards Riverton. I came down through the fields and on seeing Jack Witheridge I asked, 'Have they gone down Jack?' He said they had.

In the evening when they were loading up the hounds, Mr Smyth the Joint Master said to me, 'Norrish, be at my place at seven o'clock, I want to see you.' I thought, 'What the hell have I done wrong now?'

If you were ever called up to his house and he told you to go through the left-hand door you knew you were in for a rollicking, but if he told you to go straight ahead it wasn't so bad. When he told me to go left I thought, 'Christ, I'm in for it now'. Inside there was a big egg-shaped table. He used to sit at one end and make you sit at the other end.

He said, 'While you were hunting today, I heard you call Mr Witheridge by his Christian name.'

'Did I?' I said.

'You know you did and I heard you, and in future when you've got your red coat on, you call a farmer or anyone else "Sir" or by his surname. If I ever catch you calling anyone by their Christian name you will be for it.'

He was a stickler for that kind of discipline. I had one too many at a dance once and the next morning he had me on the carpet again and told me if I couldn't take two drinks to only have one. He would never call me John, always Norrish. A very strict man, you don't get Masters like that today, of the old school.

Colin Dayment used to jump on a horse like a cowboy and I was fascinated how he used to do it. One day we were hunting on the Horridge Valley and I couldn't close the gate from my horse, so I had to get off. When I tried to get back on I thought I would try and do what Dinky Dayment used to do but I couldn't. All of a sudden I heard, 'Norrish, what the hell are you doing?'

'Sorry Sir, I'm just trying to do what Mr Dayment does when he jumps on a horse like the Pony Express.'

'You're not in the Pony Express, you're in the bloody hunt service,' he replied.

Accepting the ways of operating in the field with the Dulverton West stood me in good stead for my next position as whipper-in at the Devon and Somerset Staghounds. I moved to Exford with Angela and my two boys Matthew and Peter, both of whom have subsequently spent time working in hunt kennels. I was working for a huntsman of the old school who expected high standards from his staff. Dennis Boyles, the huntsman, was a stickler for tradition and I had the utmost respect for him.

One season Dennis Boyles broke his leg and Mr Robinson, the Joint Master, said, 'You've got to hunt the hounds on Thursday John.' He persuaded me to do it, but I was not keen.

The next meet was at Aldermans Barrow. By the late afternoon I was stuck out over Buscombe with one hound, and

I thought, 'What the hell am I doing this for?' After a time things started to fall into place. The experience of handling hounds stood me in excellent stead for the future. I learnt a lot from Dennis Boyles.

From there I went to the South Devon Foxhounds for five seasons, gaining a lot and learning other ways of hunting. We had invitation meets, the Wynnstay, Cheshire, Cattistock, and South and West Wilts country. I gained experience hunting in those types of country – it's all jumping, a totally different sport altogether. I then went on to the Minehead Harriers.

On 1 May 1995, I took over from John Pearce as huntsman to the Tiverton Staghounds. I didn't know which hounds I could trust or rely on, so Richard Down the Quantock Staghounds huntsman gave me 3 1/2 couple of old steady hounds. They were brilliant at hunting the deer and put me right. The first hound I had from the Devon and Somerset was a dog called Waiter, an old English hound. I knew that Dennis Boyles still had Waiter and I asked to have him. He was a brilliant hound; I used him on a bitch before he got too old and have still got him. When I left the South Devon the Masters gave me some hounds and I kept breeding from the bitches. Eventually when I came to the Tiverton Staghounds I brought most of these hounds and bred on from them; they were old English hounds.

Another line I'm breeding goes back to Tiverton Foxhound Dunkery and I have been breeding that line on. I like old English hounds, but when you're breeding them with modern foxhounds you want to be careful because some of the old English lines can be a bit hard, you've just got to watch what you're doing with them. Tony Holdsworth from the Tiverton Foxhounds gave me some nice hounds that were hunting deer in their second season. They were good and I bred a litter from one of those bitches, and also from two or three bitches that John Pearce left that go back to Tiverton Staghounds Merlin and Galway old line. I haven't forgotten the Tiverton old lines and feel it is worth keeping them going. By using West Somerset Moonstone, I have produced some strikingly marked hounds, some of which are almost black with dark mottle. I have also used West Somerset Wagstaff, Partner, Barton, and Eggesford Wagstaff.

Barbara, the hound that won the championship at Honiton in 1998 was out of a bitch called Bargain from the Quantock

Staghounds. Walter Perry hunted her, she was about 10 or 11 seasons when she finished down here. Barbara hunts just like her mother.

At Honiton we swept the board and had dog hound and bitch hound champion, best bitch couple class, best brood bitch, and Richard Down won the best unentered bitch with one of the puppies I gave him. For a small kennel I only breed about four couple a year compared to the Devon and Somerset who probably breed 12–16 couple, so we did well. At Honiton in 1998 we won two championships and had one reserve champion; the only class we lost was the couple class. Richard Down of the Quantock Staghounds won that with two nice bitches. The dog hound that won the championship was called Rutland, and goes back to one of the old English lines that I bred up through from South Devon, South Devon Ruin. The bitch that won the other championship is actually the hound that we bred from Richard Down, so he was pleased in a way that through his breeding we got a win. The dog hound that came second, that was reserve champion, was from a line that went back to Tiverton Dunkery. For a small kennel like ours to win seven classes out of eight was good. It was a bit embarrassing really to keep winning. I thought half way through, 'For Christ's sake let someone else win'. I was relieved when Richard Down took the couple class, he's a good boy Richard. In the bitch class for the championship I had his breeding, with Bridesmaid winning, and the reserve he had mine, out of Ruby; so it was funny, I won it on his breeding and he had reserve champion on mine.

For some time I have been after some hounds from the Belvoir Hunt owned by the Duke of Rutland. I want to bring more English lines into the kennels. It isn't any good going just anywhere, you've got to be careful what you get and how you use it. Now I've got two nice strong Belvoir dog hounds. With a bit of luck they should fit in nicely and I will breed from them. I might put some of the bitches that have got one line of modern foxhound and the rest old English, eventually turning it back to old English, but only one line of modern in. Another bitch I might put a modern bitch on and get another cross-breed; it's a way of putting a bit more bone and substance in your pack because a lot of these modern hounds are getting too fine and that's no good for staghunting. If you're not careful with this modern breeding you can get too fine a line. It's also a way of getting a bit more nose because they've got very low scenting and you create good hounds with noses.

I was very lucky to get these two Belvoir hounds, the Duke of Rutland doesn't just give them away. One of the hounds they gave me was entered the year before and the other one had only done one season, two quite young hounds. He has also given me permission to take bitches up to the Belvoir and use their stallion hounds, you don't get that very easy now. It's an honour that he has let the Tiverton Staghounds have them.

It took 12 months of talking to Martin Thornton, the huntsman of the Belvoir, and the Duke to get these hounds. The first time I asked I got a definite 'no', but I kept on showing the interest and eventually, when they knew what I was trying to do, they let me have them. The modern hounds are getting a bit too light and whippety. Sometimes I have to go outside to use a dog because I'm getting too close with the breeding, but when I do this I find it difficult to find the dog because even the dog hounds in some of these foxhound packs are getting like bitches. They've lost the character of a good old dog hound head, that's mainly why I wanted these old English, and the Belvoir are real pure old English hounds.

Because of all the rigmarole with the ministry, you've got to go through with feeding and burning. I've worked out an area that will feed the 28–30 couple of hounds. A huntsman's job in the kennels is not just hunting the hounds, he's got to run the hunt in an economical way and cost it out to keep it running. He won't do himself any favours by running up terrific bills. The huntsman should run the kennels as his own business, even though he's working for someone else. Having said that, you don't want to cut too many corners because the standards will drop.

For five seasons we've done well. They were a very young pack of hounds to start off with and the puppies that John Pearce left me had to be virtually straight in. The first year I bred a bit heavy to get the number of puppies in. They always say it takes four years to make a pack and one year to destroy them. There's nothing wrong with staghunting if you do everything right in an orderly way. It's like Dennis Boyles said, 'You've got to do it by the book.' You mustn't go out and hunt deer like a cowboy, it must be done in a professional way.

I enjoyed the days during spring 1999 when we ran from Muddygate to North Tawton and from Meethe to Kennerleigh.

They were brilliant days hunting because nobody saw the stag from then till we fresh found it again, we had to rely on the hounds and one or two people slotting it both those days. In a way, anyone can hunt a stag when he is being seen all the time but it's harder when people don't see him and you've got to use all your skills and the hounds have got to be that much better. From Meethe we came down under with the hounds coming down the valley, twisting and doubling before they checked at the bridge. We made a cast down the river and never hit anything off, but on the way down the valley I noticed a nice bit of gorse which the deer is likely to lie up in. I cast back up again and a little bitch in her second season was feathering on. Then all of a sudden an older hound called Mason picked up the line and started speaking. He took the rest up through the wood out into the next field, coming back through the wood again, hitting the gorse and out came the stag and bayed him down under Kennerleigh.

One of the character hounds in the pack is Godfrey. He came down here in my second season. Ray Burrow gave Dennis Boyles some hounds because he was short on puppies, and then the Devon and Somerset bred this line of Tiverton on and that's how Godfrey came down here.

The key thing to staghunting in the spring and autumn is harbouring and organisation. If you've got him well and truly harboured you can go in with your tufters and get things going. Even if you don't kill but have a good day the visitors and local supporters will go back and say they've had a brilliant day with the Tiverton Staghounds and they will come again.

We have a lovely lot of puppy walkers and always have the puppies back from them very early, after six or seven months, so then I can get them trained and before they start hunting they know me and my commands. If you let the walkers have the puppies too long it's difficult because the puppies get soft. By getting them in early they will still know the walkers but will have forgotten their habits and then all they know is me. I whistle a lot; I got that habit from being a whipper-in. I was taught this instead of hollering and shouting when calling up hounds. If you're going through a wood you don't know how far the huntsman is on casting his hounds. So if you're a noisy whip coming up through getting your hounds up together or bringing on tale hounds the casting hounds may hear you and start to lift their heads and lose their concentration. We were taught as you were calling up hounds just to keep whistling and it's surprising how many will come to it. By whistling in the kennels and when on exercise they get used to it.

We have a lot of deer around the kennels and they don't take any notice of the hounds. As we go down the road in the morning they just look up and see us and put their heads down and go back to grazing. They seem to know that the only friends they have are these hounds."

Chapter Eight

Harbouring – by Geoffrey Boundy*

The harbourer is an essential official to any pack of staghounds. His role is a vital part to the day's hunting, as is the huntsman or the whipper-in. His qualifications are "woodcraft" and an intimate knowledge of the deer and the area where they live. The harbourer's business is to gather and supply information as to the whereabouts of suitable deer. This information is gained from the people who work the land and woodlands and by the harbourer maintaining a year round surveillance.

© Countryside Alliance

Harbouring is an "art" and by using woodcraft he looks for the signs of the deer. Slots are the foot tracks left by the deer as they cross the country and pass through gaps or "racks" in the hedges. The slots of the deer will tell the harbourer the sex and size of the animal he is following.

* Taken from *Hounds Magazine*, November 1999

He will also look for deer droppings, half eaten shoots of grass or other greenery. The harbourer will also look for broken twigs or barked trees or bushes, which will indicate deer activity. By using these signs he can locate a suitable sized and aged animal for the hounds to hunt, without actually seeing it. The term "warrantable" refers to a suitably aged male for autumn or spring hunting.

A lot of harbouring in the old days was done in this way, when the only transport was a horse or pony. The signs observed will give the harbourer confidence to report to the huntsman and Masters at the meet, but to actually see the deer to judge its suitability is the most satisfactory situation. Besides the signs left by the deer, a good pair of binoculars are an essential aid to the harbourer's job. He also must be sure of the wind direction when tracking close to deer, as they will scent humans and be gone. This can also apply to over-interested hunt followers who try a little unofficial harbouring and can spoil the harbourer's work and move the deer.

As hunt followers assemble at the meet, many have little idea of the work that has been done beforehand. Several mornings and evenings can be spent searching for a warrantable deer and just occasionally the harbourer comes to the meet with nothing. Yet with the help of farmers and local residents, a suitable deer can usually be located.

One of the major problems is determining when a deer enters a wood that he stays in there. Sometimes a stag can be seen going into a wood and is merely just passing through. The harbourer has to be patient and then circles the wood to see if there are any outgoing slots, or ideally, moves to some high ground to watch all sides of the covert.

There are three roles for the harbourer which are to locate the deer, report to the Masters at the meet and assist the huntsman to find it. After the right deer has been roused by the tufters, and the pack is laid on, his work is ovcr. Hc can now go home or join the hunt.

Anyone interested in the woodcraft of the deer should read *Memories of a Stag Harbourer* by Fred Goss. This is the bible for anyone aspiring to watch and harbour deer. It was written in the 1920s and records Fred Goss's unique service as harbourer to the Devon and Somerset Staghounds from 1894 until 1921.

Over the years, some stunning photographs have been taken of the deer in the Tiverton Staghounds country

Photo © S A Hesman (Scenic Prints)

Photo © S A Hesman (Scenic Prints)

© John Burston

© John Burston

© John Burston

© John Burston

© John Burston

© John Burston

Photo © Steve Rendall

Photo © Steve Rendall

Chapter Nine

Chester

Chester was an outstanding horse that the Tiverton Staghounds had for nearly 15 seasons, serving three huntsmen. I think one word sums him up, and that's what Walter Ash said to me and it stuck in my mind. He said Chester was the 'King' of the Tiverton Staghounds.

The story of Chester begins with Betty Palfrey from Bullaford Farm near South Molton. Here, she begins to describe him.

"It must be said that the most well-known horse bought was a chestnut gelding called Chester. I bought him as a three-year-old with three other young horses from two brothers that farmed in Southampton. They had a big dairy farm and bred some very good horses. Chester was a great character, I often put him out in the field and would walk back up the yard and he would jump the gate and join me and walk back into the yard and into his stable. Chester was five years old around 1970 when Mr Besley rang to know if I had a suitable horse. I described Chester as being a bit immature and a little green but I said, 'You have the right man to take him on, and if he likes him he will make it the best horse you have ever had.' That man was Walter Ash. Mr Besley came with the rest of the representative committee (Mr Venner, the late Mr Sid Gillbard, the late Mr Jack Adams and the late Mr Dick Cox) to have a look at him. Later on Walter Ash came along to give his opinion. He rode Chester and said, 'He may be a bit green but he is the best horse I have sat on and I love him.' Walter made him, being a fine horseman, and Chester turned out to be the best. I was proud to have sold him to the Tiverton Staghounds."

§

Talking with Walter Ash about Chester

"I went to see Chester at Betty Palfrey's and galloped him around this big field and, Christ, didn't he go. I said, 'Woah boy, steady down,' dropping his reigns and skidding up. That horse was coming into my hands and he was doing everything, or trying to do everything, I asked him. He was just dancing on the ground. I think at the time they bought a grey off Betty as well for £230.

One morning Chester kicked a hound and I told him off about that out exercising, but after that I did everything with him. He always went second horse and I rode him for five seasons, then when I left Ray Giles took over as huntsman and rode him for another five seasons doing everything with him, keeping the point-to-point course, parading hounds in Cornwall and at the Devon County Show.

When Ray Giles left, Ray Burrow took over and did exactly the same as I did, he rode that horse again second most every time. Occasionally I went out tufting with him one in three weeks perhaps, to ease him and give him a break, hunting him two hours in the morning then he went up into the lorry and didn't do any more. Ray Burrow, and probably Ray Giles, did the same.

Normally though, soon as ever we layed on the pack that horse went with it. I rode Chester once when we found a stag in Rifton and killed him at Waterrow, now that's a fair distance across country. Another time we found on Horridge Moor and I got lost; the wind was blowing and I went the wrong way. Someone said to me, 'The last time I saw the hounds they were crossing up at Denzil Mock's old farm on the top road by Benley Cross.' When I got there they said, 'Your hounds passed here a quarter of an hour ago,' and I said, 'Aye.' Well, it's true, I had lost them. I hadn't gone far down the road when Denzil Mock

Walter Ash riding Chester with the Torrington Farmers Hunt

came back and said, 'I've been to Lapford, your deer's gone down the railway line and the hounds have checked in the marsh.'

I said, 'You're joking.'

'I'm not joking, I wouldn't tell you a lie, you know that.'

Well it took a bit of believing, but off I went right down the Cheldon Valley flat out, up to Thelbridge, passing the race course straight through Lapford village, and I hadn't stopped galloping and trotting then on Chester. I got down to the bridge and a chap said, 'Your deer's gone in towards Lapford wood and hounds have checked in the marsh.'

I touched my horn and I blew those hounds across and they hit off the line. I said to Rob Venner the Joint Master, 'What's your horse like?'

He said, 'All right.'

'Well I've done nearly enough with Chester, I would like to give him a rest really.'

He said, 'I'll ride Chester along quietly, and you take my horse.'

I jumped on him and hadn't ridden 50 yards when the deer came back along the river and stood in front of me with all the hounds behind it and we shot the deer there. Rob came in with my horse and said, 'That was a good hunt Walter.'

When I was walking through the cover, I used to jump off Chester, put the reins back over his saddle and I used to say to him, 'Follow me, if you like someone will pick you up in a minute,' and he would walk behind me all through the cover drawing.

Before Ray Burrow left the Tiverton Staghounds in 1988, it was decided to let Chester have a steadier life and Rob Venner came up with the idea of letting me hunt the Torrington Farmers hounds with him.

In 1981 I had taken over as huntsman from Les Grills. I rode him for a couple of seasons, then my daughter Carol rode him with the Stevenstone hunt, and then I said to Rob Venner, 'It's a shame hunting this horse like this, why don't you try and sell it to a good home because the old horse has done his work,' and Chester was sold to Pam Underhill at Huxhill near Bideford. Her granddaughter Gail was riding him one day at Webbery and he threw her off, galloping nearly into Bideford, and everybody that was there said they've never seen a horse gallop like it. Then Mrs Iris Bright of Gibbon's Down, Yarnscombe bought him and said she would keep him until he died.

That horse proved he was the best horse in the country, you would never get three huntsmen to ride second horse staghunting for nearly 15 seasons: that's a horse and a half. I think out of the three huntsmen (me, Ray Giles and Ray Burrow), they will say it was the best horse they rode; he was the 'king' of the Tiverton Staghounds. When I left the Tiverton Staghounds I said to Ray Giles, 'You've got a good horse in Chester, don't go and kill him for Christ's sake, he will give you his best every day.' It's something like the Grand National horses, you won't forget him."

Walter Ash riding Chester with the Torrington Farmers hunt

Talking with Ray Giles about Chester

"When the Tiverton Staghounds bought Chester, people said at the time it was too expensive. I think he was £260, normally they were paying £150 for one. People thought he would never stick the Tiverton Staghounds country because of the roads. For a horse that wasn't going to last the season he did extremely well. I think in the 11 seasons I was there he only had two days' lameness.

I remember one year we went down to the Royal Cornwall Show and paraded hounds with Chester for three days. We had to be in the ring twice a day, that was myself and Ray Burrow, and you never saw such a show-off in all your life. When we were parading he was like a little Arab stallion, his old tale would stick right out and he would go through the field like he was the king of the ring. Raymond Brooks-Ward the commentator came up and said what a lovely horse he was and made us parade some extra time.

When you were hunting the King's Nympton end of the country there was a lot of clay and it used to stick to the sides of Chester's body fairly well. If you couldn't get to the river to clean him off properly at the end of the day then the mud used to stick to his ribs. Then it was impossible to use a brush on him because he was thin-skinned and if you did he would ripple on the side and get quite narky about it. You couldn't blame him.

In the summertime I would have visitors come, and if you had a couple novices you could put them on Chester and he would behave himself perfectly, never putting a foot wrong.

I took him out with the Devon and Somerset Staghounds once, but he didn't like being behind the hounds, he started to buck and knew his place was in front. All the time I was with the Tiverton Staghounds, he was never used as a whipper-in's horse. The first season he did burn up a bit quickly because he didn't have the stamina; once he got over the first year the stamina built up. Really he was being hunted too young, I think, for a huntsman's horse. He needed an extra year or two to build him up. We had some decent horses, but he was probably the best of them; he was 100 per cent reliable being pretty good tempered and you could do most things with him, he was a lovely comfortable ride."

§

"When I came to the Tiverton Staghounds, I whipped-in to Ray Giles for four years and I never got the chance to ride Chester because Ray rode him, but I used to look after him, he was a cracking horse.

I remember one day Ray had the flu when we were spring staghunting. He said, 'You will have to hunt them.'

I said, 'All right.'

We met at Van Post, anyway I went back to the quarry, taking out the tufters and Mr Venner said, 'I think I'd better take them on,' and I said, 'Yes, well that's all right.'

We went to Allens Down to draw, the trouble was the hounds wouldn't leave me. I thought the best thing I could do was to get out the far end, out of the way of them, but they still wouldn't draw for him. I've hardly ever heard him swear before, but he did.

'Bugger it, you better hunt them.' And I thought, 'Thank God for that.'

Later on that day they were blowing a whistle on the Emmerford Road; I was coming from the Cove side down to the main road, and was trotting on. Rob Venner said 'Steady on, you will strip the pads.' I thought, 'You don't want me to catch this deer.'

We met Mr Besley opposite Bickleigh Wood and the stag had crossed the river. Mr Venner said to Aubrey Besley, 'I think we will call it a day.'

I thought, 'Christ, you can't do that,' so I took off with the hounds, going down through the marshes and coming to this newly built stile. Now Walter Ash always told me that Chester would not jump. I thought, 'If I can get to the other side Mr Venner won't follow me, and nobody else will.' I know I shouldn't have done it, but I wanted to catch this stag, so I rode Chester as hard as I could, and I thought, 'He's either going to break his neck or he will get over the stile,' and he jumped it like a stag. Crossing the Exe and getting out on the road, the stag went around East Stoodleigh, coming back and we finally killed him in the river.

Chester would outstay anything, there's no question about that. When I took over as huntsman, I would be trotting with him and other horses would be cantering beside him. He would just get into a swinging trot and keep going. Come to the end I used to ease him a fair bit up the hills and let the other ones go on, catching them up when I got to the top, he still had a lot of life in him, there's no question about that.

I said to Mr Venner, 'I think it would be nice for Chester to have like a semi-retirement and let a hunting farmer have him so he could have a steadier life,' and he came up with the idea of letting Walter Ash have him, who was then hunting the Torrington Farmers hunt. I took Chester down there and dropped him off; I can't remember what year it was.

Walter retired from there in 1994 and I took over as huntsman. I kept asking about Chester, to see where he was because I knew he was down there somewhere. One day we were hunting at Gibbon's Down, Yarnscombe, and someone said, 'That's where he's to, in the stable.' After all those years it was marvellous really, seeing Chester again. He hadn't altered, and when we had finished hunting, I went over and Mr Bright had him on a rope and he was trotting along the road like a two-year-old.

I remember Walter Ash hunting Chester like it was yesterday. As a young horse he was like a whippet, but he filled out later on; he was something outstanding, a marvellous horse. One day we were spring staghunting and we went through Morchard Bishop. It was a hot day, and we got as far as Copplestone. I decided not to ride Chester any further because he was white with sweat and I didn't want anything to happen to him. When we got to the farm beside the main road, I took the bridle and saddle off and let him go in the field; I took someone else's horse and picked Chester up on the way home.

I had a soft spot for Chester and I can only remember him being lame once, when he had a nail prick him. He was a funny horse like that, so brave and bold, yet for all a little thing, when it came to he was a proper baby, but I've never known him sick or sorry."

Ray Burrow on Chester at the Devon County Show

Talking with Ray Dart about Chester

"I never liked Chester. At the end of the day you would have an awful job to clean him off and he was wicked – he would kick you or anything. I think he used to get sore and would crease his skin up and cringe and nearly lie down if you tried to rub him. If you got too close to the front end he would bite you and if you got too close to the back end he would up and kick you. He was a sod. When you came back from hunting you had to chuck buckets of water over him, then you would have to put three or four rugs on Chester and then go inside in the chair for a couple of hours and then go out and change the rugs to get him dry.

I remember when Ray Giles was hunting in the Cheldon Valley one day and I hadn't gone very far and I pulled a shoe. It was too early for Ray to change horses, and John Lucas said, 'Go back and get Chester, and when Ray wants to change you have Ray's horse and he can ride Chester on.' I had never ridden Chester out hunting, and I took him out of the box at Affeton Castle, and he just took off with me – all he wanted to do was to get to those hounds. I caught Ray up at Winswood Moor and I said, 'For Christ's sake have this horse.'

And he said, 'I don't want it yet.'

I said, 'You have him because I shall either kill him or he will kill me.'

Once he was up with the hounds, he was all right, he was no good behind at all."

§

Talking with Gillian Stevens about Chester

"I first met Chester in his late twenties when he was with some friends, Iris and Lewis Bright. I rode him out occasionally and he was a brilliant and energetic ride. He never stood for any nonsense and was always eager to get out and have a jolly good gallop if he could. He was always very good with any stray farm dogs who would dash out and try and nip his heels, and even when we rode under those huge electricity pylons making that awful hissing noise he would merely flip the odd ear in acknowledgement and do his usual skitter around for a minute, as he would if we met other horses, as if to say, 'I'm in charge still, so watch out!'

I tried riding him out in a group a couple of times but soon gave up on that as he always had to be in front, and I felt mean holding him back all the time, and would end up shouting, 'Sorry, coming through'. As soon as he was head of the group he was fine and would slow down a little. I moved away the year before he died and even then he was still looking strong and fit. It was a privilege to have ridden him and I was very upset when I heard of his demise. I have ridden all my life and shall always remember Chester with fondness as one of the best horses I have known."

Gillian Stevens on Chester

§

Talking with Mrs Iris Bright from Landcross near Bideford, where Chester spent his last days before peacefully passing away on 7 May 1997

"I bought Chester from Pam Underhill and I think she said she had him for five years. He was never nasty to anybody, but he did nip me in the back once when I was brushing his tummy – he didn't like me doing that. I've never known him kick, but he always gave you the impression he was going to because he would hold his back leg up, especially when I first had him, but after that he was fine. We got to know each other, and I could hold him. I knew he was very powerful and if he wanted to take off he could. My daughter was riding him once and he took off through the woods and up a steep piece. She couldn't hold him and away he went.

If anyone came to see us of an evening and it was time for his feed he would yawn and I knew he wanted them to go, but they didn't know that.

He was just one of the family, and if he was up with the bullocks and it was raining he would shout and I would open the gate and he would come in, and if he wanted to go out he would whinny. When my husband and I came to Landcross I rode him a couple of times, but that's when he started tripping and I knew there was something wrong with him, so I said, 'That's it, I can't ride you again.'

We had his teeth ground down a couple of times and when we were out at Yarnscombe Ray Squire used to shoe him and Eddy Tucker used to trim his feet here. Apart from that we never had the vet to him.

If the hounds were around we had to shut him in the stable and shut the door so he couldn't hear them; he wanted to get out there with them. He could always hear the hunting horn, you could tell because he was on his toes. When I brought him in my husband would terrify him by blowing the horn, and then he would go.

Nothing bothered him, even if a helicopter came down he was bombproof. Children would run through his legs and he wouldn't kick. He would let me know what he wanted, if it was time to be fed he would be rattling the gate with his foreleg. I spoilt him and intended him to enjoy the rest of his life anyway.

I remember at Gibbon's Down he got cold; we've got a little lake that runs down through the middle and it had rained a lot and the lake had risen about two foot in a quarter of an hour, and I'm damned if he wasn't down there stood in it up to his belly. He could have come up on dry ground on the sloping fields, but I don't know why he did it. He came in shivering and he lay down flat and I thought, 'This is it,' and I rubbed him and rubbed him, then he got up and he was fine again.

The morning of the day he died he passed our bungalow and sort of tripped and went down on his front knees. Whether he had a small heart attack then I don't know, but when I went to give him his cake in the evening he was dead. Walter Ash had always said that when Chester died we were not to bring him down to the Torrington Farmers hunt kennels. He said no way would he feed him to the hounds, which we wouldn't have done under any circumstances. We had a JCB and buried him in the field and have since planted a cherry tree there and we are talking about putting a plaque there also."

Iris Bright on Chester

Chapter Ten

The followers of the Tiverton Staghounds

Above: Bill Westacott

Right: Mrs Kathleen Lucas (left) and Marjorie Daw (right)

Helen Govier

Wagstaff greets Mrs Kathleen Lucas, mother of the Joint Master

Paul Herniman (left) and Herbert Carpenter (right)

George Stuckley

The late Ron Elstone

Clare Mock, point-to-point Secretary.
Behind are brother and sister, Peter and Julia Snell

Julie Millman, Filleigh Sawmills meet, Boxing Day 1999

Tom Drew (left) and John Dart (right)

Keith Webber (left) and Roger Gregory (right)

Brian Palfrey

Vicky Pincombe (left) and Jayne Snell (right)

Michael Snell

Peter Norrish (whipper-in 1996–1998) at The Globe in Chulmleigh

Jack Broom

Sharon Neale (left) and Pat Ellicott (right)

Lisa Lucas, daughter of the Joint Master

Jeremy Dunn and Michelle Werrett

Alison Palfrey
and
Paul Heard

Stafford Blake

1996 Centenary Puppy Show.
Right to Left:
Joint Master John Lucas;
Quantock Staghounds huntsman Richard Down;
Joint Master of Devon and Somerset Staghounds Maurice Scott; and Joint Master for the Tiverton end, Stuart Kelland
© Michael Jackson (*Hounds Magazine*)

Dave Blackford

Sue Harvey
at
The Exeter Inn,
Bampton

Verity Harvey
with
Laura Harvey
(behind)
at
the Exeter
Inn, Bampton

Catherine Milton

James Blake

Betty Long with
Tiverton Staghound
Whimsy, 1999

Three generations. Father and daughter Roderick and Rebecca Hayes, and grandfather Stanley

Tony Abraham, organiser of the 200 club, handing over a cheque for £2,000 for hunt funds to Chairman Robin Venner, right, on 1 January 2000 at the meet at the Stag Inn, Rackenford

"Putting the world to rights"
Left to Right:
Mrs Mary Greenslade, the back of Hazel Down, and Reg Down

Two authors together. Richard Lethbridge with Hope Bourne who has written many books on Exmoor. Seen here out with the Devon and Somerset Staghounds near Winsford

Daisy Webber, widow of Ken Webber, standing by one of the stags that her husband took from 1945–1958

Michelle Johnson

Brian Heard

Mother and son, Shirley and James Blake

Graham Thorne, whipper-in, 1986–1988

Centenary Puppy Show, 1996. Left to Right: Lisa Lucas, daughter of the Joint Master; Francis Kelland, Joint Master's wife; Angela Norrish, wife of the huntsman © Michael Jackson

Stephen Cole

Kennels meet. Father and daughter Maurice Greenslade and Margaret Giles

Michael Heard

Mrs Grania Phillips

Kennels meet. Father and son John and Victor Burston.

Julian Selby

Kath Turner

Molland Common.
Left to Right:
Geoff Boundy,
John Richards,
Shirley Blake

Bill Hill

Kennels meet.
Geoff Hurford (left)
and Norman
Webber (right)

Gardners End.
Left to Right:
Michael Webber,
Brian Gill,
Stuart Bowden

Les
Greenslade

Ann Heard

Paul Herniman (left) and Chris Babb

Maurice Greenslade (left) and Henry Webber at the kennels meet.

Gilbert Ayre

The late
Mary Besley

Michael Webber
(Hon. Treasurer)

Ken Blackford

Mr Desmond Bale

Left to Right:
Emma Lashbrook,
Douglas Bailey,
Ruby Arnett

Last Meet for Robin Venner as Joint Master of the Tiverton Staghounds in 1985 at Swinehamhill. Left to Right: Ray Burrow (huntsman), Robin Venner (retiring Master), Ray Dart (whip), Walter Ash
© Robert Venner

Pat West and her late mother Iris

The Hyde Park Rally in 1998. Left to Right: Joan Ellis, Shirley Pincombe, Nora Tucker, Pam Hammet

Monica Ashton (left) and Cynthia Palmer (right) at the Stag Inn, Rackenford

Outside the Stag Inn, Rackenford. Left to Right: Tim Laman (Secretary), Ivan Webber, Terry Nicholls, Christopher (Kipper) Heywood

Lloyd Govier and Sharon Neale

The late Mrs Mary Besley with her faithful dog Nettle

Adrian Pillivant

Linda Blackford

Former whipper-in John Ellicott (right) with his brother-in-law Bill Saunders

"That Condor Moment"
Left to Right:
Grenville Woollacott,
John Beer,
David Bevan, kennel huntsman of the Torrington Farmers

Stuart Kelland (left), and John Lucas (right), Joint Masters

Mother and daughter,
Joyce and Bridget Rowcliffe

Harold Eastman (left) and George Slee (right)

"Identity Parade"
Left to Right:
David Gillbard,
Martin Gillbard,
Kevin Vickery,
Tom Brock,
Jonathon Brock,
Dick Keenor,
Johnny Hooper

"Time to cool down"
Left to Right:
John Richards
Bob Saunders
Steve Bucknell

Mr Frank Turner, Joint Master of the Tiverton Staghounds, 1985–1986
© Robert Venner

Jennifer Condon on Lydacott Moon ex pointer, 15.1, won the Ladies Open at South Tetcott and the Torrington Members (1987). Retired and then used by Jennifer for pony club and country and show jumping. On Lydacott Moon she won the Tiverton Staghounds 15+U from the age of 12 to 15 (4 years in a row)

Honiton Show, taken in 1985. Left to Right: John Lucas (Joint Master), David Ford (whipper-in) holding hounds, Ray Burrow (huntsman). Hounds: Derrish and Fiction

Landlord Robin Hogg gives Keith Webber's horse a drink outside the Butchers Arms, Alswear 15 April 1976

The Tiverton Staghounds hunt staff. Left to Right: Joint Master, Joint Master, whipper-in, huntsman

Hunt officials

The Tiverton Staghound kennels
A sketch by Terry Gable

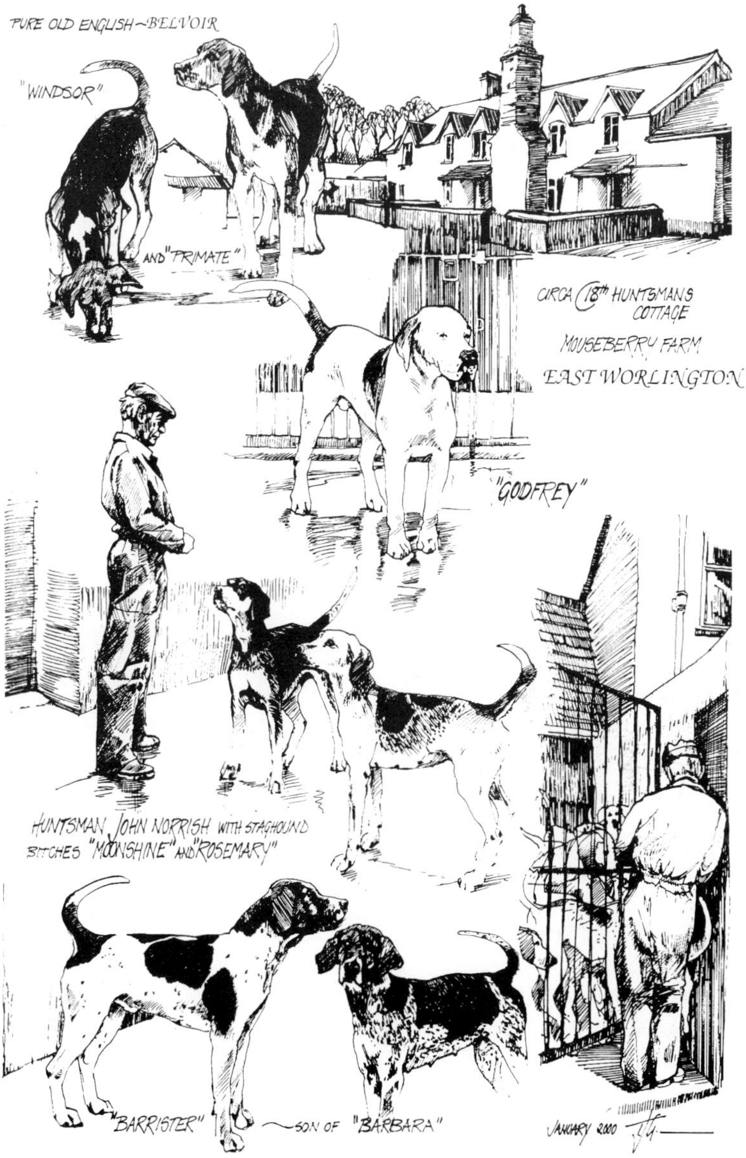

A cartoon from the *North Devon Journal* © Jane Taylor

Chapter Eleven

Bruno

Geoff Boundy of Rackenford talks about Bruno, a stag which appeared on the scene around 1990

"He had an unusual head of protruding points and was very distinctive. He ruled over the Rackenford Manor hinds and was king of the forest being feared by other stags and he had a very deep roar. He first appeared at Worthy Moor and came to this spot for the rut for two or three years before moving into Rackenford Manor woods. He became famous and was a film star on camera, but he was a very easy target for the poacher and had a prized head. He was in the rifle scopes on several occasions but was reprieved for several years. He was even protected from the Tiverton Staghounds, though he really should have been taken out because he was serving his daughters. Inevitably he had to come to a bad end and so it proved, as he died in a secluded valley near Witheridge in 1999.

After the rut he would stay around the Manor until Christmas before slipping away to quieter quarters, reappearing the following rut. He had an outstanding head, and was the centre of attention in the rutting season when people came from miles to see him along with his harem at Rackenford. Some people thought he was a farm deer that had escaped, as he surely was not afraid of anybody, and would walk boldly up to Worthy Folly House nearby, the home of Dick and Simone Williams, walking onto their lawns even with the dogs barking.

Bruno the Rackenford stag

I was lucky enough to pick up one of his cast antlers in April 1995. Unfortunately someone else found the other one, and it was not until May 1999 that I managed to acquire it. I now have them mounted together on a shield, a trophy worth having.

Local video maker Johnny Kingdom caught Bruno on film and said he was the king of Rackenford.

'I used to wait till the end of September to see him and I'd follow him until November filming him. He's chased me many times, but I've been able to get close to him. Bruno was a symbol to me, he was a challenger. It was my challenge to get out there and get close to him. I have been so close to Bruno, whose antlers weighed a huge 14lbs, that at times I did not know whether to run or stay put when he focused on me. A particularly dangerous situation to be in as a stag is capable of killing a person. On one particular occasion during the time of the rut, I captured a fight between Bruno and his son. I saw him challenge Bruno which lasted for six minutes and the clash of antlers was deafening. The reason why Bruno survived for so long was because of the watchful eyes of Dick and Simone Williams, with a friend of theirs giving him his name, and they frequently let him use their garden. The last shot I ever took of Bruno was of him going to sleep at the end of the rut.' "

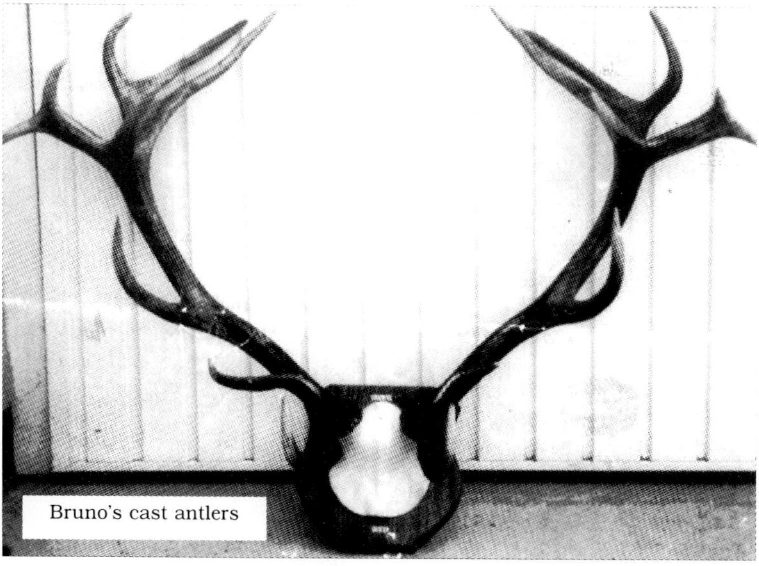

Bruno's cast antlers

Chapter Twelve

Tiverton Staghounds motorbikers

Above: "The Wild Boys"
Left to Right: Charlie Howard, John Beer, John Bolt, and Richard Lethbridge (the author)

Left: Richard Trehern in festive mood at Filleigh Sawmills meet, Boxing Day 1999

Above: Father and son Alan and Robert Seatherton

Kevin Loosemore, with Peter Benn bringing up the rear

A conference between Steve Rendall (left), and Stuart Guscott

Stuart Guscott with his son Ben

Above: Steve Rendall

Below: Ken Knowles

Left: Paul Angel

Below: John Bere

Below: Steve Grant (left)
and Alan Stapleton (right)

Chapter Thirteen

The Loyal Tiverton Staghounds Cappers – who come out in all weathers

Above: Shirley Grant at Filleigh Sawmills meet, Boxing Day 1999

Below: Brenda Cole

Above: Donald Moore (right), ready to pay his cap money to Norman Ellis at Chulmleigh

Right: Sheila Blake

Left: Nora Tucker

Chapter Fourteen

Hunt Characters

The late Dudley Down was a notable character who lived on Exmoor and was a regular follower of the Quantock, Tiverton, and Devon and Somerset Staghounds. I spoke to Ray Burrow about his memories of Dudley.

"I remember going to a meet at Knowstone Moor, riding a horse I bought off Cyril Luxton called Caranatic Lass, a thoroughbred. Aubrey Besley was hunting the hounds and I must have been 17 or 18. Dudley Down took out his pocket knife cutting off so much of the tail of my horse and he said, 'There you are young man, that's put a hundred pound on him.'

When I was hunting the staghounds we had a doghound called Morquis from the Beaufort hunt by Newforest Megan, very light-framed. To be honest, the first two seasons he was really useless. The only thing I liked about him was when you let the pack go he would stand there, and they would be gone two fields away and all of a sudden he would take off after them. I didn't get rid of him because I knew he would come to it, and after two seasons he started shining and doing a lot of work. I decided to put Morquis to a bitch called Lemon, and Dudley Down said, 'What a bloody specimen.' Anyway she had a lovely litter and whelped 11 in all. They were like peas in a pod. I took one of them, Lantern, to Honiton Show, and he beat the foxhounds in the Devon, Somerset, Dorset and Cornwall area. As I came out of the ring, Dudley was there and he said, 'Well done Ray,' because of what he had said about the father being a bloody specimen. I replied, 'What a bloody specimen Dudley,' and he said, 'Now come on Ray.'

He was a good old character, there's no question about that. One of the old school. I remember him driving a little sports car at one time (a red Healy Sprite) with a slide-back canvas roof and Dudley would be wearing a deer stalker hat with a feather sticking out of it, he was a real dandy.

He rode second horse a bit to Aubrey Besley, and Mr Besley said he didn't always get his horse because the nearest television ariel Dudley saw he would be watching the racing. I can remember riding behind Dudley as a kid when I used to have a pony. When I came to go uphill I would jump off and run beside him, then when I got to the top I would jump on again. I have ridden behind Dudley many a time. I said to him once, 'How do you keep so fit?', and he said, 'I have garlic every day.'

There was just something special about him really. He was always concerned before he went home that I had all my hounds and to see which ones were missing. He lived on his wits, he was a crafty devil mind, and very cunning.

One of the places where Dudley used to house-sit on Exmoor was where the late Duke of Beaufort used to stay when he was hunting with the Devon and Somerset Staghounds. Coming to the meet one day, we couldn't help but laugh because he said, 'I slept in the Duke's bed last night!' "

The late Dudley Down

In 1997 Halsgrove Productions produced a cassette tape on characters of Exmoor by John Burgess who had recorded Dudley on tape.

John Burgess introduces Dudley

"Dudley Down, when he was alive, provided a unique service to the farming families on Exmoor, he would move in and take charge so the farmer and his family could move out and take a short break and have a holiday. Let's hear him tell the story.

'I always remember going to friends of mine at Exford, a jolly nice couple, they were going stalking and the wife said to him, "Why on earth don't you get your hair cut before you set off?"

I said, "Don't bully him, I've got a pair of scissors in the car, and I will cut it for him.'

They looked at me in astonishment, both of them thinking I was telling them a fairy story. Anyway I got the scissors and I cut his hair and I've cut it ever since, and this was about six years ago. I never learnt hairdressing, I simply thought I would have a go. I used to cut girls' hair sometimes.

Another family, the wife said would I come and I said, "What have you got there?" and she said, "Dogs and cats." Two dogs, she never mentioned the number of cats, and I said, "How many cats are there?" She looked and hesitated, and then she said "Ten." Having a little terrior of my own, I wondered what will he think of these ten cats? Anyway, he took no notice of them. When I arrived they were all there in the back kitchen, awaiting my arrival, and my terrior took no notice of them, but they all disappeared knowing he was a strange dog.

Once I had four people that wanted to go on holiday at the same time, and I hated disappointing them, so I went from one place to another, luckily they were quite near, within a mile or so. I used to feed the dogs and cats and some nights I would sleep in one house and the other's another night. A friend of mine said, "How on earth do you manage to sleep in strange beds?" and I said, "Not a bit of difference, one bed to the other, if you go to bed tired you will sleep." I much prefer double beds to single ones, especially when the dogs and cats want to sleep. When you think these are strange dogs and cats and they want to sleep on my bed, I think it speaks for itself.

I don't charge anything, I wouldn't think of doing so, I do this for fun and something to do. And I meet a lovely lot of people, and everywhere I go they're always pleased to see me and treat me well and I love doing it.

There is a story behind the hat that I wear. Betty, my daughter, and I, went to see the National and we knew Ryan Price, the jockey, and met him several times on the race course and when we arrived at Liverpool, we went to the Eldelvy which is the hotel for the racing crowd. Ryan Price greeted us and said, "Hello you old so and so, what are you doing up here?"

I said, "I've come to see you win the Liverpool hurdle,"

And he said, "I'm going to bloody well win it."

"Well," I said to Ryan, "if you do, will you give me your hat?"

And he said, "Yes, I bloody well will."

And sure enough he won it and gave me his hat. Anyway I've had the same kind of hat for quite a number of years and I treat them the same as old Ryan.' "

§

Another character of the Tiverton Staghounds is Walter Reed. He was 85 years old when I had a chat with him about his hunting days.

Walter Reed

"I was born at Cole Park near Chulmleigh, and I have ridden miles with the Yandles. The first stag I saw them kill was at Chulmleigh Bridge when I was 11 years old. They could hunt the hounds, Bert Yandle was the best huntsman I ever saw in my life. He could blow the hunting horn, no one else could equal him. I heard my father say scores of times that Bert Yandle was the best huntsman but Percy Yandle would kill the most deer.

When Bert was hunting the hounds, Percy would always wear an ordinary jacket and vice versa, they never rode two red coats together, but the other two brothers, Ernest and Jack, always wore red coats.

My father had a lovely mare, Ladybird, that the Yandles gave to him, before that Sir Ian Amory owned her.

Tiverton Staghounds head presented by the Yandles to Edmund Reed (Walter's father) who harboured the deer for them

John Symons from King's Nympton had a transport business with his father and when Ken Webber was huntsman he would transport the hounds and horses for him. He also transported for the Yandles. Once, John had to take his lorry to George Guard's at East Week where Ken Webber had killed that day. Bill Westacott and myself were up at King's Nympton at the time when he was driving his lorry out and he asked us if we would we like a ride. So we went with him and when we got there they loaded the stag in the back and Ken Webber sat in the front. There was no room for me and Bill and they put us in the back of the lorry with the hounds and the stag. John Symons drove to Chulmleigh first to drop off the carcass at Mark Lake's the butcher to be cut up. Then we went on to the Eggesford Foxhound kennels to drop off the hounds (at the time they were kennelled there alongside the foxhounds). After dropping off the hounds he took me and Bill back to King's Nympton and then took Ken Webber home.

The breeches I wear out hunting are 62 years old. I had them made by Percy Gill at King's Nympton and there wasn't a better tailor in England. When my breeches were 32 years old I had to take them back to Percy Gill to be repaired and he put in a different colour material and lined them with leather inside.

I remember years ago when John Lake was a lad, he bought me a hunting horn for letting him ride my ponies a time or two out hunting. He got it in Yendells in Barnstaple for £2, but I wouldn't let him pay. I've still got it, and I've blown it scores of times at sheep fayres, dances etc."

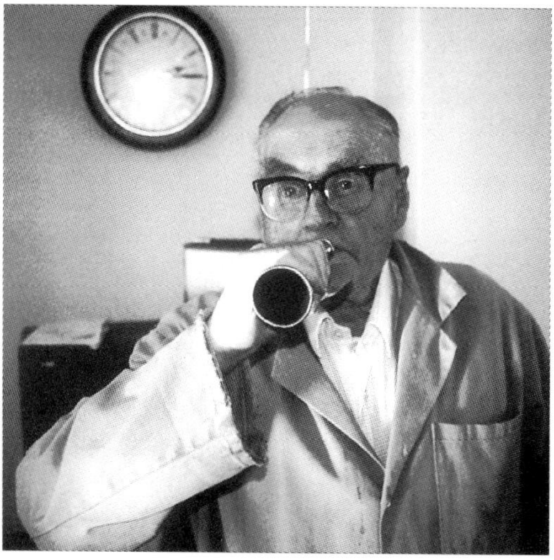

Left: Walter Reed with the hunting horn John Lake gave him many years ago

Walter Reed in his bowler hat with his dog Rosy, and granddaughter Gillian Meadkidd alongside at Witheridge

§

The late Jack Sing was another notable character who lived at Ash Mill and hunted with the Tiverton Staghounds for many years. Ray Burrow starts off with a few stories about him.

"The summer of 1976 was very dry. There were stags coming in behind the kennels eating Derek Elstone's potatoes. The Tiverton Staghounds started hunting on 2 September and Ray Giles was hunting the hounds. That day we found at Muddy Gate and killed at Coleford Water. The following Saturday we met at Benley Cross finding there again, killing the stag just down from Chulmleigh Bridge. We had opened the stag up and I was up on the bank and Jack Sing was going in to wash off. I could take you to the exact spot now in that water. The following story is the gospel truth.

Jack came down on his chestnut horse, reins going everywhere, you would hardly know which one to pull. Then he went down off a ledge, going right under the water and all you could see were a few bubbles, then there was nothing. I said, 'Can anyone swim, because Jack Sing's in there,' and everyone looked at me as if I was stupid. Dudley Middleton and Clifford Bridgeman were there. Then all of a sudden you saw like rings come up on the water, and it was like a submarine, he came up and you saw his hat first with all the water dripping off. It was just like something in the movies. Jack and his horse never panicked, they walked out the same place as they went in and Jack was still sat on him. I said, 'Good God Jack, I thought I was going to come to your funeral.'

He said, 'You would have picked some dandelions for the grave wouldn't you?' That's true as I am here. How the hell he didn't drown I don't know, there must have been like a whirlpool there, really deep.

When we met at Knowstone Wood, Jack did the harbouring for that area. We would be waiting, like we always did, and all of a sudden you would see him coming along the road and he would pull up beside me and say, 'I don't know, I don't know, I've been up looking.' Anyway, one day he turned up on this bay horse that had a hood on him like a racehorse and I said, 'What have you got that on for, Jack?'

'Oh,' he said, 'he's shying, I'll stop him.'

Then we went into Beaples Lane, down in Knowstone Cover, down the path and all of a sudden Jack said, 'Hang on, we've got to go down over here.'

It was a little path cut out down over the steep, and his horse wouldn't go. I said, 'Hang on, I will give you a lead.' At that moment, the horse went backwards and I saw that where his eyes looked out of the hood, the holes were stuffed full of hay. The horse couldn't see anything – he had come all that way blindfold and I said, 'Good God Jack, you've got hay in the holes where his eyes should be looking out.'

'Yes,' he said, 'that will stop him from shying, he can't see nort.'

So then we had to stop and take this hay out so the horse could see to go down over the cover, and it's true as I am here. Jack would never ride a made horse, he would buy something from a knacker's yard that nobody else could ride, like old Twister.

I heard Jack tell of the time he was hunting with Ken Webber, and Jack said, 'I was riding Twister and I jumped out over this hedge and Ken didn't have too much heart and he never followed. We killed the hind out to Stogumber Station, and a chap came in with an Austin Seven to take it away and I asked him where the nearest hayrick was because my horse was hungry and wanted something to eat. The horse stayed up there that night and the next morning he was taken on the train down to Dunster and I collected it from there.'

He was a good old bloke and had been hunting for years and years, when it came to, his ideas were different to mine. 'You chaps,' he said, 'will keep stopping those leading hounds. That's fatal, you will never catch deer like that. You wouldn't see Percy Yandle doing that.'

I used to stop them sometimes to let them get together because you would have them strung out from here to kingdom come."

Talking with John Lake about Jack Sing

"Two of Jack's horses were Twister and What Next. He would buy horses of unknown quantity and with What Next it virtually was that. One day when the hounds were hunting near the turning to Bycott, they started going through this hazel hedge. Suddenly, from a standing start this What Next took off, ripping Jack's cap, coat and everything, but he stayed on. That's the sort of horses he used to ride. What Next was good tempered but was unpredictable as can be, and you didn't know what he was going to do next. Twister was a bad-tempered horse, he would kick or do anything."

Talking with Ray Dart about Jack Sing

"Jack Sing was a dear old chap, he taught me the way across Exmoor when he hunted with the Devon and Somerset Staghounds and taught me a lot about the Tiverton country.

The last horse I remember him riding was a chestnut and he had so much old tack on him to stop one thing or another.

I pulled a shoe once and he told me to jump on his horse. He had a piece of rope on the bit and he said, 'If he arches up his back you just pull the rope or he will have you off.' I changed over onto his horse at the Eggesford Foxhound kennels, and I thought he should be all right now he's got this far. I hadn't gone very far and he arched his back and I didn't pull the rope up quick enough and the horse nearly had me off.

Jack told me once that his horse Twister wouldn't go hunting so he pulled him out of the stable with a tractor and rope.

Once, we had a good hunt from Rackenford and killed at Waterrow and when we were coming back in the lorry, Jack was in front of us. As his lorry came down the road to Shillingford and around the corner, the whole container came off, with the horse still inside. Of course, Jack had gone a fair way down the road before he realised what had happened. Coming back the road, he didn't seem too concerned about it. He said that the day before he had collected a load of straw in the lorry and when he put the container back he must have forgotten to screw it down. There wasn't a mark on the horse."

Talking with Betty Palfrey about Jack Sing

"Jack Sing was a great character. He would take me hunting in his lorry on the Quantocks once a fortnight. It was a hair-raising ride to get there across country. We would approach Four Cross Ways and I would always pray because Jack would go straight across without looking left or right, and when he parked the lorry he would reverse until he was touching something and then drive forward enough to pull down the ramp."

§

The late Denzil Mock from Cheldon was another character. Often when the Tiverton Staghounds were hunting in the Cheldon area Denzil would be standing by the gateway close to the church. He had a dry sense of humour and spoke in broad Devonshire dialect. Everything he said he turned around, making it fun to listen to and even though it was a lot of old rubbish you couldn't help but laugh and laugh again. I caught him on video a few times and this is the sort of conversation I had with him.

27 March 1993

"Beautiful weather now Mr Mock."

"Proper. We won't get no snow until June now; most times if you get it then it's invisible. I saw the hounds early on, hunting an upright. He looks to me like he's disregarding the normal routes altogether; he could soon be in Taunton I should think."

"How's everybody in Cheldon? Keeping them under control?"

"Oh all right, but not so busy up here now they've closed down Woolworths, the cinema's done away with and they've stopped the big bus depot. There's nothing wrong with the area, but it's the inhabitants that take a bit of putting up with. Although it's a privilege now they've done away with cannibalism, the last 30 years they don't eat each other now."

"Do you get a lot of strangers coming to live in Cheldon these days?"

"There is a few sometimes that my father used to call imported people if they come from ten miles away."

"They've got to live several years in the parish before they're locals."

"Yes, anything up to two centuries. They live out here to such an age, before all their teeth fall out they haven't got to be taken out."

"Oh well, I better go and find these hounds."

"Well I will tell you one thing for certain, they're most certainly still in Devon. I shouldn't think they've gone across the Channel. One thing different, they should have a fair day because this morning when I saw them the deer seemed to be in front of the hounds which I suppose is unusual really."

"I will see you again Denzil."

"Yes I reckon."

The late Denzil Mock

January 1994

"Did you have a nice Christmas Mr Mock?"

"Oh near enough, but I'm still taking feathers out of my mouth. Apparently I didn't understand it but you've got to put the turkey in the oven after he's plucked not before. You always learn as you get older. The first night I tore abroad most of my toys, I had the teddy bear's two eyes out and one of his ears has gone, youngsters like myself get wild you see. I didn't understand there was a Christmas this time, I thought it was 12 months ago, but apparently it's an annual thing." (Gilbert Ayre comes into the field where Denzil is standing.) "Can't come in here boy there's filming going on."

"Where's the deer gone?"

"Oh up past Clayparks."

"Do you think they will kill this deer today, Denzil?"

"No, get out no, the way he was going just now I should think he could last them three weeks, put down a stick when they go home tonight."

Chapter Fifteen

Whist Drives and Dances

(Mid Devon Gazette)

21 April 1931

By the kind permission of the management of the Belgrave Hotel, Torquay, Stan Pavton's famous "New Era" Casino Dance Orchestra (winners of the Devon County Dance Bands Contest, awarded Silver Cup and Gold and Silver medals) will be in attendance at Wonham House at the Subscription Dance in aid of Tiverton Staghounds on April 23rd.

23 April 1931

Subscription Dance for the Tiverton Staghounds

In spite of a gale of wind and rain there was a large attendance at a subscription dance in aid of the Tiverton Staghounds held at Wonham House, Bampton on Thursday last, by the kind permission of Capt and Mrs M.A. Kennard. The event was a variation from the usual hunt ball, and its success should lend to requests for similar functions in the future. Among those who brought parties were Col and Mrs Wiggin, Sir John Amory, Capt and Mrs Aspinall, Mrs and Miss Chamberlain, Mr and Mrs Pugsley, Mr and Mrs White, Mr Le Bas, Mrs Pertwee, Col E.J. Harrison, Lady Davidson and Mr J.B. Harman. Donations were received from Colonel Capper, Mr A Capel, Gen Livingstone Lermont, Mr E.P. Row, Mr E.L. Hancock, Mr Cecil Smith, Mr Lloyd Mauder and many others. Messrs Thorne Bros, Ellertons Stores, and Mr J.A. Goggs of Tiverton also rendered kind assistance. In no small degree the success of the evening was due to the arrangement made by Capt and Mrs Kennard for the comfort and entertainment of their guests and the fact that dancers and non dancers alike found plenty to occupy their attention. An excellent band and a perfect floor were sufficient and in themselves for the most energetic visitors, so much so that the night was not very old before additional floor space was brought into use. Bridge was in progress for those who did not wish to dance, while from time to time, an amateur Cinema display of considerable technical merit was shown in the billiard room illustrating the activities of the Tiverton Staghounds. An enjoyable evening was possible for those who neither danced nor played cards. The collection of hand painted pottery in itself was sufficient to justify a visit to Wonham, and the paintings of Capt Kennard showing the infinite variety of Icelandic mountains and streams drew many people away from the strains of the band. It was specially appropriate that a hunt dance should take place amid trophies of rod and gun secured in all parts of the world. An intriguing competition was arranged further to benefit the funds. Briefly, an unknown lady had been kissed by an unknown man, in an unknown locality. Clues were freely scattered throughout the house. For the benefit of amateur sleuths desirous of running the mystery to earth. Promptly at midnight the successful lady who incidentally had to pay the forfeit of the competition was revealed, Mrs Stapleton having been successful in discovering the medallion secreted at the scene of the crime. She was rewarded with a stag's slot. Admirable parking arrangements were supervised by the local AA road patrol, the subscription dance resulted in a most handsome and welcome contribution to the hunt funds.

30 April 1935
Hunt Ball at Wonham
Brilliant scenes in ideal setting

At Wonham House, Bampton on Tuesday night the hunt ball went with a swing and was universally popular. The setting for the dance was ideal for Wonham is essentially a hunting house, massive antlered heads gaze down from the walls with a kind of friendly tolerance, the look of one good sportsman to another. A silver stag, with head proudly raised, keeps guard in the dining room. The pink coats, the sound of music, the chink of glass and laughter from odd corners, where many a hardened old stag is being hunted over again, mix sweetly with the mellow lights and calm dignity of the house. There was a large number of people there, Stan Payton's popular band from Torquay provided the dance music, and kept things going merrily to the last.

31 December 1937

A whist drive in connection with the Chawleigh hunt ball was held in the schoolroom, 12 tables being occupied. The MC was Mr E Baker, and the following were the winners. Mrs T Rippin, Mrs Horwill, Miss Elston, Miss Westcott, Mr T Rippin, Mr A Hosegood, Mr T Pennington. The prizes were presented by Mr B Yandle. The sum of £20 was realised.

Cove Whist Drive, 1937

There were 19 tables in play at a whist drive at Cove village hall in aid of Tiverton Staghounds, Mrs T Smythe presented the prizes and thanks were expressed by Mr A.L. Hosegood, Mr W.H. Gregory was MC.

Winners were ladies: 1, Mrs Lovett (Exford), 2, Mrs Gooding (Withleigh), 3, Mrs F James (Exford), 4, Miss E Wyatt (Tiverton), High Miniature Master R Hill (Stoodleigh), Low Miniature Miss K Bere, Consolation Mrs W Rowe (Calverleigh). Gentlemen: 1, Mr J Skwisecznski (Halberton), 2, Mr F.A. James (Dulverton), 3, Mr J Dymond (Oakford), 4, Mr C Mills (Cullompton), High Miniature Mr G Greenslade (Witheridge), Low Miniature Mr R.P. Crook (Witheridge), Consolation Miss E Middleton. Competition winners, Messrs J Dymond, K Tucker (Clayhanger), A Williams (Dulverton), S Vincent (Morebath), W.H. Gregory, Mrs Greenslade (Witheridge).

Dec 31st 1937

CHAWLEIGH'S FIRST HUNT BALL

Two Hunts Combine for Successful Evening

LARGE GATHERING

A hunt ball was held on Wednesday in the Jubilee Hall, Chawleigh, in aid of the North Eggesford Foxhounds and the Tiverton Staghounds, was a great success. It was the first Hunt Ball ever to be held at Chawleigh.

The hall was tastefully decorated, hunting colours being predominant in the artistic scheme. Trailing festoons and trophies of both Hunts adorned the walls. That the ball was attended by nearly 150 guests from a wide area indicates the popularity of the Hunts.

The joint organisers were the Misses D. and M. Ford, of Nethercott, backed by a strong committee. The refreshment buffet was in charge of Mesdames E. Baker, F. Partridge, W. Reed and A. G. Hill, assisted by Mrs. N. Prettyjohns. Raffling competitions for a bottle of port and a tin of biscuits realised nearly £4, and were won by Mr. R. Bates, of Chulmleigh, and Mr. W. H. Reed (Fiddlecott). Novelty dances were well supported, the winners being Miss M. Wills, and Mr. R. Webber (Alphington), Mr. and Mrs. Headon (Mountcombe) and Miss A. Penfold and Mr. V. H. Coaker (Cheldon). Mr. Aubrey Webber was M.C.

The master of the North Eggesford Hunt (Mr. D. F. B. Stucley), in a short address, thanked the organisers and all the sporting people who had made the evening a success. He went on to say that to date he had accounted for 30 foxes and he hoped to make it 30 brace by the end of the season. Mr. T. Kippin thanked Mr. Stucley.

Feb 8th 1946

CHULMLEIGH WEEK

HUNT BALL-A profit of £68 10s was realised at the Hunt Ball, held at Chulmleigh Week, and this has been equally divided between the Eggesford Foxhounds and Tiverton Staghounds. The hard-working committee consisted of Messrs A. Rowcliffe (organizer), B. Hurford (chairman), W. G. Rice (hon. treasurer and secretary), B. Mock, C. Rogers, E. Pincombe, David Wale and Ian Mock, who tastefully decorated the Jubilee Hall with trophies of the chase.

The winners of the draw were T. Shopland (Chulmleigh), C .Webber (Chulmleigh), J. Phillips (Cheldon), A. Gard (Chulmleigh), Ginger (Okehampton), F. Dockings (Chulmleigh), F. Jones (Worlington), F. Hill (Chulmleigh). The ladies who ran the refreshment buffet were B. Mock (supervisor), E. Wale, Rogers, A. Hammett and E. Routcliffe

Chulmleigh Hunt Ball
will be held on
Tuesday, March 5th,
1946 - 8 p.m. to 1 a.m
.NORMAN PINCOTT'S BAND
(7 Players)
Proceeds for Tiverton Staghounds and Eggesford Foxhounds.
Tickets 6/6
Refreshments at moderate charges
V. K. Reed (Hon. Sec.)

Tiverton Staghounds
HUNT BALL
at
BLACK DOG
On Thursday, March 1st, 1951
9 p.m.-1 a.m.
Music by Ernie Gregory and His Band (Exeter)
TICKETS 5/-; Door 6/-
Tickets obtainable from L.Bradford, Black Dog

March 1st 1946

£177 For Tiverton Staghounds

Tiverton Staghounds ball at South Molton was a great success, and as a result a cheque of £177 has been sent to the Hunt Funds.

The committee responsible were: Messrs. S. Andrews (chairman), W. J .Berry, H. and R. Bowden, J. Purchase, H. Elworthy, E. Webber, J. Sing, and W. Tapp, Misses P. Purchase, F. Elworthy, with Miss R. Hancock as hon. secretary and treasurer.

South Molton Women's Institute undertook the refreshments.

Winners of the draw were: Pig or £2, Mr. W. Burnell (Bremridge), who kindly gave the £2 back to the funds; Mr D. Sing, Kingsnympton; Miss G. Palfrey, South Molton; Mr. Crudge, West Anstey; Mrs. Thorne, Rackenford; Mrs. Clarke, South Molton; Mr. Kingdon, South Molton; Mrs. Boundy, Knowstone.

1948
TIVERTON STAGHOUNDS

HUNT BALL
at
South Molton
on
Tuesday, Now. 16th

Dancing 8-1 :: Adm. 10/-
Secretaries Please Note Date
Tickets can be obtained from:
Miss R. HANCOCK

Tiverton Staghounds Hunt Ball at King's Nympton, 1951.
3rd Left, Frank Heal (Master of Torrington Farmers hunt),
2nd Right, Ken Webber (huntsman of the Tiverton Staghounds)

WORLINGTON

A HUNT BALL
will be held in
THE PARISH HALL
on
Friday, Feb, 8th, 1952
Dancing from 8.30 p.m. to 1 a.m.
to the music of the
Blue Ribben Dance Orchestra
Adm, 7/6 (Refreshments included)

A HUNT WHIST DRIVE
will be held in
THE PARISH HALL
on MONDAY, FEB, 11th, 1952
commencing 7.30 p.m., sharp
14 PRIZES
Adm, 3/- (Refreshments included)
by Ticket Only (limited number)
Tickets may be obtained from the Hon. Sec., G. D. Keenor, or any member of the committee.

Proceeds in aid of the Eggesford Hunt and the Tiverton Staghounds

CHITTLEHAMHOLT

HUNT BALL

March 5th, 1952
8.30 p.m. to 1 a.m.
Ray Carter and his Rythmets

Tickets 6/-

Refreshments at Moderate Charges.
Proceeds for Tiverton Staghounds and
Eggesford Hunt

TIVERTON STAGHOUNDS

Annual Hunt Ball

will be held in the New Assembly Rooms
South Molton

on
Tuesday Dec 9th 1952

Dancing from 8.30 p.m. to 1.30 a.m.
to Les Gales Dance Orchestra

Tickets 10/- (including refreshments)

WORLINGTON
A HUNT BALL
will be held in
THE PARISH HALL

On Monday, Dec. 7th 1953
Dancing 8 p.m. to 1 a.m, to the

music of
Don Bowles Orchestra
(Tiverton)

Adm. 7/6 (refreshments incl.)
Proceeds in aid of the Tiverton
Staghounds and the Eggesford
Foxhounds

BLACK DOG

HUNT BALL

AT MEMORIAL HALL
On THURSDAY, FEB, 12th, 1953
from 8.30 p.m. to 1.30 a.m.
Les Gale's Dance Band
Tickets 5/- (at the door 6/-)

Tiverton Staghounds

HUNT DANCE

At the ANGEL HOTEL, WITHERIDGE

On Friday, FEB. 12th, 1954, 9 p.m. to 1 a.m.

THE GAY NINETIES ORCHESTRA (from Braunton)

M.C.: WILF DUNN - MODERN & OLDE-TYME DANCING

TICKETS, 7/6 inclusive, obtainable from: R.S. Brendon, Newhouse, Witheridge (phone 249); J.F. Partridge, Lower Park, Witheridge (phone 463); or members of the Organising Committee.

TIVERTON STAGHOUNDS

HUNT DANCE 1954

New Hall, Tiverton - Thursday, March 4th

9 p.m. - 2 a.m.

COLIN DAY (late Pianist to Donald Peers) AND HIS ORCHESTRA

Tickets 7/6 (limited) Bar (license applied for)

Refreshments at moderate charges

Tickets obtainable from : Boars Head Inn, Tiverton; White Horse Inn, Tiverton; O.J. Hillyer, Fruitere, Gold Street, Tiverton (Phone 2906)

4 March 1954

There was a company of nearly 400 at the new hall, Tiverton on Thursday March 4th. The hall was beautifully decorated with red and white artificial flowers and on the stage was a rhododendron thicket out of which a stag appeared. Dancing was to Colin Day and his band and MC was Mr G Sellick, refreshments were served by a ladies committee under Mrs A Besley and Mrs O Hillyer. Organising Committee Mr R.E. Heard (Chairman) Mr O.J. Hillyer (Secretary) Mr A Besley (Treasurer) and Messrs G Sellick, F Philp, F Cook, F Church, C Turner, C Heywood, T Arnold, A Redwood, W Lewis and L Durman.

NOVEMBER 26, 1954

To-night ! To-night !

Don't forget the

HUNT DANCE

At Chulmleigh Week
9 p.m. to 1 a.m. Admission 5/-

Skylarks Dance Band

Proceeds in aid of Tiverton Staghounds

29 November 1955
A hunt dance was held at Oakford parish rooms in aid of Tiverton Staghounds. The skylarks band provided the music, the room was tastefully decorated by Miss Shirley Dymond, assisted by Miss Heaton and members of the ladies committee.

Eggesford Foxhounds
Tiverton Staghounds

C H E L D O N
H U N T B A L L

At Waltingbrook Hall,
CHULMLEIGH

On Wednesday, Jan. 22nd

BLACK DIAMONDS DANCE BAND
(7 Pieces)
Dancing 9 p.m. to 1 a.m.
TICKETS 7/6
Licensed Bar — Refreshments

March 23 1960

Novel decorations at hunt ball

SPECIAL decorations, including a hand-painted skit of a fox dancing the cha-cha with a Christmas turkey, were much admired at the Chulmleigh hunt ball last week.

The £134 profit will be shared between the two local hunts. Among those present were the joint masters of the Eggesford Fox Hounds, Capt. and Mrs. P. N. Coombe, and the joint masters of the Tiverton Staghounds, Mr. A. H. P. Besley and Mr. A. Hosegood. The M.C. for dancing was the chairman of the ball committee, Mr. A. E. Kingdon.

The draw was organised by Mr. and Mrs F. Sanders, and winners' names were drawn by Mrs. Besley and Mrs. Coombe. Conveners of the cold buffet were Mrs. M. E. Beer and Mrs. E. Stevens, helped by Mrs. J. Millman, Mrs. A. M. Hammett, Mrs. F. Richards, Mrs. A. Turner, Mrs. C. Brownscombe, and Miss J. Mortimer.

The Wallingbrook Hall had been decorated by Mrs. J. M. Wingfield (joint hon. area secretary to the Foxhound Committee), Wing Cmdr. E. Mortimer (hon. secretary to the Staghound Committee), and Mrs. M. E. Kingdon.

Prize winners were: Carole Sanders (Lapford), David Alexander (Rose Ash), W. F. Board, H. R. Pincombe, R. Sanders (Lapford), D. Earl (Bondleigh), Bridgman (Winkleigh), W. J. Ridd, and R. Black.

TIVERTON STAGHOUNDS HUNT BALL

will be held at the

NEW PARISH HALL, WITHERIDGE

on FRIDAY, DECEMBER 4th, 1964

Rhythm Kings Orchestra

TICKETS 10/6 (inclusive) :: Licensed Bar applied for

WITHLEIGH HUNT BALL

FOR TIVERTON FOX AND STAGHOUNDS

Wednesday, January 15th

9 p.m. to 1.30 a.m. 1969

at WITHLEIGH VILLAGE HALL

CY EASTMOND AND HIS BAND

Admission 15/- inclusive

Chittlehamholt Hunt Ball 1970, Left to Right: Harold Eastman, Frank Congram, Walter Ash (huntsman), John Pincombe, Robin Venner (Joint Master), Ray Giles (whip), Ron Darch, Les Baker

TIVERTON STAGHOUNDS SUPPORTERS

are holding their 2nd Annual

BARN DANCE

at

Parsonage Farm, Chulmleigh

(By kind permission of Mr. and Mrs W. Crocombe)

on Friday, June 4th, 1971

Licensed Bar applied for

Dancing from 9.30 to 2 a.m. to TWO BANDS

SKYLARKS DANCE BAND

and FERGUSON DANCE BAND

Tickets £1·10 (22/-) — Limited

includes CHICKEN & SALAD SUPPER and a chance to win a

WEEK-END FOR TWO IN PARIS (valued at £60)

★ At least 25% of the proceeds will be donated for the treatment of cancer at the Royal Devon and Exeter Hospital

TICKETS obtainable from Organising Secretary, J F. Partridge 1, East Burrow Close East Worlington, or C. Parish, Langley Gardens, Chulmleigh, W. Crocombe, Parsonage, Chulmleigh 420; W Saunders, Hole, Chulmleigh 479 W. Lucas, Lakehead, Chulmleigh 339; J Hurford, Wixon, Chulmleigh 438; R. Pincombe, Sheepsbyre, Chulmleigh 436; Mrs. M. Slade, Southcott, Chawleigh Chulmleigh 296; G. Smith, Dobbs Moor, Chulmleigh 327; E. Stevens, Brooklands, Chulmleigh 441; G. Alvis, Durdon, Winkleigh 328; C. Shapland, Thurle, Chulmleigh 207; and others.

1896 *1996*

The Tiverton Staghounds

Centenary Hunt

Dinner and Dance

at

Cobley Farm

Worlington

Dancing to:

Sapphire

Friday 9th August, 1996

Toast List

Loyal Toast
given by Mr. T.R.S. Venner

★★★

Welcoming Remarks
Mr. T.R.S. Venner

★★★

THE TOASTS

"The Tiverton Stag Hounds"
Proposed by Mr. T. Yandle
Responded by Mrs. C. Mock

★★★

"Guests"
Proposed by Mr. T. Hamlin
Responded by Mr. J. Lee

Whist drive, Cholt Village Hall, 1997.
Left to Right: Vera Bucknell, Myrtle Partridge, Ivy Bucknell

Final whist drive 1998, South Molton Assembly Rooms.
Left to Right: Jim Partridge, Amy Bowden, Vera Bucknell

South Molton final whist drive, 1998. Right to Left:
Russel Bowden alongside the late Mr Michael Wort

South Molton final whist drive, 1998.
Shirley Bowden (left) and Elaine Summers (right)

South Molton final whist drive, 1998.
Left to Right: Donald Pile, Edna Dunning, Jean Beer.
Looking across from the other table, Colin Taverner

South Molton final whist drive, 1998.
Left to Right: Rowland Dayman, Pat Skipper, Henry John Summers

South Molton final whist drive, 1998.
Left to Right: Wilf Butt, Michael Cooper, Rick Rickard, Fred Carter

South Molton final whist drive, 1998.
Left to Right: Brenda Cole, Vera Bucknell, Reg Bucknell

Chapter Sixteen

Point-to-Points

Point-to-pointing started in this country as a hunt race from church steeple to church steeple. There was no set route and riders got there just as fast as they could over fences, along lanes or through gates. "Just get there first" was the message. Life then was based round the Manor and that is where the pack of hounds would be kennelled. Point-to-points developed as part of the life of the local hunt.

In the following pages are the results of the Tiverton Staghounds point-to-point races starting with Sir John Amory, the earliest one I found being 1891.

Also in this chapter are details of the many different venues where the Tiverton Staghounds have had their point-to-points and interviews with jockey Luke Harvey who started his early days riding with the Tiverton Staghounds and has just retired and gone into commentating for the race channel. Also an interview with local jockey Neil Harris.

Winners of Point to Point Races

STAGHOUNDS.

England.

SIR JOHN AMORY'S.

1899. Open Race, 8 starters: Mr. E. Dorse's Gladys.
Light weights, 12 starters: Mr. J. Butt's Stag (Mr. G. Coulson).
Farmers' Race, 10 starters: Mr. J. Butt's Stag (Mr. G. Coulson).

1891. Open Race, 6 starters: Mr. E. A. Stanley's Aplin (Farrant).
Pony Race (14'3), 10 starters: Mr. J. Moyle's Miss Perkie (Mr. H. Newman).
Light weights, 7 starters: Mr. J. C. de las Casa's Mrs. Pike (owner).
Farmers' Race, 6 starters: Mr. J. Bucknell's Moonlight (owner).
Consolation, 4 starters: Mr. Watkins' Lady Dina Doe (Mr. J. C. de las Casa).

1901. Open Race, 6 starters: Mr. E. A. Stanley's Aplin (Farrant).
Pony Race (14'3), 10 starters: Mr. J. Moyle's Miss Perkie (Mr. H. Newman).
Light weights, 7 starters: Mr. J. C. de las Casas' Mrs. Pike (owner).
Farmers' Race, 6 starters: Mr. J. Bucknell's Moonlight (owner).
Consolation, 4 starters: Mr. Watkins' Lady Dina Doe (Mr. J. C. de las Casas).

16 April 1901

Tiverton Point-to-Point Steeplechases

The annual fixtures of the Tiverton Hunt point-to-point steeplechases which was held at Chevithorne Barton on Saturday afternoon proved as popular and successful as any of the previous meetings. The weather forecast was distinctly discouraging, a drizzling rain falling nearly the whole of the morning. Soon after noon however, the sun shone out brilliantly and the elements continued favourable throughout the afternoon. The race card consisted of an open race, tenant farmers race, pony race, hunt race and a consolation race, a programme which secured 34 entries. There was an excellent attendance both of the sporting fraternity and the general public.

The state of the course – about three miles in length was rather unfavourable for racing, the rains of the previous days making the "going" very heavy. Fortunately with the exception of a few minor spills, no accident marred the enjoyment of the afternoon's proceedings.

The following acted as stewards, Sir John Heathcoat Amory Bart MSH, Messrs W.C.L. Unwin MFH, T.C. Daniel, W Renton, H.J.W. Coulson, A De las Casas, C.D. Harrod, J.C. Hill, L. Corbet, Ian H. Amory MSH, C. Carew MH, E.H. Dunning, N. Chichester, T. O. Lazenby, M. De las Casas, T. W. Charlton, J. R. Holland, L. Mackenzie, and Ernest Hancock. Colonel Garrat MFH acted as judge, Captain Harry Heathcoat Amory starter and Messrs W. Renton and F.C. Boles officiated as clerks to the scales. Great credit is due to the honorary secretary Mr J.C. De las Casas for the success of the meeting. The racing started soon after one o'clock, the following being the results and the order in which they were contested.

Open race – a sweepstake of £2-2s, second to save his entrance fee, catch weights over 11st 7lbs, open to any horse, about 3 miles.
Mr E.A.V. Stanley's "Aplin..." (J. Farrent) 1
Mr J.C. De las Casas' "Mrs Pike" (owner) 2
Mr Jarvis Bailey's "Kidare..." (A De las Casas) 3
Also ran Mr M. De las Casas' "Harpford" and Mr W.T. Watkins' "My Honey", Mr J. Butt's "Stag" and Mr L.H. Amory's "Solomon" did not run.
Betting evens "My Honey" and "Mrs Pike" 3 to 1 against, "Aplin" 4 to 1 against, "Harpford" 6 to 1 against "Kidacre".

Tenant farmers race – silver cup or £10 given by Sir John Amory Bart, W.C.L. Unwin MFH, Mr Ian Amory MSH and Mr. C. Carew MH and £5 for the second and £2 for the third, for horses the property of tenant farmers or their sons over whose land the Tiverton Foxhounds, Sir John Amory's Staghounds or Harriers &c Hunt, farmers or their sons riding allowed 7lbs catch weight over 12st.
Mr J. Bucknell's "Moonlight" (Bucknell Jun) 1
Mr H. Haydon's "St Blaize" (Haydon) 2
Mr H. M. Crosby's "Colleen" (owner) 3
Also ran Mr H.M. Crosby's "Blarney", Mr Abel Blake's "Little Eva" and Mr H. Matthew's "Tommy'.
Betting; Evens "St Blaze", 5 to 1 againt "Moonlight", "Little Eva", and "Tommy", 6 to 1 "Blarney" and "Colleen".

Pony Race – Value £10 for ponies 14 hands 3 inches high to carry 11st 7lb, allowed for every clear inch under. Conditions same as hunt race, second to save his entrance fee about 2 1/4 miles.
Mr J A Moyles' "Miss Perkie" (H Newman) 1
Mr J D Renton's "Phil" (Je de las Casas) 2
Mr Abel Blake's "Little Eva" (Atkins) 3
Also ran Mr T W Charlton's "Joe", Mr J C Hill's "Midge", Mrs Watkins' "Lady Dinah Doe", Mr J A Moyles' "Cornish Lass", Mr M de las Casas' "Gipsy", Mr R S Pethick's "Ptolemy" and "Pancake"
Betting: 2 to 1 against "Lady Dinah Doe", 4 to 1 "Miss Perkie", "Joe" and "Phil", 6 to 1 "Ptolemy" and "Pancake", 8 to 1 "Ridge".

Hunt Race – Value for horses which have been fairly hunted with the Tiverton Foxhounds, Sir John Amory's Staghounds or Harriers, the property of persons who reside within the limits of the above hunts. Catch weights, over 11st 7lbs, about 3 miles second to save his entrance fee.
Mr J C De las Casas' "Mrs Pike" (owner) 1
Mr M De las Casas' "Sportsman" (owner) 2
Mr J W Please's "Her Grace" (Bucknell, Jun) 3

Also ran Mr J C Hill's "Greek Girl", Mr H Haydon's "St Blaize", and Mr J Farrant's "Falcon".
Betting: 2 to 1 againt "Sportsman", 3 to 1 "Mrs Pike", 4 to 1 "Falcon" and "Her Grace" 10 to 1 others.

Consolation Race – steeplechase of £1-15 for beaten horse, catch weights over 11st 7lbs, ponies 10st 7lbs.
Mr W T Watkins' "My Honey" (C De las Casas) 1
Mr J Farrant's "Falcon" (owner) 2
Mr Watkins' "Lady DInah Doe" (Hill) 3
Mr J A Moyles' "Cornish Lass" (newman) 4
The best tanks of competitors and spectators are due to those who so kindly placed their farms at the dispersal of the stewards viz, Messrs N Cook (Crazelowman), R Cook (Chevithorne), Luxton (Pileywell), Westcott (Little GFornhay), and H Haydon (Chettiscombe).

§

23 March 1928

Our Letter Box

Tiverton Point-to-Point Races

To the Editor of the *Western Times*

Sir, the members of the Tiverton Hunts – both foxhounds and staghounds, wish, in return for the hospitality they have received from the farmers of the district, to invite them to bring their cars on to the course on the day of the Point-to-Point races this year without charge and to partake of some refreshment in the tent.

Will any farmer who lives within the boundaries of either of these hunts and who proposes to attend the races, write before Sunday 8th April to General Lesley Butler at Loxbeare House, Tiverton, or to Mr John Yandle at Fordlands, Tiverton, saying for which members of his family he would like tea and refreshment tickets, and whether he would like a pass for his own private car.

Or if it is more convenient for him will he call at Captain Leslie Stagg's office in Bampton Street, Tiverton, on any Tuesday or Saturday between 10 and 1 o'clock before Sunday 8th April, and give these particulars to him. We shall do our best to send invitations to all farmers of the district who apply for them in either of the ways mentioned above – but we hope that everyone will realise that because the plans hitherto adopted have led to confusion and to the omission of some whom it would have been our wish to invite, no invitations can this year be given except in accordance with the above plan.

Yours, etc,
NOEL RUSSEL
Hon Sec., Tiverton Foxhounds.
JOHN YANDLE
Master, Tiverton Staghounds
LESLEY BUTLER
Hon. Sec., Tiverton Point-to-Point Races.

The Eggesford Hunt
and
Tiverton Staghounds

POINT- TO -POINT STEEPLECHASES

(over BIRCH FENCES) will be held at
WILLEY, STICKLEPATH, OKEHAMPTON.
On Easter Monday 22nd April, 1946
First Race 2.15 p.m

Eggesford Hunt and Tiverton Staghounds Members' and Farmers' Race
Winner (Members) £6, 2nd £4, 3rd £2.
Winner (Farmers), Cup and £6, 2nd £4, 3rd £2.

Nomination (Open) Race
Winner £20, 2nd £12, 3rd £8

Adjacent Hunts' Maiden (at closing) Race
Winner £12, 2nd £7, 3rd £4.

Adjacent Hunts' Lightweight Race.
Winner £15, 2nd £10, 3rd £5

Adjacent Hunts' Pony Race.
Winner £12, 2nd £7, 3rd £4

Weight 12st, or over 7lb, allowed for every clear inch under 15h.h.

Adjacent Hunts-Eggesford, Dulverton, Stevenstone, Silverton, Tiverton and East Devon Foxhounds, and Tiverton Staghounds.

Further particulars, schedules and entry forms from Lt.-Col. Derek F. Brown, Okehampton Tel 16.

April 11th 1947
Alteration of Date
TIVERTON STAGHOUNDS
POINT-TO-POINT
STEEPLECHASES
will be held at
THELBRIDGE
(by permission of Messrs. Troake and Hosegood)
SATURDAY, MAY 3

2 p.m. - Farmers' and Members' Race. 1st Cup and £12; 2nd, £8; 3rd, £5
2.45 p.m. - Nomination (Open) Ladies Race. 1st, £20; 2nd, £10, 3rd, £5.
3.30 p.m. - Adjacent Hunts' Maiden Race. 1st, £15; 2nd, £10; 3rd, £5
4.15 p.m. - Adjacent Hunts' Race. 1st, £15; 2nd, £10; 3rd, £5.
5 p.m. - Adjacent Hunts' Pony Race. 1st, £15; 2nd, £10; 3rd, £5.
Entries close Saturday, April 26th, at 6pm

Adjacent Hunts-Dulverton, Stevenstone and Torrington Farmers, North Cornwall, Silverton, East Cornwall, Four Burrow, Tetcott, Eggesford, Tiverton, East Devon Foxhounds, and Tiverton Staghounds.

The totalisator will be staffed and operated by Racecourse Betting Control Board, and tickets value 2s, and 10s, respectively, will be sold, to win only. Racecourse officials will be in attendance.

Refreshment Bar and Buffet on the Course.

N.B.-The course, which adjoins the main road from Thelbridge Cross to Chawleigh, is very easy to access for motor vehicles, and the whole can be viewed with ease, the parking fields providing a natural grandstand.
Car Park £1

Particulars and entry forms from: Hon. Secretary, J H H Parkhouse, Higher Ford House, Chawleigh, Chulmleigh, N Devon. Telephone: Chulmleigh 37.

22 March 1960

Pay-Out on Wrong Horse at Tiverton Staghound Point-to-Point

After bookmakers had paid out on a horse they thought had won the last race at Tiverton Staghounds course at Loosebeare on Saturday they found that another horse has passed the post first.

Like most of the race goers, the bookmakers watched the finishing line, and from the angle it appeared that the favourite Mr R.E. Keenor's Uncle Rob had won at 4-5 on, despite a strong challenge by Mr R.N.V. Williams' Muveran. About half a dozen of the bookmakers present paid out on a win for Uncle Rob before the judges announced that Muveran had won by less than a head at 3-1.

"I have paid more that £20 on Uncle Rob, and a couple of us have paid around £100," said Harry Smith, an Exeter bookmaker. "We shall never get the money back unless the punters return it," he said eyeing the rapidly emptying course.

"It's the last time I shall pay out before confirming the results," said another bookmaker. "It has been a wasted afternoon for me, everyone thought Uncle Rob had won."

The last race was the only one not won by the favourite in an afternoon of heavy going following overnight rain. In the first race G.O. Keener's bay gelding Vinke was going well with the favourite Rising Way when it ran out at the eighth race. Jockey N. Anseil circled the horse to bring it back into the race and finished third. Rising Way won by a length. Mr Bertie Hill won the adjacent hunts maiden by a length on Agonistes after a long tussle with Mr C.J. Sampson's Merry Chace.

OFFICIAL CARD **PRICE 2/6**

THE TIVERTON STAGHOUNDS

Joint Masters: Aubrey Besley, Esq., M.S.H., Aubrey Hosegood, Esq., M.S.H.

Point-to-Point Steeplechases

to be held

ON SATURDAY, MARCH 17th, 1962

at LOOSEBEARE MANOR on the Crediton - Torrington Main Road

(Two miles from Lapford Station, S.R.)

By kind permission of L. Quick Esq., and the Eggesford Hunt.

FIRST RACE AT 2.15 p.m.

This Meeting is to be subject to National Hunt Regulations for Point-to-Point Steeplechases, Rules 5 and 163-167 (Disqualification of Persons and Corrupt Practices), and appendix B of the National Hunt Rules.

Horses whose names are registered under any recognised Rules of Racing or Steeplechasing, or which have ever run in a Point-to-Point Steeplechase, or at a meeting under the recognised Rules of Racing or Steeplechasing in any Country, shall be run under the same names in these Steeplechases.

(When the name of a horse has been changed or altered on registration, the name under which he has previously run in Point-to-Point Steeplechases, as well as his new name, must be given in every entry during the current season).

No person or horse who is disqualified under any Rules of Racing or Steeplechasing shall be eligible to take part in these Steeplechases.

1962 LIST OF OFFICIALS 1962

Judges: Sir Dennis Stucley, D.L., J.P., C.A., R. L. Pugsley, Esq., M.F.H.

Stewards: Capt. A. W. Budgett, Capt. P. N. Coombes, M.F.H., A. Hosegood, Esq., M.S.H., L. Quick, Esq.

Starter: F. W. B. Smyth, Esq.

Assistant Starter: W. Nott, Esq.

Clerks of Scales: G. W. Blackman, Esq., O.B.E., W. Yendell, Esq.

Hon. Surgeons: Dr. J. M. Wingfield, Dr. J. D. Cox

Hon. Veterinary Surgeons: C. B. Turner, Esq., M.R.C.V.S. C. P. V. Jones, Esq., M.R.C.V.S.

Hon. Treasurer: Wing Comdr. E. Mortimer

Hon. Secretary and Clerk of the Course: Stanley Andrew

TIVERTON STAGHOUNDS

POINT-TO-POINT

STEEPLECHASES

VENFORD, DULVERTON

(4 miles north-west of Dulverton, on the Devon and Somerset Border, and 12 miles from South Molton).

SATURDAY, MAY 18th

2.30 p.m. — Tiverton Staghounds Subscribers', Members', and Farmers' Race.

3.10 p.m.—Open Race.

3.50 p.m.—Adjacent Hunts' Ladies' Race.

4.30 p.m.—Adjacent Hunts' Maiden Race.

5.10 p.m. — Adjacent Hunts' Moderate Steeplechases.

Entries close Saturday, May 11th, at 8 p.m.

STANLEY ANDREW, Hon. Sec., Northam House, South Molton (Tel. 20), from whom schedules may be obtained.

TIVERTON STAGHOUNDS'

Point-to-Point

STEEPLECHASES

will be held at

Three Hammers, Worlington

(On B3042 Witheridge - Chulmleigh road, 4 miles from Witheridge 4 miles from Chulmleigh)

Saturday, May 21st, 1966

2.30 p.m.—**Members', Subscribers', and Farmers Race.**

3.10 p.m.—**Open Race.**

3.50 p.m.—**Open Ladies' Race.**

4.30 p.m. — **Adjacent Hunts' Race.**

5.10 p.m. — **Adjacent Hunts'** Moderate **Race.**

Car Parking £1. Special enclosure £1-10-0

Entries close Saturday, May 14th, 1966, at 8 p.m.

Further particulars and schedules from the Hon. Secretary :— F. H. Stacey, "Trelawn," Bishopsnympton, South Molton Phone Bishopsnympton 388

TIVERTON STAGHOUNDS

Point-to-Point

STEEPLECHASES

SATURDAY, MAY 16th, 1970

at BISHOPSLEIGH, MORCHARD BISHOP

First Race 2.30 p.m.

Official Totalisator will be in operation by the Horserace Totalisator Board

Tiverton Staghounds 18 May 1974. Mens Open. Martin Pipe riding Clock Corner (Third) from Eric Wonnacott riding Owls Roost (Fourth) © Baths Photographic

Talking with jockey and trainer Neil Harris at his Westbridge Park Stables, Bish Mill, South Molton

"When I left school I wanted to go into the hunt service and the late Podge Roberts got me a job interview with the Eggesford Foxhounds when Christopher Gill was Master. I didn't get the job because Mr Gill thought I was too small to get on his horses. Thinking no more of it, I continued hunting with the Tiverton Staghounds on a motorbike and, for a couple of seasons when Ray Burrow was huntsman, I hunted my uncle's ponies.

I suppose my point-to-point career really started as a result of hunting. One day, out of the blue, Mike Tricky from Sannacott Farm, North Molton, phoned me up. He was looking for someone to work for him; he was still riding point-to-point then. I took the job and after a couple of years Mike asked me if I had ever thought about racing myself. I said, 'No, I haven't really, but I would like to have a go at it.' Anyway, he gave me my first ride on a horse called Anna's Spirit – I managed to jump three fences before I fell off! My second ride was on a horse called Dark Image, owned by Jack Down from High Bickington. I got a bit further before falling off her, and she was going nicely too. It was that ride that really got me into point-to-pointing; from there things took off, and before long I was getting between a dozen and 20 rides a season. But it was

Neil Harris with his horse Oneovertheeight, now retired and in his thirteenth year

about six years ago when I really started to make an impression in the point-to-point field and my partner and I decided to train pointers for other people in our own yard. Now I have 80–90 rides each season.

The best horses I've ever ridden would have to be Cillipour, Butler John and Magnolia Man; they really stand out and I think between them I've had about 30 wins. Magnolia Man retired two years ago, going back to the hunting field where he will spend the rest of his days. I was sorry that he retired as we trained him ourselves and his success really put our yard on the map. We have got some good horses now, but a horse like that will be hard to find again.

In order for the horses to be able to run point-to-point they must be qualified with a hunt first. To get a certificate, each horse should be hunted seven times, this must be signed by the secretary or the Master of the hunt to prove you are qualified and you send this off to be logged at Weatherby's. You can run the horses after two weeks of it being logged.

There is a lot of work involved in a point-to-pointer. Most of the horses come into work around September when they are given a good month to six weeks road work, just walking and trotting. Then you can introduce them to tracks where they start cantering. The technique of training has changed over the years with more and more people using all-weather gallops, but this is the way we do it. Once they have done the track work we start hunting them. We do hunt our horses hard, some will hunt seven times, some more. It depends if they enjoy hunting or if they are a nuisance in the hunting field; if they are a nuisance then we try and stay out of the way, but I usually like to get in the thick of things.

For some people point-to-pointing is one big party, they take their picnics to the meetings and it's real good fun, which is how a hunt fundraiser should be. We get all the owners to come back to the lorry at the end of the day and have a drink, and we all get a lot of fun out of it."

Neil Harris on 11-year-old Butler John, with 28 career wins behind him. (Trained by Gerald Dartnall and owned by Nick Viney, Master of the Dulverton West hounds)

§

Talking with Luke Harvey who hunted with the Tiverton Staghounds in the 1970s, later to become a jockey, and is now commentating on the racing channel.

"Ever since the age of four I have been horse mad and Mother and Father saw fit to buy me my first pony when I was around six.

Our farm is situated just outside Bampton, which put us in the perfect position for hunting. Within a ten-mile radius we had a variety of packs to choose from. The Dulverton East and West, the Devon and Somerset Staghounds and the Tiverton Foxhounds and Staghounds.

Our favourite was always the Tivvy Stag because of the friendly atmosphere. When I was eight I was riding well enough that I was allowed to go hunting on my own. My pony was a 12.3 hh palomino called Sundance, which my parents bought at Exeter Market.

The first meet I recall attending on my own was at Kissing Gates, Stoodleigh. I used to leave very early, in fact it wasn't uncommon for me to arrive so early that no one else had arrived. Then I'd panic, worrying that I'd gone to the wrong place.

I always remember being fascinated watching the hounds work and I never went home early. Rarely was I home before dark.

Because I have a terrible sense of direction, I used to follow a particular person that lived nearby which meant I used to end up in some strange locations. I can remember on one occasion having to hack home from near South Molton.

Sundance was a very willing pony and soon built himself quite a reputation of being a front runner and having a mind of his own.

He was a very impatient pony and I remember once the field queuing to go through a hunt gate. Sundance had other ideas and galloped headlong into the other horses catapulting me into a gatepost head first. My next recollection was being taken by Land Rover to hospital.

Through hunting I became friendly with Debbie Bemrose who lived at Holmingham Farm near Cove and we often hacked to the meet together for company.

My favourite venue was New Bridge near Stoodleigh because the deer would often run along the fields adjacent to the river, which enabled us to get a decent view. It was at New Bridge that I was given my first slot, a treasured possession I still have to this day.

I hunted every Saturday with the Staghounds and would hunt Wednesdays as well in the holidays.

Hunting was my life until I left school at 16 to join Captain Tim Forster (who also liked to follow hunting) to become a jockey.

I recently retired as a jockey, in order to work in television for the Racing Channel.

During my riding career I rode over 250 winners including one at the Cheltenham Festival and also the Welsh Grand National. I attribute a lot of what I achieved as a jockey to what I learnt riding with the Tiverton Staghounds."

Luke Harvey
© Eric Gibbs (Race Course photography)

Luke Harvey on Just Blake at Newton Abbot
(trained by John Roberts)

TIVERTON STAGHOUNDS

LAST POINT TO POINT OF THE CENTURY

at

BRATTON DOWN

Saturday 12th June 1999

First Race at 2pm

★ Excellent viewing on Exmoor location
★ Catering, Extended bar
★ Tote
★ BBQ & Music after racing

Results and photographs of the 1999 Tiverton Staghounds point-to-point races at Bratton Down courtesy of the *Mid Devon Gazette*

Tiverton Staghounds' rearranged meeting at Bratton Down, overlooking Exmoor, closed the 1999 season with one of the largest crowds and an abundance of horses seen throughout the year.

Nine races were the order of the day and all were put back 30 minutes because of an accident on the M5, where many horseboxes and jockeys travelling long distances were held up.

The meeting started with a disqualification in the opening race that left Mr and Mrs Fred Hayes' Master Kiwi (NZ) shrewdly ridden by the new area men's champion, Cullompton-based Leslie Jefford, the winner.

The Intermediate attracted 10 runners and was seized by eight lengths by Welsh raider Moon Tiger qualified with the Llangeinor and ably ridden by David Jones. Second was It's Stormingnorma, which travelled from the Gelligaer Country and was piloted by Jamie Jukes.

The West Country Classic Race with a first prize of £300, provided punters with short-priced favourite Jalcanto, from the North Ledbury, ridden by David Mansell to a two-lengths victory over Oliver Carter's successful home-bred gelding Heading North. Also in this race ex-champion lady rider Shirley Vickery collected the Stafford Babbage Cup for the first woman home.

Carter's 14 year-old Abbotsham, ridden to perfection by Ian Widdicombe from South Devon, took top spot in the Confined Hunts race, only by a head from Link Copper and Polly Curling.

Favourite was the late Capt Tim Forster's Tuskar Flop, but as in the Members' race earlier, horse and rider Dominic Alers-Hankey took the wrong course. Stewards inquired and explanations were accepted.

The restricted race divided on the day produced a 14-runner first division and saw the popular fawn and maroon colours of

Martin Salter – carried by Vansell and worn by Leslie Jefford – seizing the prize money by one-and-a-half lengths from the Proud Pound, ridden by David Dennis.

Second division winner came from the Berkely, owned by Dick Bainbridge, Rap Up (USA), under record breaking 1999 champion Julian Pritchard, managed a length victory over North Cotswold's Fiddlers Knap ridden by John Hobbs.

Open Maiden Division One attracted a maximum 18-runner field. Although he was left many lengths at the start, Dominic Alers-Hankey made no errors aboard Butterwick King (IRE) and made amends to cruise to a six-length advantage over Paul Tylor's fancied Cornish Fort, trained by Keith Cumings.

Division Two part one provided ex-jockey Mike Biddicks' six-year-old Peyton Jones a clear foot perfect race under the talented Alec Charles-Jones who has been in the winners' enclosure many times this season.

Division Two part two, the final race, was won by Scallymay, an eight-year-old grey mare for the West Shropshire Draghounds, giving owner S Edwards and rider Mike Munrywd a long awaited season's win.

Shedoes, also long-travelled and from Warwickshire, finished second.

Tiverton Staghounds thank all supporters and sponsors for making this final meeting of the season a huge success.

Results

Tiverton Staghounds Bratton Down:

Members – 1 Master Kiwi (NZ) (L Jefford); 2 Nearly All Right (I Widdicombe); 3 Master Buckley (Miss K Cook), 10L/15L 6.33, 6 ran.

Intermediate – 1 Moon Tiger (D Jones); 2 It's Stormingnorma (J Juke); 3 Belitlir (Miss S Young), 8L/6L. 6.16, 10 ran.

Mixed Open – 1 Jalcanto (D Mansell); 2 Heading North (I Widdicombe); 3 Flying Maria (C Heard), 2L/4L. 6.16, 15 ran.

Confined – 1 Abbotsham (I Widdicombe); 2 Link Copper (Miss P Curling); 3 Hensue (Miss C Prouse), HD/8L, 6.24, 7 ran.

Restricted Division One – 1 Vansell (L Jefford); 2 The Proud Pound (D Dennis); 3 Ballina (M Harris), 1 2/2L. NK, 6.15, 14 ran.

Restricted Division Two – 1 Rap up Fast (USA) (J Pritchard); 2 Fiddlers Knap (J Hobbs); 3 Morchard Milly (K Rixon), 1L/6L. 6.19. 13 ran.

Open Maiden Division One – 1 Butterwick King (IRE) (D Alers-Hankey); 2 Cornish Fort (Miss J Cumings); 3 Alpine Castle (IRE) (Miss S Young), 6L/NK, 6.21, 18 ran.

Open Maiden Division Two part one – 1 Peyton Jones (A Charles-Jones); 2 Porters Lodge (P Griffiths); 3 Dunston Slick (J Barlow), 6L/8L. 6.26. 12 ran.

Open Maiden Division Two part two – 1 Scallymay (M Munrywd); 2 Shedoes (Mrs C McCarthy); 3 Madam Rose (IRE) (Miss J Congdon), 15L/20L. 6.26. 11 ran.

Adam Jones followed by Leslie Jefford
Photo © Marcus Thompson, courtesy of *Mid Devon Gazette*

Jalcanto under David Mansell, outpaces Heading North with Ian Widdicombe aboard to win the West Country Open
Photo © Marcus Thompson, courtesy of the *Mid Devon Gazette*

It's close as Welsh combination David Jones and Moon Tiger (right) move through the field on the way to winning the Intermediate race at Tiverton Staghounds Point-to-Point, the final meeting of the season, at Bratton Down, near Barnstaple. The Welsh combination is passing David Dennis on Big Seamus (left) and P J Millington aboard Court Thyne. Photo © Marcus Thompson, courtesy of the *Mid Devon Gazette*

Cup of Cheer. Owner and trainer Jenny Hayes holds aloft the Members Race trophy. The race was awarded to her horse Master Kiwi ridden by Cullompton based Leslie Jefford. Jefford who also won the first division of the restricted on Vansell, clinched the area men's title for the first time. Also pictured are her husband Fred and daughter Tess
Photo © Marcus Thompson, courtesy of the *Mid Devon Gazette*

Results and photographs of the Tiverton Staghounds point-to-point at Bratton Down on 22 April 2000
Courtesy of *Mid Devon Gazette*
Double for Jefford in Staghounds' meeting
Point-to-point with SOS

Hail, rain, and mud were the order of the day at Bratton Down on Saturday when Tiverton Staghounds held their annual point-to-point, making it a third year of inclement weather.

Nevertheless, the stewards decided racing should go ahead on Friday evening.

The first race, the hunt, was greeted by a massive hail storm with seven runners going to post.

Local businessman Stuart Redwood's Valnau (FR) 4/5 fav took the race by a margin of 25 lengths not to trouble judge Peter Wakeham.

Only three horses were declared for the intermediate race, but this gave the judge far more trouble as Claude de Berry's Ardbei (IRE) won by a neck only, with the golden jockey Les Jefford aboard, from Basil Young's Fossy Bear ridden by his daughter Susan.

The Westcounty Classic race with £500 prize money attracted eight runners, and the favourite was the David Pipe-trained Horus unbeaten in the last three outings.

But with ground described as bottomless, Edward Retter's Black Dante (IRE) obliged by five lengths under the stylish Alex Charles-Jones. Horus finished a gallant fourth under testing conditions.

The Pipe-trained Iranos (FR) obliged in the next, the confined, under Les Jefford, his only other competitor Cool Clown ridden by Ben Trickey. Charles-Jones' double of the day came on Sarah Prouse's home-bred gelding Shobrooke Mill in the confined restricted, an impressive winner by 15 lengths.

There was a disappointing entry of only 33 horses because of the severe conditions.

RESULTS
Tiverton Staghounds at Bratton Down:
Hunt, 7 ran – 1 Valnau (FR) (C White) 4-5F; 2 Master Kiwi (NZ) (G Richards) 12-1; 3 Mayhem (M Sweetland) 4-1.

Intermediate, 3 ran – 1 Ardbei (IRE) (L Jefford) 5-2; 2 Fossy Bear (Miss S Young) 2-5F, only two finished.

Mixed Open, 8 ran – 1 Black Dante (IRE) (A Charles-Jones) 100-30; 2 Wibbley Wobbley (Miss J Cumings) 7-2; 3 Red Parade (NZ) (D Alers-Hankey) 20-1.

Confined, 2 ran – 1 Iranos (FR) (L Jefford) 1-4F; 2 Cool Clown (B Trickey) 3-1.

Confined Restricted, 1 ran – 1 Shobrooke Mill (A Charles-Jones) 2-1F; 2 Jabiru (IRE) (D Alers-Hankey) 3-1; 3 Fursan (USA) (P Philips) 8-1.

Confined Maiden, 3 ran – 1 Tony's Time (N Harris) 9-4; 2 North Newcombe (T Greed) 10-1, only two finished.

Above, David Ridge riding, and left, Nicky Dickenson parading, Another Bula (Ire). Another Bula is jointly owned by Nicky Dickenson and Dene (Dino) Richards

Carol Norman, right, parading her horse Mutual Memories owned by herself and Ray Burrow, with a helping hand from Jean Keenor

Smiling through the rain
Angela Norrish (left) and Barbara Walton (right)

Elaine Babbage, wife of Stafford, presents Jo Cummings with the Stafford Babbage cup for the first lady rider past the post in the Westcountry Classic Mixed Open race sponsored by J. Cole and Sons and Kemira Fertilisers © Baths Photographic

Near side, Dene (Dino) Richards and Nicky Dickenson's horse Another Bula (Ire) ridden by Mr D Ridge in the Tiverton Staghounds Members Race sponsored by Winston Pincombe Land Rovers © Baths Photographic

Number 10, Valnau (Fr) ridden by C White. Number 9, Ru Bidding ridden by Mr R Emmett. Number 6, Mutual Memories ridden by Ray Burrow © Baths Photographic

Ray Burrow fulfils his ambition by riding in his first point-to-point race on 22 April 2000

Former huntsman of the Tiverton Staghounds Ray Burrow fulfilled his ambition by riding in their point-to-point this year in the members race at Bratton Down on his horse Mutual Memories owned by himself and partner Carol Norman. Ray works at the East Burrow stud near Worlington for John and Sarah Haydon spending much of his time with much loved former racehorse Double Trigger. Ray always had a great interest in point-to-point racing and would have loved to have ridden between the flags. This year, the opportunity finally presented itself and his ambition was achieved at the age of 53. Ray led the race over the first fence and completed the course to tremendous cheers from the crowd, which he acknowledged by standing up in his irons and waving his whip in delight on the run-in. Well done, Ray! A perfect way to end this book on the Tiverton Staghounds.

Ray Burrow on Mutual Memories, at the Tiverton Staghounds point-to-point 2000 © Baths Photographic

Left: Ray Burrow and Carol Norman, owners of Mutual Memories © Baths Photographic

Right: Ray Burrow on Mutual Memories © Baths Photographic

Left: Ray Burrow and Carol Norman, with their horse Mutual Memories. The expressions of joy, satisfaction and relief on completing the course

THE END